PENGUIN BOOKS

Southern Winds

Sebastian Smith has won two prizes for his reporting of the war in
Chechnya, including France's highest award for journalism, the Albert
Londres. His previous books are *Allah's Mountains* and *Channel Crossing*.

Southern Winds

Escaping to the Heart of the Mediterranean

SEBASTIAN SMITH

PENGUIN BOOKS

For Z

PENGUIN BOOKS

Published by the Penguin Group
Penguin Books Ltd, 80 Strand, London WC2R ORL, England
Penguin Group (USA), Inc., 375 Hudson Street, New York, New York 10014, USA
Penguin Books Australia Ltd, 250 Camberwell Road, Camberwell, Victoria 3124, Australia
Penguin Books Canada Ltd, 10 Alcorn Avenue, Toronto, Ontario, Canada M4V 3B2
Penguin Books India (P) Ltd, 11 Community Centre, Panchsheel Park, New Delhi – 110 017, India
Penguin Group (NZ), Cnr Airborne and Rosedale Roads, Albany, Auckland 1310, New Zealand
Penguin Books (South Africa) (Pty) Ltd, 24 Sturdee Avenue, Rosebank 2196, South Africa

Penguin Books Ltd, Registered Offices: 80 Strand, London WC2R ORL, England

www.penguin.com

First published by Penguin Books 2004
1

Set in 11/13 pt Monotype Dante
Typeset by Rowland Phototypesetting Ltd, Bury St Edmunds, Suffolk
Printed in England by Clays Ltd, St Ives plc

Vagrancy is emancipation
Isabelle Eberhardt

Acknowledgements

With thanks to David Godwin and Simon Prosser, Pegram Harrison, Siobhán O'Connor and A. C. Smith; Camilla Geddes, Graham Prince and Kirsty Ritchie; Peter de Jersey; all those who brought love and tinned food on the day we left; and, most of all, my brave, beloved Adèle.

List of Maps

The Mediterranean Voyage

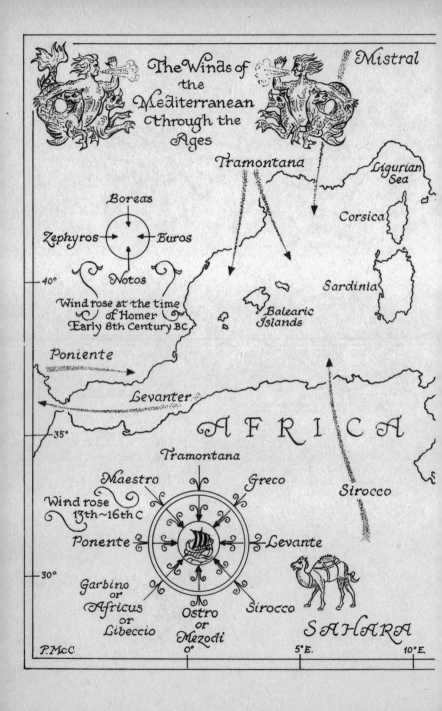

The Winds of the Mediterranean through the Ages

Mistral

Tramontana

Ligurian Sea

Corsica

Sardinia

Boreas

Zephyros — Euros

Notos

Wind rose at the time of Homer
Early 8th Century BC

40°

Balearic Islands

Poniente

Levanter

35°

AFRICA

Tramontana

Maestro   Greco

Wind rose
13th~16th C

Ponente   Levante

Sirocco

30°

Garbino
or
Africus
or
Libeccio

Ostro
or
Mezodi
0°

Sirocco

SAHARA

P.McC

5° E.

10° E.

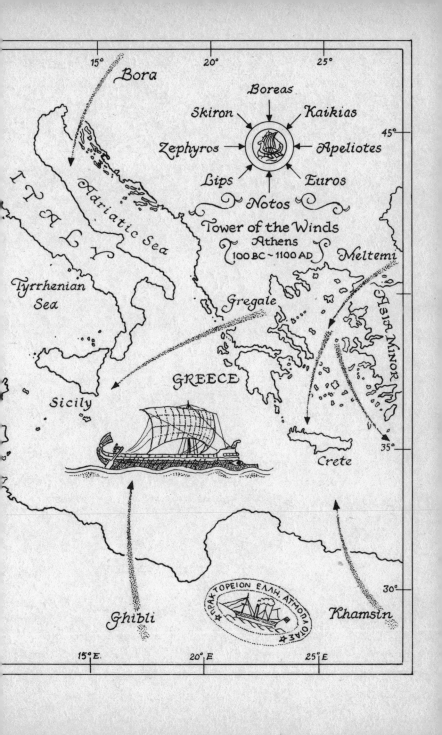

I

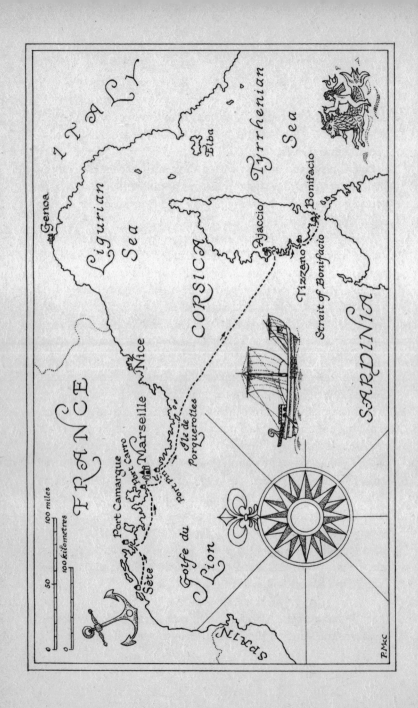

Embarking

'I wouldn't go out today,' Monsieur Beauton said, with a jerk of his thumb over the harbour wall. 'Winds here are treacherous.' I peered into the sky.

Beauton's friend, a giant with a short moustache, clasped my arm. 'He's right. The Mediterranean's not like other seas. Winds you can't trust and breakers as you've never seen – a boiling cauldron, I tell you.'

We were on the quay of the old port in Sète, starting point for a sea voyage around the Mediterranean. My boat, *Shamaal*, tugged at her mooring lines, and a stiff breeze hummed through the rigging. Adèle was aboard, making final preparations. It was true a gale had been forecast for that night, but we were only heading a short distance, just up the coast to Port Camargue, and the day had barely begun. I wished the two Frenchmen farewell. They looked mournful.

'Wait until the wind becomes stable. Another week, perhaps.' Gently, I freed my arm from the giant's grip.

It is impossible to tire of the excitement of leaving harbour. Sails are bent on, charts laid out, the anchor lashed. Frozen while in port, the compass needle suddenly awakes. Life jackets and oilskins emerge from lockers, their bright colours and battered fabrics redolent of dramas past and promises of trouble to come. A last look at the sky. The engine kicks up like approaching thunder. Dirty mooring lines come loose and the boat, before an appendage of land, becomes an island. You are alone. Chugging from harbour into open sea. Adèle and I glanced back. Beauton and the giant were still there, tiny now. Ahead stretched southern France and a world of quivering blue.

If at the heart of the Mediterranean is the sea, then at this sea's heart are the winds. I didn't need Beauton to tell me that – he was echoing Homer and every Mediterranean man since. Where some bodies of water are renowned for vastness, powerful currents or strange creatures, the Mediterranean has always been the sea of winds – not always strong, but defying prediction, full of surprises, tricks and, maybe, as Beauton said, even treachery.

The ancients worshipped the winds and gave them names, many of which endure. The turn-of-the-first-century Greek geographer Strabo said of the mistral, which still sweeps the Golfe du Lion, '[it] hurls men from their chariots, breaks their limbs and strips them of their clothes'. The sirocco brings madness and Saharan dust. In the Adriatic, the bora, known in classical times as *boreas*, has been recorded as accelerating from calm to storm in fifteen minutes. The zephyr, from the old Greek name *zephyros*, may be soft and gentle, but the meltemi can turn the sea white. Tramontana, libeccio, poniente . . . there are many others.

The gods on Mount Olympus were so afraid of the winds they put them under the guard of Aeolus, who kept them in a cave on his floating island. In Homer's *Odyssey*, Aeolus tried to help Odysseus, or Ulysses, by trapping the contrary airs in a sack so that the Greek hero and his lost band would be able to sail directly to their home island of Ithaca. In the words of Odysseus: 'This bag he stowed in the hold of my ship, securing it tightly with a burnished silver wire to prevent the slightest leakage. Then he called up a breeze from the West to blow my ships and their crews across the sea.' After nine days, Odysseus' men were within sight of Ithaca. Homer's tale of a traveller's return might have ended there, except that Odysseus now fell asleep and his crew, mistakenly believing the sack to contain more earthly valuables, untied the silver seal. The subsequent storm drove them back to Aeolus' island, and this time there was no welcome. They were cast out with a curse and ten years would pass before Odysseus, the sole survivor, was to reach home.

The Odyssey recounts the first and greatest Mediterranean voyage ruled by winds. Setting sail from England earlier that summer, Adèle and I had embarked on another. The wind would be sometimes friend, sometimes foe, but always our guide – to the heart of the sea and, for a footloose pair, perhaps to an Ithaca of our own.

Shamaal heeled and leapt through the chop towards Port Camargue, our first taste of the Mediterranean. We'd already covered 1,000 miles of English Channel, Bay of Biscay and French canals to get this far, yet it was only here in the Golfe du Lion that our real travels commenced. From Port Camargue, we'd continue up the French coast to Marseille, then Corsica, Italy and the rest of the great, lopsided cross we hoped to describe over the next sixteen months, heading south to Africa, east to Greece and west to Gibraltar.

Sète and the low-lying coast soon dissolved in our wake. Adèle, eyes wide as the sea, took the long, wooden tiller under her arm. Rigging tightened and strained, but held, a miracle of collective strength and loads well spread. Sails found their natural curve. The scuppers spat out water that found its way on deck. And in the cabin, the items that made that cave home rattled and hopped, not quite breaking free. We were away.

Despite the gale, a mistral, being forecast to hit in about eleven hours, the sky remained deep aquamarine and the sea slight – less a 'cauldron' than the placid, toothless Mediterranean so familiar from postcards and holiday ads. The newly arrived mariner especially might be forgiven such a thought. The water is gem clear. The near absence of tides means a boat will go where it is pointed, most of the time at least; that coastlines do not alter silhouette by the hour; and that the plug won't be pulled twice daily from the bottom of harbours. After the twisting currents of the English Channel, navigation is astonishingly easy. 'Not a real sailor's sea,' as John J, an Englishman we met in Sète, had put it. John, whose towering white body and uneven sunburn gave him the look of a striped lighthouse, was leaving after a week's sailing holiday in which six days had been calms.

Yet I'd already heard and read enough to know that Beauton

and his doom-filled friend might be right. The Golfe du Lion, set in southern France like the jaws of a circus lion (we were now in its throat), is the most gale-ridden area of the Mediterranean. 'Notorious for bad weather, sudden and violent gales, and a heavy confused sea,' warned the British Admiralty in a nineteenth-century guide. Modern sea guides, known as pilots, said much the same. So, regardless of the gentle first reception we were getting, Sète's sailors had the experts on their side. Besides, in their mistrust, almost loathing, for the wind and waves lay something ancient that we outsiders might do best not to mock.

I'd got an inkling of these emotions the previous Sunday at the cathedral in Sète. It was the local fishing fleet's day of blessing, the Grand Pardon de Saint Pierre. Many of the fishermen in Sète are of Italian descent and their boats bear names such as *Louis Nocca*, big tuna hunting vessels with crews of up to ten men. Revelling in their Catholicism, they'd filled the cathedral and spilled into the streets to hear the Mass. The gospel, predictably, was that old favourite about the apostles being unable to catch fish until the appearance of Jesus, but the sermon had made me prick up my ears.

'In faith,' said the bishop brought in from Montpellier for the big day, 'as in life, we have a choice. We can hug the coast, keeping a foot in port, yet telling ourselves that this is enough, that we have done all we can. Or, we can head *au large* – offshore, into the deep. You all know that this can require courage. To lose sight of land and shelter, to risk storms, can be a fearful thing. Yet the fisherman knows that often the rewards he seeks lie far away. And so it is with faith. Sometimes for true faith there is no option but to go out there – *au large* – to abandon comforts, abandon pretences and seek God the hard way.'

After Mass, there'd been a procession of fishermen, brass bands and a tottering statue of Saint Peter before the real business of the day got under way: a sortie by the whole fleet to throw wreaths of remembrance on the sea for lost sailors. Away from the street celebrations, away from the bishop, away from the Japanese agents waiting on shore to pay silly money for live tuna, the fishermen were doing their best to appease an angry god.

Our first hop was almost at an end. From seaward, the flatlands of the Languedoc-Roussillon region appear as a smudge, making progress along the coast almost impossible to judge by eye, but the log, a device gauging speed and distance through the water, measured twenty-six and a half miles from Sète. That could only mean we had arrived. Adèle climbed on to the cabin roof and danced a jig in celebration, while I scanned for our refuge in the coming storm. Soon enough, the bulk of purpose-built Port Camargue loomed from the marshland of the Rhône estuary and in less than an hour we were moored.

The Master

Every corner of the Mediterranean claims a wind that causes the most havoc. Vying for the title might be the simoom, or 'poison wind', of North Africa; the arifi, the 'scorcher', of Morocco; the trapez-okairos, or 'table weather', which interrupts meals at outdoor cafés in Greece; and the bora, the 'ruffian' of Shakespeare. Or why not the cold south-easterly that the Berbers call mezzer-ifoullousen, the 'chicken plucker'? The Spanish have the descuernacabras, the 'remover of goats' horns', and matacabras, the 'killer' of the same. In the western Mediterranean, though, and above all in the Golfe du Lion, the mistral is what sailors fear most. The *magistralis*, or masterful, of the Romans may not be blowing hard, indeed it may not be blowing at all, but you never forget in whose territory you are. The landscape bears the scars, the locals talk about little else and, already, the hand of the master was on our shoulders.

We woke early the next day to palm fronds beating frantically and triangular waves scurrying past the quays. A boy howled as the wind threw his beach ball into the water. Two teenage girls ran down a flight of steps screaming. *Shamaal*'s wire rigging shrieked and the ropes down the mast hammered without rhythm. Adèle and I sheltered in the cabin, then pushed ourselves up to the port's observation balcony, where we watched the sea gallop against the beaches. Within a minute we had to retreat, eyes watering, ears aching, exhilarated.

A few in port claimed it was not the mistral, but the tramontana. They are similar winds, with similar effects. Both are born of northern European depressions that track east across France until, like a marching band in a dead-end street, they meet either the wall of the Alps or the high ground of the Massif Central. In the first case, the storm whooshes down 150 miles of the Rhône valley, emerging as the north or north-west mistral. In the second, the wind turns for Toulouse, flips over the tail of the Pyrenees, and catapults into the sea as the more westerly tramontana.

The twins, famous for their unpredictable effect on human nerves, have been credited with outlandish feats. Marseille folklore has it that the mistral once blew a train backwards, while the tramontana is said to have hurled all manner of unlikely objects, including a church font and a Spanish *guardia civil*, clean through the air. If this is hyperbole, then it is in good company, for as long ago as 195 BC, the Roman statesman Cato wrote that the tramontana could 'throw an armed man and a loaded wagon to the ground'. So when a two-masted yacht with an Italian flag limped into port in mid storm, I strolled around for a look. There were four on board: a leathery old captain, his wife and two strapping youths. Their faces were flush with the elation and exhaustion that follow danger. 'Got caught out trying to get over from Corsica,' the captain said. 'This is a big boat, but there were times I was really starting to wonder . . .' And well he might. As we talked, Adèle came with news that a large catamaran had broken in two that afternoon about ten miles out to sea.

The fact that anyone tried to counter such winds – and that the Italians succeeded – testified to the efficiency of modern sailboats and liberal use of powerful auxiliary motors. In the past, ships could only turn and run. A mistral of 1569 is recorded as scattering a squadron of twenty-five Castilian ships from the Golfe du Lion to as far as Sardinia and, in one case, all the way to the tiny island of Pantelleria off North Africa, fully 600 miles off course. Later that century, the Genoan diplomat Cesare Giustiniano, just days from Spain where he was due to present his credentials as ambassador to the court of Philip II, was blown by the mistral from the gulf to present-day Algeria. Before he could even begin to resume his journey, a week camped in a deserted bay, a further diversion east in his damaged ship and a hitchhiked passage to Sardinia awaited. So much for the Mediterranean of simple navigation.

Traditional wisdom has it that both the mistral and the tramontana always blow for a number of days divisible by three, but ours blew for only two. We left Port Camargue during the middle of the night, catching the tail end of the bad weather to get a head start.

There is always a whiff of mystery and secrecy when a yacht goes to sea, particularly at night. Where are they going? Why now? (Also, because this is the sea: what will happen?) Seeing a boat depart always made me wish instinctively that I were on it. Adèle's reflex was much the same. All our lives we'd been travelling in some way – Adèle from sheer curiosity; I as part of a peripatetic family and only later because I understood this was what suited me, too. When Adèle and I met while working as journalists in Moscow, this rootlessness was one of the first things we realized we had in common. And if it were only quite recently that we'd taken to sailing, there was nevertheless something about being afloat that felt natural. We were born stowaways.

So while the rest of the harbour slept, we rose, put oilskins over T-shirts, drank coffee with condensed milk and, with the boat's night-lights glowing red and green, eased *Shamaal* from her berth. By 2.30 a.m. the engine was off, the sails were up and in the darkness we sped east. I thought of the jolly German man and his young son next to us in that motor boat at Port Camargue. After a couple of days sheltering together from the same gale, we'd become quite familiar, neighbours. But we hadn't told them we were leaving and they'd have found only empty water at our berth this morning.

For half a dozen hours we sailed headlong, the wind fresh, *Shamaal* playing a scherzo through lively waves. At dawn we were still making tracks, but by late morning the wind had evaporated, the waves deflated and our rush slowed to a jog, then a walk. We let out more sails, shed clothes and watched the coast transform from the flat Camargue to the scented crags and rocky outcrops so typical of southern France. By midday, the lazy sun and light breeze made it hard to remember the gale.

The advent of hot weather also underlined how *Shamaal* had not been designed exactly with the Mediterranean in mind. A hair under twenty-six feet long and built in the old-fashioned, low, narrow way, she had living space below decks like a telephone box on its side. Instead of plenty of opening windows to create air currents, there were only two hatches: a circular escape hole at the bow, which was closed while at sea, and the main entrance, an archway that required a nifty swinging manoeuvre to negotiate. There was no fridge, nothing like standing headroom, no shower, a tiny loo and an antiquated two-burner stove that ran on paraffin – temperamental and a swine to start. Modelled on a Nordic sailboat and built in England, *Shamaal II* (her official name) was definitely of northern inspiration.

Yet the rakish lines and blue hull had caught my attention when I'd found her for sale in an Essex boatyard a few months past. She was inexpensive – less than what many people spend on a small car – and hardly more complicated to handle than a dinghy. There was room, just, for two to live. Above all for a voyage on the wind, *Shamaal* was seaworthy – 'bombproof', as someone back in England put it – and should we ever find ourselves caught out, by a mistral for example, we'd be glad. I'd bought her on the spot.

Within a few months of fitting out and training ourselves in the swirling North Sea, Adèle and I had left our North London flat and moved aboard, with us a miscellany ranging from Adèle's film camera to fuel canisters, glues, paints, varnish and other toxic bric-a-brac, sextant, charts, knives, flares, a library . . . The day we embarked from the muddy River Crouch for the Mediterranean, there'd been a party of London friends to see us off. Also a few horrified expressions: 'What, no fridge? That's the loo? Where do you *sleep*?' Adèle and I had also wondered on occasion how we would cope, but the freedom of being at sea made such concerns insignificant. *Shamaal* was our dream boat. Even the name – bestowed by the first owner twenty-five years earlier and, as is customary, never changed – was fated. Shamaal, meaning 'north' in Arabic and Persian, is a wind: the northerly of the Arabian Gulf.

The port of Carro is a simple, laid-back place featuring fishermen, the odd visiting summer fair, and evening rounds of boule at the harbour front. It was during a stop here that we learnt something of the trick to predicting a mistral. Many claim they read the skies, but Pino the fisherman was one to trust. 'There may well be no usual indication of bad weather,' he said, palming a cloud of cigarette smoke away to illustrate the point. 'The air becomes beautifully clear, but then you get clouds like little balls. Clouds like plates, or some say cigars, are another sign. But stay alert: when these balls start to explode and scatter, the mistral will soon be upon you.'

A friend in London, a French television cameraman working with Adèle, had put us in touch. He and Pino had been childhood friends. 'You'll find him there in a kind of club, Le Cercle des Pêcheurs. Just say that "Chocolat" sent you.' The word had indeed been all we needed, Pino breaking into a fishing-net smile and agreeing at once to join us in *Shamaal*'s cockpit for a chat.

'Chocolat was my best friend. As boys we'd hang around the harbour catching fish in the rocks. Chocolat – that's what he was always called – went and became such a success, but we never forgot him and he's never forgotten us. We were quite a gang. There was another, a fisherman named Marius who used to lend us nets so that we could learn. He was a good friend to us, but he drowned after falling off the back of a fishing boat *au large*. Took a while to find him and you know, when we did, it was not a pretty sight. Seems he'd just gone to take a crap when he fell. Just like that.'

About the mistral, Pino had little good to say. 'It burns, pure and simple. It burns the coast, it burns the woods, it burns the sea.' But, as with the English when it comes to rain and Russians with snow, the people of Provence had learnt to live with the wind. Streets in towns are positioned at right angles to the mistral, as are the long, sloping roofs of farmhouses. Farmers have learnt to shelter fields with stands of thick yet permeable cypress trees. 'When the mistral blows,' wrote the region's happily named poet Frédéric Mistral, 'it rocks only the cradle.' Sailors have their own trick. A small boat can safely leave some southern French harbours during a mistral provided it clings to shore, so allowing the gale to blow overhead. Watch out, though: the whole top layer of water in the Golfe du Lion is pushed eastward during a mistral, and along France's coast the yellow underwater rocks which seemed safely distant only the previous day may now be snatching at the keel.

Before pressing on to Marseille, we took Pino's suggestion of visiting the local semaphore station, a form of coastguard that monitors shipping, records the weather and keeps watch over nearby seas. We had only to chug around the bluff from Carro into the next cove, drop anchor and row ashore in our rather tattered old rubber dinghy. The station, a white stone tower, was a short walk through the pine trees on a piece of high ground over the beach.

After overcoming his initial military reserve – or most of it, given that he preferred not to reveal his name – the commander, in the naval uniform of the *sémaphoriste*, invited us in for a tour. I asked him about something Pino and another fisherman had mentioned: that the mistral was changing character, becoming erratic, even that the flight path of birds on their annual migration down the Rhône valley had been affected. 'I've heard these rumours, too, and they are difficult to pin down,' the commander said. 'Anecdotally, I can tell you one thing. The tradition always went that the mistral blew three days, six and so on, right up to twenty-one. Well, no one talks about the twenty-one any more. The periods may be frequent, but they are shorter. Why? There are different possibilities, but some say the heat from the motorways, or industry, has affected the flow of air in the Rhône, actually deflecting the mistral.'

The commander proudly led us about the sparse interior of the tower. Turned out he'd come to his profession the way that a young jeweller might take over the family shop, adding '& Sons' to the sign. His father and his wife's father had been *sémaphoristes* – indeed, his wife was born in a semaphore station. He showed me a small poster pinned against the curved wall. '*SIGNAUX VISUELS D'AVIS DE TEMPETE*,' it read over diagrams of black triangles. Storm signals. They were an old method of warning sailors and fishermen of coming gales. Large shapes, mostly triangles, would be hung from a mast at the top of the tower, signalling the forecast to those at sea. According to the poster, two black triangles pointing up signified a north-easterly gale, two pointing down a south-easterly, one pointing up a north-westerly and one pointing down a south-westerly. There were also a black ball, a stubby, black cross and various black flags symbolizing near gales, storms and even expected shifts of direction.

'Of course, they're not so in demand,' the commander said. 'Most boats get weather warnings over the radio, but they remain part of our official duties and they still matter to some people, the ones in very small boats who go out for the day, for example. I'm in favour. There's something ancient about them.'

As we descended the tower's spiral staircase to return to the boat, I noticed what looked like a punchbag. 'The ball signal,' the commander said, 'the one warning of near gales. It's just been delivered – a replacement after the last one fell apart!' I paused before the mysterious object. In its repose before the storm, the ball possessed something magical, something, as the commander said, that was ancient. I thought of Homer's description of Aeolus' sack – 'a leather bag, made from the flayed skin of a full-grown ox, in which he had imprisoned the boisterous energies of all the winds'. I looked again at the ball. It could have come from the same workshop.

The Debate

Between Carro and the eastern corner of the Golfe du Lion, the cliffs grew higher, the winds lighter. On the chart, the pencil line of our journey clung to mustard-yellow southern France, while I wanted to be in the white spaces between. The 'vast sea' of Homer remained vast, only now, instead of gales, our path was blocked by calms. Progress in these conditions could be pathetically slow, a mile an hour, a mile in two hours, nowhere at all. There was always the engine, but the shake and rumble of the one-cylinder machine could be as dreadful in the heat as sitting motionless under sail.

We drifted into Marseille on a carpet of fog. The ships, gantries, churches and steep streets of the great port were invisible until the last minute. From every direction came the woeful, bovine cry of foghorns. We were glad – and maybe lucky – to dock safely.

From Marseille we squeezed through the sheer rocks of Cap Croisette, bobbed along, sails flapping, over Plateau des Chèvres, and hours later were cheated by false breezes on the far side of Ile Riou. We stopped offshore, let down the rope ladder and dived overboard. Adèle basted herself and roasted on deck, wearing not even sunglasses, while I sank deeper under straw hat and long-sleeved shirt. We whistled, we cursed, we prayed and we fidgeted with the ignition key. We scanned for any sign, the start of the thread that might lead to movement – a tuft of cloud over the cliffs, a ripple of water far away, an unexpected caress of breeze on the cheek – and received little reward. How long had we been trying to round that headland? Where were the sea breezes the pilot book promised? Was the whole Mediterranean – we'd covered only 100 miles – going to be like this? A blip in the placid waters was enough to make us believe our luck was changing, but blips were too often just that.

Floating into Port Pin, not a port, but a simple *calanque*, a gash of air and water in the cliffs, I thought once more how hard it was to reconcile this Mediterranean with that of Beauton – and not only Beauton. Pino, recalling the death of his friend Marius, had issued the same warning: 'They say the Mediterranean is safe, but it's a traitor – *une traîtresse.*'

We decided to stay a while in Port Pin. Umbrella firs shut out the heat and the world, sprinkling pine scent and needles over the water. Sunbathers came through the woods around the cove in the mornings and perched on the rocks, then vanished with the sun. The odd tripper boat tripped past, overloaded with people and cameras, gone as quickly as it came. Only *Shamaal*, anchored at the bow and tied from the stern to a rock, stayed. In the evenings, apart from another boat or two, we were alone. Dusk coated the land and water in a delicious cool, and at night the sky wheeled in U-shaped segments, framed by the cliffs of the *calanque*.

One evening, reading by the soft glow of oil lamps, I turned to a description by Chateaubriand of a journey made under sail from Alexandria to Tunis in 1806. The trip, recounted with the Frenchman's characteristic mix of wry humour and grand thoughts, began in calms and contrary winds, then hit a devastating series of December gales in which his ship was driven as far off course as Rhodes, where he witnessed the sinking of a felucca.

He wrote: '*Notre navigation ne fut plus qu'une espèce de continuel naufrage de quarante-deux jours, ce qui est un peu long.*' ('Our sailing was not more than a sort of forty-two-day continual shipwreck, which is a little long.') Instead of the two, maybe three weeks that might have been expected in normal conditions, the passage dragged on for six.

The account seems to confirm the difficult, if not downright perverse, nature of the inland sea, yet it came at a time when the new, soft image was already in vogue. To a large extent, this was due to Byron, champion of Greek independence and one of the first northern tourists. In the lovers, sultans, sailors, pirates and landscapes of his verses, Byron caught the spirit of the romantic, leisurely Mediterranean we still have today. Don Juan's reception by nymphs after he is shipwrecked is an example:

> They looked up to the sky, whose floating glow
> Spread like a rosy ocean, vast and bright;
> They gazed upon the glittering sea below,
> Whence the broad moon rose circling into sight;
> They heard the waves' splash, and the wind so low,
> And saw each other's dark eyes darting light
> Into each other – and, beholding this,
> Their lips drew near, and clung into a kiss . . .

Byron, though, was a landsman, and I wondered: what would a writer who knew sailing, one who spent days *on*, not *by*, the sea, have to say?

Highly strung, inveterate Lothario and egotist Guy de Maupassant might not have been the easiest of shipmates. In *The Story of San Michele*, published in 1929, the Swedish doctor Axel Munthe recounted meeting de Maupassant aboard *Bel Ami*, the novelist's elegant yacht of about thirty-three feet, in the south of France. 'I well remember our sitting up the whole night talking about death in the little saloon of his *Bel Ami* riding at anchor off Antibes harbour. He was afraid of death. . . . He was particularly insistent in questioning me about death at sea. I told him my belief that death at sea without a lifebelt was a relatively easy death, with the lifebelt perhaps the most terrible of all.' Whereupon de Maupassant, who would die of syphilis at a Paris insane asylum, aged forty-two, vowed to rid his boat of all life-saving equipment.

Yet de Maupassant, familiar both with the Mediterranean and the English Channel where he was raised, was passionate about sailing and that, with his love of freedom, made him worthwhile. For him, as for me, sailing was less about technical bits and bobs than about escaping the drudgery of life on land. To a dreamy northerner, a native of soggy and muddy Normandy, the light and exoticism of Mediterranean shores were a revelation. 'On this sea-tossed boat, which a wave can fill and overturn,' he wrote in *Sur l'Eau* in 1888, 'I know and I can feel how the things we know about are as nothing, for the earth floating in a void is even more isolated, more lost than this barque on the waves.'

In another part of *Sur l'Eau*, an account of sailing trips made along the French Riviera in the 1880s, de Maupassant describes how he and his crew have to wait for the wind off the Côte d'Azur – in a place not so far from Port Pin. Suddenly, I thought I could see through to the kernel of the Mediterranean riddle:

What a character the wind is to sailors! They talk about it as of a man, of an all-powerful ruler, sometimes terrible, sometimes charitable. . . . You don't know him at all, you landlubbers! It is we who know him better than our fathers and our mothers, this terrible, invisible, changeable, cunning, treacherous, ferocious person. We love him and we fear him, we know his tricks and his rages, which the signs in the sky and the sea slowly teach us to forecast. He makes us think about him every minute and every second, for the struggle between him and us never breaks off. . . . In a sailor's soul there reigns, just as in a believer's, the idea of an irascible and mighty God, the mysterious, religious, never-ending fear of the wind, and respect for its power.

He is the master of the sea, he who can be used, avoided or fled from, but who can never be tamed.

Scattered

Another day of drifting, of swaying like a metronome in the waves of far-off ships and eventually of using the motor brought us to the prickly island of Embiez, where we fought unsuccessfully against mosquitoes and heat. However, we left at dawn in high spirits: this next hop, to Ile de Porquerolles, would be our last before crossing to Corsica.

We made Porquerolles without touching the engine, even sailing out of the rocky anchorage in which we'd stayed at Embiez. But this was still no weather for the 130-mile passage across the Corsican sea, so on the north side of the island we again dropped anchor and settled down to await a favourable breeze.

One evening after dinner we rowed ashore in the dinghy for a walk on the beach. Myrtle, oak and eucalyptus trees made a forest behind the sand and it was here, as dark fell and the area became deserted, that to our surprise we found a man erecting a white screen. Working carefully, he first put up a frame about the size of a blackboard, then stretched over this a sheet of white material. For the first time the man noticed us. He was brown and sinewy, like biltong, and he wore glasses, a khaki shirt and shorts. 'I'll give you three guesses,' he said.

'Outdoor puppet theatre?' Adèle tried.

'*Non.*'

'Photography?'

'*Non.*'

'You're a painter. "Forest at Night".'

'*Et, non.*'

Our strange friend went to his pick-up truck parked in the track nearby and flicked a switch. The screen glowed purple. 'Ultraviolet light. Still can't guess? OK, I'm collecting insects – they fly into my screen thinking it's the moon. Get them on the sheet and, *voilà*, I catch them in my net.'

Odd as it seemed for a professional entomologist, Antoine was already suffering the attention of many mosquitoes, but I was intrigued by his task, which was to survey the insect population and see how it differed to that on the French mainland. 'There are big fluctuations as a result of strong winds,' he said. 'Often it happens that non-native species are blown by a mistral from the mainland to the Mediterranean islands. Other times, the same strong winds will so scatter the population of some species that their breeding pattern is totally disrupted and numbers fall dramatically. That's what I try to monitor.' I felt for the poor devils lured to that screen, their instinctive navigational devices befuddled by the ultraviolet trap. 'Last year,' Antoine continued, slapping in the dark at his calf, 'I put screens high up in the trees, but a mistral blew and sent the whole lot crashing down. Winds cause trouble. Oh, excuse me' – he struck again at his leg – 'but, of course, they also bring new life.'

Homer could not have put it better. Winds scatter. Winds bring trouble. Winds bring life. I thought of the insects that survived the wild journey over the sea and made Porquerolles their new home. Many would die, but a few must have shaken the salt from their wings, buzzed around a little and set off to restart their lives. Without Antoine, this drama would have gone unrecorded. Among people, it was hardly different: the most anonymous families went through incredible disintegration and rebirth. My relatives were famous to no one, yet both sides had been in movement for a century – from Russia to Germany, from Germany to anywhere but Germany, from one ocean of America to the other, from Europe to America and back again. Adèle's family, too, had blown this way and that. Few hadn't. Traipsing between jobs and homes as a journalist, I'd sometimes envied the ones who stayed put, taking time to learn that even their stability was illusory.

The adventures of the insects also underlined the particular geography of the Mediterranean. As its name – 'between land' –

suggests, this is an intimate sea. Its essence lies in the puzzle of jagged, golden coasts, a landscape the remarkable uniformity of which reinforces the sensation of a small, self-contained world, what the ancients liked to call *mare nostrum* – 'our sea'. There are vast empty spaces – the Ionian, for example – but it is the relationship between sea and land – the Iberian, Italian and Greek peninsulas, the long wall of North Africa, the big islands in the west and the peppercorns of the Aegean – that counts. Although 2,200 miles long, the Mediterranean is narrow, a wriggling collection of minor seas in which a boat is never more than 250 miles from land, and often far less.

So this is a sea of landfalls. Perhaps the most famous is the biblical Noah's, his trick of releasing a dove to look for land – it eventually returned to the Ark with an olive branch – being retained by later Mediterranean sailors and into modern times by the Polynesians. Herodotus tells the remarkable story of Colaeus, a merchant captain who'd been on his way from the Greek island of Sámos to Egypt in about 650 BC, when the wind blew him off course to the site of present-day Derna in Libya. This setback was still reversible; however, when Colaeus set out again to retrace his steps, a huge easterly gale blew him across the entire Mediterranean and through the Straits of Gibraltar – in those days, practically off the edge of the world. 'By a piece of more than human luck', as Herodotus puts it, Colaeus found himself among the people of Tartessus, in the south-west corner of Spain. These people had never met Greeks, nor seen the Samian pottery and wine he had in the hold. They were, not surprisingly, delighted, and the silver they offered in return made Colaeus a rich man.

Larger scale voyages in the same spirit – wandering the Mediterranean in search of better fortune – are a common theme in the sea's literature and history. In *The Aeneid*, the Roman poet Virgil recounts how refugee Trojans made their way to Italy to establish Rome. It is a fictional account, but accurate in the sense that in antiquity many peoples did take to the sea in order to find new lands. The Phoenicians and the Greeks, with their trading colonies stretching from Spain to Crimea, are the chief examples. Virgil's story of the Trojans led by Aeneas may echo that of the Etruscans, a tribe some believe to have migrated from the eastern Mediterranean to Italy's Tyrrhenian coast well before the birth of the Roman Empire. Insects, in other words, who took the first wind that blew and opened their wings.

And it is against that background that we taste the bitterness in the scene of Odysseus' failed return to Ithaca. 'For nine days and nights we sailed on,' Odysseus recounts, 'and on the tenth we were already in sight of our homeland, and had even come near enough to see people tending their fires.' Here is the description of an ideal approach. The navigation has been good, the winds fair; the emergence of beacons, signs of habitation and people on shore, is headier still. Aeolus may even extend a small welcome: with the right wind, the crew will scent the herbs and flowers of the maquis. But in Odysseus' account, it is just after catching sight of Ithaca that he relaxes his guard over the ox-hide sack. Within minutes the crew, suspecting Odysseus to be using the bag to hide treasures for himself, has undone the silver seal:

Evil counsels prevailed. They undid the bag, the winds all rushed out, and in an instant the tempest was upon them, carrying them headlong out to sea, in tears, away from their native land. When I awoke my spirit failed me. I debated within myself whether to jump overboard and drown or stay among the living and quietly endure. I stayed and endured.

That horror of the open sea is palpable.

The day after meeting our entomologist friend Antoine, a gentle wind sprang up. Rounding Porquerolles in the afternoon, we set a course south-east and by evening had left the overcrowded, suffocating Midi astern.

Running my finger over a pocket atlas map of the Mediterranean, I traced the route to come. It would be good to make

Tunisia before October, ahead of the season of gales. Tunisia was right about in the middle of the Mediterranean. The winter would be warm and, with *Shamaal* mothballed, Adèle and I could dip our feet in the sand sea of the Sahara. Next year we'd sail on to Greece, the Ionian, the rocky Aegean and all the haunts of ancient gods and winds. Then from there, we'd begin the great trek west back to Gibraltar and the Pillars of Hercules . . . But I was getting ahead of myself now – small-scale maps were dangerous that way.

For now, it would be enough to escape the Golfe du Lion and its leonine breath. The seabed here, even well out, lay just eighty metres below the keel. We were still attached to France, to the whole of northern Europe – even, by way of the shallow Dover Straits, to England. Time to head out to sea: our path to the great South, the furnace of southern Europe and North Africa. The South of vagabond northerners, of shimmering mountains, heavy blue skies, heat, cicadas, glass seas, white walls and dark eyes. We were on our way now, dipping into the night.

Bearings

As *Shamaal* slid towards Corsica, I squeezed myself in by the chart table, brass dividers, ruler and pencil to hand, and went through my sums. At least, I did my best. Lines on charts are drawn straight, but boats follow twisting, random paths that cannot be recorded. An hour had passed since my last estimate. Corsica was still about 115 miles off. We were moving at a pitiful two knots, or nautical miles, an hour. The wind, though, was starting to pick up. Our course was 120 degrees. We should be just *there*, right over the 200-metre depth contour. How about the current? On the map showing Mediterranean surface currents, the arrows swirled anticlockwise from Gibraltar to the Levant, all the way along the northern rim, then back past Gibraltar into the Atlantic. At our position, a thick, black arrow pointed down:

the sea pushing us sideways – south. I couldn't be sure. In tidal waters, currents come and go like trains, the times of departure and destination tabulated years in advance, while in the almost tideless Mediterranean the hydrology is complex and unreliable. Here, the constant mixing of fresher Atlantic water with salty, heavier Mediterranean water sets up the basic flow described in that map. But a few days of strong winds can create one current, annul another and double the strength of a third. As always, it is the wind that counts.

Adèle was asleep, curled up in the bunk opposite the chart table. Probably in the middle of some crazy dream – a blank night was unknown on this boat. I climbed back on deck to keep watch. We did this in three-hour shifts, short enough for whomever was outside to resist and long enough, almost whatever the circumstances, for the other to catch some sort of sleep. Midmorning to late evening we were usually both up, but from dusk our separate lives began. There'd often be little to do on watch other than scan all around for other boats, occasionally adjust the sails and keep an eye on the compass and wind.

Most of the time, a wind vane connected to the rudder did the steering. Sailors often refer to these devices as extra crew, or two or three extra, for they will steer through all weather (provided there is wind), never feeling heat, cold, hunger or fatigue. Just two wooden paddles, one attached underwater to the back of the rudder, one sticking in the air over the stern rail, and, between, a system of levers: that's all there is to the wind vane. No need for electricity or any other artificial power. The upper paddle senses the wind and the underwater paddle responds, turning the rudder. Even without someone on deck, the boat sails on, akin to the magical Phaeacian ships described in *The Odyssey* – ships that 'have no helmsmen or rudders such as other craft possess [yet] know by instinct what their crews are thinking'.

Soon we'd be out of the Golfe du Lion. I watched the stars in the sky and the starry trail in our wake: phosphorescence from the last shallow water. Our speed up to four knots, we were jumping right off the continental shelf. It ended abruptly out here – 100 to 1,000, then 2,000 metres deep, just like that – and *Shamaal*'s dragon tail of green and gold withered away.

The night sky suddenly flowered. Polaris spinning on its toes, Cassiopeia looming in an untidy cluster and the Great Bear circling the firmament, to be stalked for much of the night by Leo and the Lynx. Under the keel moved the less predictable constellations of the deep. The sea revealed itself only in a flash of foam or momentary thud of water against the hull, but somewhere below there'd be schools of tuna, swordfish, dolphins, maybe a blue shark. Dolphins love small boats and often surface alongside. We'd hear the sound of a snorkel being cleared and the laughing whoosh as the creature arched out and back into the sea. At night, the gunmetal grey of the dolphin might become luminous, leaving a fiery wake as it shot under the bows. A scraping, thrashing sound up by the mast? Another flying fish. Big ones are good to eat, but these were miniature. If we got to them in time, we'd throw them back before their wings were damaged. Sometimes we found them in the morning, lying dead on deck, still beautiful.

Everything free, everything in flux, but all the while, as the stars and the fish went through their motions, as Adèle and I rose and slept, and *Shamaal* traced her thin, grey line across the Admiralty chart, the cockpit compass gave its stern, unchanging orders to us all.

Purists argue that the compass made slaves of early sailors, and there is a shred of truth in this, but today even the magnetic needle seems terribly old-fashioned. Once a luxury, the global positioning system, or GPS, is now available for the price of a mobile phone, and almost no yacht, much less medium-sized fishing boat or commercial ship, goes to sea without one. Apart from informing the sailor of his position down to the nearest few metres, the satellites of the GPS instruct the helmsman's every move, suggesting a minute turn this way or that. Link the device to an electronic autopilot and the boat will take itself to any chosen spot as surely as if it had been reeled in on the end of a line. The cockpits of some boats begin to resemble those of aeroplanes.

We had a GPS on *Shamaal*, but it was the smallest, simplest version sold and was hidden by the chart table. It worked only on AA batteries, not through the boat's electricity supply, and the batteries wore out quickly, so we rarely used it. Besides, I liked to remember the sea is a vague landscape. We make tracks that immediately disappear. Wind, which guides the wind vane and therefore the boat, shifts constantly. The stars and planets follow their own seasons. Even north is not what it seems – the position of the magnetic pole wanders each year. Navigation has always been the art of useful approximation. That the GPS provides instant, absolute facts might seem only good; certainly it is most useful. But in relying on this magic box, this book of answers, we risk no longer understanding the labyrinthine nature of the sea. Adèle and I were new enough to sailing not to be interested in shortcuts: we were still learning and willingly so. Where possible, we'd follow the North Pole, the sea below and the winds above and, when I mastered the sextant, try abandoning that electronic screen for the stars.

Shamaal dived into the thick night, faster now. There is a joy, a knee-shaking, heart-bursting joy, in this kind of sailing. The wind vane knows nothing of magnetic fields or satellites, listening only to the wind across its sensitive face. Every now and then I'd glance at the compass or that star hanging up there in the rigging, just to be sure, but *Shamaal* blazed her own path. A few more minutes and it would be my turn to sleep – and to dream.

Mapping the winds

At dawn I rose again and swapped places with Adèle. The sun had scared off the wind and, even after raising all sail, the log showed a speed of only two and a half knots. Still, we'd made good ground during the night – we were coming up to halfway to Corsica – and the sailing would be easy. No spray, none of that terrible racket that went through the cabin during rough weather, and plenty of time to ourselves. Adèle would have her sleep and later we'd sit together, drinking tea from tin mugs. She could film the dolphins if they came. We might even dive over for a swim. A lazy day – or as long as the weather allowed.

No VHF forecasts reached us here and the weather guides we carried proved of little use, their photographs and explanations of Atlantic conditions, not the irrational Mediterranean. The glowing blue sky was as expressionless as ever.

For the initiated, there are always clues, and in the beginning all sailors would have known where they lay. Today, few do. Used to living on land, barricaded behind car windows, double glazing and climate control, our old connections to the sky are almost gone. We know street corners where there are gusts, where we should brace and turn our faces. We are aware, without questioning why, that on some days we hear distant sounds that on others we don't – the rumble of trains, the peal of bells, the roar of a stadium crowd. Our language is full of images of wind direction. Of pissing *against* the wind, of being gone *with* the wind, of blowin' *in* the wind. Ill winds blow no good, we get wind of something, there are winds of change. We can be winded. In every language, weather-forecast terms have a double entendre of an almost philosophical nature. A situation may be calm – *calma* in Spanish and Italian, or *calme* in French – or turn stormy, a word always meaning more than bad weather. The translation in Spanish of a strong gale is *muy duro* – very hard. In French it is *fort coup de vent* – a strong blow or strike of the wind. The word storm (*Sturm* in German, *shtorm* in Russian) is wonderfully evocative.

But these are only fragments of knowledge, echoes of a time when the earliest sailors were so familiar with the sky that they navigated not by GPS, sextant or even compass, but by the very wind itself.

The essential was straightforward. If a wind blows constantly, it gives a navigational reference no worse than that of a compass, the wind playing the role of the needle. Provided one knows the direction of the target at the beginning, very little else is needed: keep the wind at the correct angle to the boat and double-check on progress through the stars at night and the sun during the day. This is what happens in Homer when Odysseus sails east for seventeen days on the boat he built at Calypso's island. She gives him 'a following wind so that you may reach your own country safe and sound'.

But in the Homeric era, about the early eighth century BC, no more than the four cardinal directions had been identified, meaning north was anywhere in the region of north, west anywhere to its left, and so on. This was too crude for navigational purposes, so soon enough the Greeks began subdividing the circle of the horizon into smaller and increasingly accurate segments, using the sun's east–west movements, rather than the still unknown magnetic north, as the base for their calculations. (It was not until the twelfth century AD that the magnetic needle entered use in Europe.)

The most dramatic expression of this science was the Tower of Winds built in central Athens by Andronikos of Kyrrhos (argued by some to be from Syria, others Macedonia) in the first century BC. Still standing among the ruins of the city's Roman marketplace – with luck, we'd sail there next year – the tower has eight marble walls, each depicting a wind personified as a winged god. This and similar towers would have been public centres of learning in ancient Greece, their roofs used for celestial observation, their sides adorned with sundials and some, like the one in Athens, also sporting a water-driven clock. The frieze of the winds circling Andronikos' tower reveals the Greeks' enormous progress. It is no coincidence that northerly Boreas, westerly Zephyros and their friends are shown flying anticlockwise around the edifice: in the northern hemisphere, this is the pattern of a typical bad weather system, spinning so that easterly winds give way to southerlies, then westerlies and finally north-erlies before moving away. Most striking, though, is the detail and precision in the directions of the winds, Boreas precisely matching north, and so on: a thousand years before the magnetic needle and already the horizon had been perfectly calibrated.

A portable, paper version of the Athens tower became common. Called 'wind roses', these were diagrams of the horizon displaying the names and directions of each wind. From Homer's early four petals, the rose bloomed rapidly to eight, then twelve, sixteen and thirty-two. Armed with this map to the empty hori-zon, the mariner could begin picking routes across the sea. Sailors now refer to the compass course – south-east, for example – they need to get *to* somewhere, but in the age of wind-hopping they would discuss the direction *from* which they wanted the wind. So, when Pliny described the journey from Carpathus to Rhodes, he said it was 'fifty miles with *africus*'. In other words, a sailor wanting to go from Carpathus to Rhodes had only to wait for the south-west wind called *africus* to blow, then follow it for fifty miles. Strabo wrote that Chios to Lesbos was '200 stadia with *notos*', the south wind, while another survey advised that from Paphos to Alexandria was a journey of '3,800 stadia with *boreas*'. This way of thinking literally brought the sky down to earth.

The first and most prosperous of these wind highways was between Crete and Egypt, a bustling conduit for everything from Canaanite jewellery and Egyptian scarab gems to fishing nets, coral, hippopotamus ivory, ebony and Cypriot pottery. The route began on mainland Greece and in the Aegean islands, using the summer etesian (a moderate to strong north wind, meaning 'annual') to sail to Crete. From there, the route continued over 300 to 350 miles of open sea to Alexandria and the Nile. The return journey was assured by the khamsin, a burning Saharan wind that blows back to the north. Along the Nile those same traders might enjoy a similarly convenient pattern: sailing up-stream with the prevailing northerlies and downstream, sails furled, with the current and oars.

From such simple beginnings, Mediterranean sailors, all of them from the eastern basin, rapidly spread out – 'like frogs on a pond,' as Plato said of the Greeks. In *The Haven Finding Art*, E. G. R. Taylor describes how captains eventually came to consider the winds a sort of network across the sea. One wind, such as the etesian, took you in a certain direction, another somewhere else, but a journey might combine different winds to reach a new destination altogether. This was wind-hopping, similar to changing bus several times in order to cross a city. For all the coast-hugging that surely took place, many remarkable journeys were being made, and the Old Testament idea of the Mediterranean as a wilderness – the 'Great Sea' – was on the retreat.

'Sebastian! Look!' I was in the cabin, deep in my notes, when I heard Adèle cry out. Notepad, photocopies and pen tumbled, and I was through that hatch. 'Look!'

A whale, quite a bit larger than *Shamaal*, had surfaced thirty metres astern. Gently up and over it went, a little spout of air and sea water shooting from its breather hole, a real picture-book fountain. It did that three times, and after the third arch vanished. Adèle had just put the camera away after a spell of filming that morning, but in any case we were too fixated on the disturbed patch of water to care. The whale had gone but, long after the sea closed around its great tail and stubby fin, its presence remained. Would it surface again? Was it right below us now? What would it make of *Shamaal*? We moved from gunwale to gunwale, the cobalt water suddenly full of expectation. I'd heard stories of whales scratching their backs against keels, even of falling in love with boats. Just stories probably, like the story of Ahab's white leviathan. But we felt suddenly privileged, as if from the submarine world a secret had been revealed.

By the time I'd gathered my materials and settled back down in the cabin, leaning on a sail bag, I understood what I'd seen: a glimpse of a younger world. The sea had once been a mysterious, desolate, alarming space. Often, myths filled the vacuum of facts.

Yet it was that same lack of hard information that nourished the early sailors' receptiveness. We consider ourselves advanced, but are we? Where we merely purchase information, the earliest navigators made their own; where we read digital screens, they read the sea and sky, studied the water and tasted the air. Winds were named not just because of a fondness for mythology, but for the same reasons we name any part of nature with which we are intimate. Invisible though they were, winds were as real a presence as any mountain, river or sea.

Even today, sailing does not have to mean subordination to man-made instruments. In fact, it was on this same route to Corsica that Bernard Moitessier, the record-breaking French sailor of the 1960s and 1970s, would astonish students aboard his boat *Joshua* by navigating in the old manner. Moitessier had learnt the skill from fishermen on Gulf of Siam junks in the last days of French Indochina. In *The Long Way*, he recounted how 'the taicong would tell me, for example, "Keep the swell two fingers off the quarter, and you should always feel the wind behind your left ear, looking forward."' So it was that Moitessier insisted that instead of 'bearing 110 degrees to Corsica my crew had to steer with the mistral swell very slightly off the port quarter. At night, it was the Pole Star one small hand abaft the port beam. And if there was neither distinct swell nor star, we made do with whatever we had. I wanted it that way, because concentrating on a magnetised needle prevents one from participating in the real universe, seen and unseen.'

GPS will blind many sailors, but the old pathways are still marked. I was learning. Didn't I already keep one eye on the skies, searching for the cloud or change of blue that might signal a new wind? Hadn't I registered the pattern of low swell striking *Shamaal* from behind? And now, after the whale, didn't I spend as much time thinking about what might be below *Shamaal* as above? I certainly hadn't given up looking at the compass, and I was still awkward with the sextant. But I had begun to tune in.

*

Adèle's keen eyes picked out the beacon first – three white flashes over the Iles Sanguinaires, the 'Bloodthirsty Isles', that guard the way to Ajaccio. Dawn and first sight of the tawny Corsican mountains soon followed.

Time to disconnect the wind vane and steer by hand. There was a narrow pass to negotiate through the rocks and suddenly a lot of boats to avoid. Time for intricate upwind work, for large-scale charts, the depth sounder, binoculars. Like a nomad, the wind vane loved open spaces, not the confusing world inshore.

Arrivals always bring mixed feelings. Excitement at the soaring landscape, relief at the thought of quiet sleep and, already, loss at leaving the sea. I could still picture the burning sky, the moon, stars showering through the rigging, the surfacing whale, the hypnotic rhythm of *Shamaal* in the waves. This was not the arrival of which Odysseus dreamt, the kind where the boat might then be hauled out for good – we were not ready for that. This marked the end of one journey only so that another could begin.

Tramping

Ajaccio is a long-established resort, but the jazzy waterfront restaurants and air of southern comfort didn't quite mask an unease. Maybe this was to do with the drip-drip of violence associated with Corsican independence groups. Two men had died that week – not attacking the French but, as was more usual, in some internal bloodletting of their own. Wherever an incident took place, the ripples inevitably spread to Ajaccio, seat of French authority. Sirens howled up and down the main road beyond the marina at all hours, while outside the ferry port the gendarmes had an unusually alert mien. In addition, Ajaccio suffered from the more banal problem of being the main port and town on an otherwise intimate island. Sailors came here mostly in order to go somewhere else, a hard fact that no doubt explained why the marina and its associated businesses were so rapacious.

Soon enough, we crossed the bay to the promontory of Porticcio, anchoring at dusk near a dark sickle of beach, from which the flicker of campfires and the sound of laughter came late into the night. Daylight showed us to have inadvertently halted over the wreck of a fishing boat, its algae-covered structure wobbling up through crystalline water. Fortunately, though, our anchor had not become entangled, and so after our morning swim we set sails and departed, using an unsteady breeze to round the submerged rocks of the promontory and turn south.

With luck, we'd make the little harbour of Porto Pollo by afternoon and, if not, we wouldn't care: there were coves and inlets where we could stop almost every step of the way. There are only forty miles or so direct to Bonifacio on the southernmost tip of Corsica, but this extends to about sixty-five in tracing the gap-toothed line of the shore, and Adèle and I had in mind to take the long route and take it slow.

From now on, at least for a while, we'd be coast-hugging in the old Mediterranean way.

It wasn't always that the old mariners feared losing sight of land – though they often came from societies that did – rather that the attractions of keeping close were too great. Along many parts of the Mediterranean that strip of coastal sea could be as prosperous and bustling as a great river. In *The Mediterranean*, his magisterial work first published in 1949, Fernand Braudel holds up the logbook of a sixteenth-century vessel from Ragusa to illustrate a typical trading voyage of the time: 'a matter of buying one's butter at Villefranche, vinegar at Nice, oil and bacon at Toulon. Or as a Portuguese chronicler puts it, of travelling from one seaside inn to another, dining in one and supping in the next.' This butterfly's progress, Braudel wrote, was typical not only for traders, but nobles bound for some more distant port as well, travelling 'from one coastal town to the next, taking time for festivities, visits, receptions, or rest while the crew was loading the boat or waiting for better weather. This is even how the fighting fleets travelled, doing battle only in sight of land. The word that springs to mind as one studies the itineraries or *Arti di navigare* of the period, which are from beginning to end a description of the coastal route, is the humble word "tramping".'

Much as Adèle and I would tramp in *Shamaal* down the west Corsican coast, pausing to swim at Porticcio, watching an outdoor film in Porto Pollo, purchasing croissants and motor oil in Propiano . . .

Corsica's leathery, broken coast would have looked deceptively similar in the sixteenth century, but there'd have been no confusing the scene on the water. Instead of millions of pounds' worth of dinky pleasure boats, we would have seen voluminous carracks laden with barrels of foul-smelling produce, feluccas with their long, diagonally boomed lateen sails, the odd war galley – a trireme maybe – its wretched manpower switched on and off by the cry of the captain. The smell from such craft was said to have been so vile that other ships did their utmost to pass to windward. One French officer described a floating hell: 'The creaking of the blocks and cordage, the loud cries of sailors, the horrible maledictions of the galley slaves, and the groaning of the timbers are mingled with the clank of chains. Calm itself has its inconveniences . . . [given] . . . the evil smells which arise.'

In fact, the ease of coastal sailing is often exaggerated. Help may be closer than when offshore, but so are the perils, and in bad weather a modern, well-found boat is often safer out to sea. For galleys and tramping merchantmen this was not such an option, making certain Mediterranean headlands, such as Cape Maléa in southern Greece, infamous lee shores – shores against which a boat could be pinned by the wind. Light summer conditions pose their own test, the wind along shore becoming almost as varied as the geography of the coast itself. Sea breezes sucked off the water by hot land come and go with the sun. Cool air from high ground cascades in katabatic gusts, bursting in on supposedly sheltered anchorages. Anabatic winds promising to waft a boat back to land expire as they hit the coastal mountain wall. Channels between islands become barrels for gusts. Two opposite winds may even run into one another. A former coast-guard we'd met on the beach in Porticcio had seen this happen: 'Two yachts, both with the wind right behind them, both flying their brightest spinnakers, and both heading towards each other. Figure that out! Just when they began to draw close to each other, their sails, more at less at once, collapsed – from opposite winds to no wind at all.' The phenomenon was marked enough for the Admiralty to put a special note on 'Opposing Winds' in its 1894 *Mediterranean Pilot*. 'It is observed in the western basin that counter winds are frequent, often blowing simultaneously from opposite quarters at no considerable distance apart, there being at the time a cloudless sky.'

It was midday when we finally rounded Pointe de la Castagna, just six miles from Porticcio. Sailing boats passed us regularly under motor, all canvas furled. So far, we'd managed to resist the temptation – this was a chance to see how the old-time trampers managed – but the sense of such powerlessness took getting used to. The facts were these: Porto Pollo was still twelve miles away and, at speeds of around one knot, twelve miles meant twelve hours – far slower than walking. When the wind died altogether, *Shamaal* also stopped. A slight puff and we might gain another 100 metres before halting again, Corsica as out of reach as if we'd been adrift mid ocean on a raft. More from habit than hope, we spent the afternoon tweaking sails, adjusting the weight by moving to one side, and whistling all manner of daft tunes. Even when cat's-paws began ruffling the water we were cautious and kept whistling. Then, something approaching a steady breeze. Could it be? Sails filled, rigging tightened and, miracles, *Shamaal* crept away.

In the end, we could have made Porto Pollo just before dark – provided we weren't fooled again by the wind – but the fight in us was gone. Instead, we'd break the journey in nearby Anse de Cacao, a dark cove under cliffs and the ruins of a Genoese watchtower. Coasting, there was always the temptation to go too far, especially here, where one headland offered itself up after the other. Arrive early enough and, if the place were inhabited – Porto Pollo, for example – we could row ashore and buy cold beer, fresh milk or any of the other luxuries that did not keep without a refrigerator on *Shamaal*. Or in deserted spots, such as Anse de Cacao, there'd be time for a swim, maybe a snorkel over the underwater caves and secret places where the fish liked to hide. Adèle was happy. My urge usually was to take the lure of the next bay.

Anchored with us in Anse de Cacao were three other vessels, one of them a substantial motor boat. Instead of the standard white, this had a silver sheen and the hull swept back at such an angle that the craft, even at anchor, appeared to be passing in a blur. 'Looks fast standing still,' as John Harty, my distant Irish relative and a champion horseman, once said of a sleek steed.

Every big Mediterranean harbour has a section devoted to these gas-guzzlers. This boat, named a Pershing, was big, but there were bigger still – boats more like ships, smug, gleaming ships. With veranda-style doors, showers, air conditioning, satellite films, freezers and fancy taps in the bathrooms, these marked the latest step in man's conquest of hardship. They made irresistible viewing. Usually moored stern to the quay, their innards lay open, and small groups of tourists would hang around half-watching, half-pretending not to, like people catching TV through a shop window. The pampered residents played a parallel game, pretending not to notice they were being watched, but doing nothing – including putting on more clothes – that would make the attention die. Most vessels and crews fell into one of two categories. There were the sunbathing machines where more or less beautiful, more or less youthful passengers turned themselves on a spit. And there were the floating executive hotel rooms, their saloons as desperately impersonal as the five-star suite, everything just so and just not. The Pershing was unusual both for its shape and ship's company. Sections of the deck had been opened in the same way a flying beetle raises its shell, and beneath, instead of wings, there was a fully equipped gym. Here, a bare-chested man of quite some age, but prodigious strength and fitness, strode away on the cross-country skiing machine. Nearby a young woman did sit-ups, while another man lifted weights. Down on the side decks, a pair of young men in white, evidently the crew, burnished those already shiny railings. An aura of wealth, eccentricity and something faintly evil surrounded the boat.

For audacity and style, we had to admire the Pershing, but this was an exception, for we'd come to consider motor boats the enemy. They brought the spirit of the big car to sea, literally driving, not sailing, their skippers too often forgetting the fraternal rule in which the captain of a dinghy equals that of a ship. Each day over the VHF radio the French coastguard pleaded for motor boats to keep their distance from slow, small craft, and each day these requests were ignored. The wash from a gin palace going ten times the speed of *Shamaal* simulated a miniature storm without wind. Food left plates, sails collapsed, unstowed binoculars took flight.

So monsters, then. Yet, even I had to admit, monsters that had an impeccable pedigree – the true descendants of the venerable galley. Not much resemblance, one might think, between these frivolous tubs and the sprightly Homeric warship, or the Roman quinquerime. But from a purely seagoing perspective, many qualities were shared: both a liability in storms, yet ideal for coast-hopping and shallow water; both swift, yet costing a fortune to run (slaves or diesel); and, above all, both truly independent, unlike we on *Shamaal*, from the wretched caprices of the wind.

Out from a supply stop at Propiano and across to Campomoro, a compact, cheerful and palm-shaded village under a castle, I could reflect how well the tramping life suited me. I liked the temporary nature of it all. I liked the leaving as much as the arriving. I liked always being a visitor. I'd have liked those professional coast-hoppers. Only, what on Earth was I trading? 'Every sailor, from captain to cabin-boy would have his bundle of merchandise on board,' Braudel wrote. 'It was not unusual for the master of a Corsican boat to arrive at Leghorn with a few casks of salted meat and a few cheeses, which he would sell in the streets of the city, regardless of the protests of the local shopkeepers.'

I hadn't sold anything in the streets since unloading twenty metres of unwanted anchor chain for a few quid back in Dover. Most business went the other direction. The wind may be free on a boat, but nothing else is. Not the many varied pieces of stainless steel, aluminium and bronze you find fixed to a boat. Nor the dozen or so ropes, some blue, some white, some red or green, snaking along the mast and deck. Not engine parts, nor the most humble, U-shaped shackle. Not a single strip of teak, not winch grease, marlin spikes, paintbrushes, wire ties, anodes, valves, fairleads, gimbals, nuts, glues, pumps, sea cocks, lanyards, bungs, bulbs . . . not the tiniest rivet. From a distance, the sailboat appears to be a simple machine. You could draw one without once removing pencil from paper. But those elegant lines mask a snarl of competing elements, their only common goal a long, inevitably losing campaign to resist the sea. Ultraviolet in the sun picks at every surface, burning, bleaching and weakening. The wind shakes loose sail stitching. Salt and dust worry at the interior of ropes. Sea water leaves nothing unharmed, worming beneath the skin of the hull and encouraging electrical currents that eat through submerged metals – a bronze propeller here, a chunk of stainless steel there. Damp spoils electronics. Teredo worms hunt greedily for anything wooden.

Indeed, we had far less reason than the sixteenth-century crews to rush ashore. Besides, we were happy in our little, floating cocoon. Who would disturb us? No one other than, perhaps, the occasional yachtsmen.

There is camaraderie among sailors based on the fact that at sea, as opposed to land, all are equal and bound to support one another. (A mayday call, to take the extreme case, legally obliges anyone within range to offer help.) Some yachtsmen, though, will extend this to mean a state of chumminess that, once on a boat, can be hard to escape. Socializing of this type often split down national lines. Americans, being generally gregarious and relatively rare in the Mediterranean, were most active. The arrival of a second yacht flying the Stars and Stripes in an anchorage was sure to spark a buzzing of dinghies and calls of 'How y'all doing?' Italian boats, always carrying what seemed to be too many people, could not bear to be separated. Swiss sailors, with the instinct of self-perpetuation occurring in unlikely creatures, were also not long kept apart. Many people do not sail for solitude – quite the opposite – and, for them, coasting is the very thing. The Red Ensign (*Shamaal* was registered in Britain) was what landed us in trouble. 'Saw the Red Duster and thought I'd just pop over to see how you were,' a complete stranger announced in Campomoro, his sunburnt face appearing over the side of our deck from his dinghy. 'Just being nosy, really,' explained another from under a white sun hat, cornering us into a session of small talk.

I fended off these visits as best I could. I wished sometimes I was more clubbable, but the nature of the tribal get-togethers made me uncomfortable. A scattered family had given me the passport of one country, accent of another, birth certificate of another, and names (and middle names) from at least three. To which ex-pat club should I belong? I preferred none, and in Adèle was lucky to have found the perfect accomplice. She, too, had a natural disinclination for pigeonholes. In England, she'd play up her French style; abroad, she'd often make first contacts in English. After half a lifetime living in Russia and England, she found the lines easy to blur. I'd long been used to people becoming confused over my origins, but in Marseille I witnessed the same thing happen to Adèle: a Frenchman with whom she was speaking French asking which country *she* came from. I was amazed and felt slightly guilty – as if she'd caught my disease.

Even British-built and -registered *Shamaal* was no longer so sure of her roots. Boats traditionally display their home port below the ship's name. 'Southampton', 'Cape Town', 'Newport', 'La Rochelle' – these words appear on sterns of cruising yachts all over the world, testimony to their origins and promises of eventual return. *Shamaal* used to have something similar: a wooden plaque bearing the initials of a Suffolk yacht club. But Adèle and I had no home port. The harbour we used in Essex had been only a staging post, easy to enter, easier still to leave. And, in *Shamaal*'s stern, just two empty screw holes remained.

No, we'd no need to envy those ashore in Campomoro: neither the tourists in the cafés, nor the locals waking to this enchanting scene every day. It was fine to stop for a day or a week, even better to have the freedom to leave. Ten kilos of anchor and a mound of chain and rope sound impressive enough, but swim over the anchor in the sand, trace that umbilical cord up through the water to the boat, and you soon see how tentative the whole arrangement is. It suited me well.

Leave or stay? The weather forecast would decide our fate. And not just ours: look around other boats at the time of the announcements on the VHF radio and there was never a soul to be seen. Every skipper was below, hoping for something good. Deadpan talk of a gale and the nerves tingled. A collective groan met the announcement of calms. This morning, in particular, they were promising good sea breezes: real winds, yet winds that by their nature must die with the sun that evening. Already the sun had rolled above the horseshoe cliffs. My trunks were dry from the morning dip. Not a moment to waste.

Just about every boat was getting ready to depart. Not knowing that we'd all just listened to the morning forecast, an onlooker on shore might well have wondered what had happened. He might give a nervous look about. Anchor winches grinding, chain rattling, sails snapping – the little squadron was clearing out. Off we all went, on down the coast, all tramping, all with our eye on the next place to call home.

A meeting

Warnings of a new mistral the following day sent us scurrying into Tizzano, set on a finger-shaped creek prodding into Corsica's southern flank. As soon as *Shamaal* had been safely anchored in the lee of a ruined fort, we set out in the rubber dinghy to explore. There was little to Tizzano. Rowing along the creek, we saw one partially paved street, two restaurants, a few summer villas and a half-dozen fishing boats bobbing under the harbour wall. Further, the water became shallow, less than half a metre in places, and the woods closed in on the sides. The inlet ended in an area of marshland surrounded by olives, oaks and giant reeds.

We had paused by a scrap of beach near the head of the creek when an ageing, bearish man, dark eyes in a massive head, emerged from the trees, probably, I thought, to tell us we had no right to land. Instead he smiled, reached into a bag and proffered three tomatoes. 'I saw you arrive in your boat and thought you might like these,' he said.

His name was Emile and he lived somewhere up beyond the ledge of rock overlooking the creek. His boat, a rickety skiff, was moored nearby. 'I'm a fisherman, retired now, but I still go out to lay nets,' he said. 'Just this and that for the table and my friends.' We asked about the reports of a mistral. Emile nodded. 'Looks that way and it could come down hard, but Tizzano is a good spot, so don't worry.' Turning on a pair of much-voyaged sandals, he disappeared through the bamboo and trees.

As predicted, the mistral hammered away the next three days, sweeping all in its path, from the rare cloud in the heavens to the dirt in the one street of Tizzano. *Shamaal* swung and yanked at her anchor chain. A much larger yacht lay parallel with us in the anchorage and, when the swinging brought our two boats to their closest point, we exchanged waves or raised a glass with the crew. A third boat arrived as the wind grew strong, and her crew made four increasingly desperate attempts to anchor, first dragging towards us, then towards our neighbours, then the rocks, before finally being pinned safely to the ground.

The second morning, we again bumped into Emile. As much the gentle giant as on the first occasion, he began to say we were welcome to fetch vegetables from his garden, then, as if he'd just remembered a previous idea, changed the invitation to dinner.

That evening, we rowed back to the head of the creek and pulled the dinghy ashore. The wind made a dervish of the dusty ground as we climbed up through the trees. Olive branches and reeds rasped like sea shingle and, above, a solitary bird glided through the eddies. Emile's place lay just along the path through a gate in that fence made of fishing nets. Our host was waiting. In the twilight I saw little until we were seated at a long, outdoor table lit by guttering lamps and candles. Guests, all of them fishermen, came shortly, one bearing home-made wine, another a boulder of goat cheese, another cigars. Cicadas and songbirds struck up, Emile's gnarled hand cracked the top on a huge bottle of pastis, and the moon drifted across the horizon.

As my eyes grew accustomed to the half-light of candles, oil lamps and moon, I was able to take in the surroundings. There was no house at all, yet nothing lacked; no walls, but many rooms; no windows, but the most charmed views . . . That fishing-net fence, itself glittering as if from some underwater grotto, had opened on to an enchanted scene. On one side, the little cliff descended to the creek where *Shamaal* hid from the mistral. On the other rose the myrtle- and rosemary-scented maquis of the Corsican mountainside. We sat in the middle, the table resting under a sheet draped between olive branches. Behind loomed an old caravan, apparently Emile's sleeping quarters.

Across some grass, bathed in the heavy musk of a fig tree, was the kitchen: a table and gas cooker from which sweet vapours snaked into the night. A pair of stone steps announced a terrace of gardens. Here beds of aubergine and tomato lay attended by harems of yellow and blue flowers. A long sofa stretched between vines.

Oil flames danced, trees swayed around the table. I asked Emile to explain how anyone could navigate in such winds.

'As a sailor you can't choose your wind and sometimes it will blow hard. Like now. In fact, all the people at this table have been caught out at sea in a mistral. Fearful times: boats rising and falling like toys, water pouring over the side, cabins breaking, men falling, fish crates sliding. Yet they must accept that this is the life of a fisherman. Anyway, it's also adventure, and I've always said that adventure is the only way to live, *n'est ce pas?*' Emile expounded with a relish not all his old cronies around the table seemed to share.

'Me, too,' I replied, 'I love adventure. But I don't know these winds enough. I get blown this way, that way, or nowhere at all. A devil of a sea to sail.'

'Ah, it's not in one day that you learn the secrets,' Emile replied. 'And what you see here in Tizzano is nothing. Go to the Strait of Bonifacio. It's said that's where the winds are born.'

Anyone who has travelled in the Mediterranean – away from the tourist parts – knows the feeling. A sight, a sound – and suddenly images of the ancient past, like buried memory retrieved in a dream, re-form. Tumbled columns, but just as easily a row of black cedars, can make millennia fall away. A remote chapel may well be constructed from the same blocks used for the Roman temple once there, itself originally a Greek shrine. These stones are the DNA of one family. There is timelessness in the features of a smallholder in deep rural Greece, his cottage, goats, donkey and dogs themselves transferred from a Homeric farm scene. And one only has to spend time in harbours, or better yet on boats, to glimpse the faces of the men that voyaged with

Odysseus. Feasting in this strange abode on ragout and roast wild boar (shot in the maquis by one of Emile's friends), it was this very sensation that I now had.

There was something heroic in the remnants of Emile's strength and in his tales of the sea and wind. Also in the style, poor as he was, in which he managed to live. This was not dinner in the orderly, slightly calculating way to which we in the north were accustomed, but a feast – a full-blooded feast in the spirit so dear to old Mediterranean man, or, rather, to the gods that he worshipped. Apparently these gatherings were a regular occurrence and, when it wasn't wild boar, it was lobster, mullet, octopus. Emile lived as if land and sea were under his charm.

'Maybe he's not even one of us,' Adèle whispered. Maybe not. If it had been antiquity, when mortals often encountered gods, I would have paid close attention to a man such as Emile. Sometimes the gods descended from Mount Olympus in recognizable form – Hermes in his golden winged sandals, Artemis with her bow and arrows – but often they came in disguise. Lusty Zeus had been known to transform himself into an ant, swan or beaver in pursuit of unwilling lovers; a young shepherd boy might turn out to be Aphrodite; a street cat, Artemis. Why not a fisherman? Between sips and gulps of pastis, Adèle and I began discreetly to trade names.

Zeus? I shook my head: Emile didn't look like one of the Olympus jet set. He lacked the refinements of Apollo or the cruelty of Ares. He was not enough of a smart arse for Hermes.

Dionysus? I tried. Yes – almost! We had only to sit drunkenly between the vines and sea to imagine the arrival of wine-swilling goat-men. Maybe something, too, of Hephaestus, who for all his ugliness and humiliations possessed the strength and spirit of invention so clearly present in Emile.

But surely, Adèle whispered, it had to be a sea god. Poseidon? Emile had the broad chest and raging hair – the temper, too, on occasion, one suspected – and as for the trident, well, any Corsican fisherman was as comfortable hunting with the instrument today as his ancestors had been millennia ago. Yet haughty Poseidon, brother of Zeus and ruler of a great part of the world, would never have been so gracious.

I recollected the picture of a Roman mosaic I had in a book back in England. Emile was missing the beard, true, but in every other respect the features matched that image. The same unruly locks, the bull neck, fierce eyes and a mouth that was easy to imagine issuing a mighty gale. Aeolus. The coincidence was only more striking with regard to descriptions in *The Odyssey*. For, apart from imprisoning the winds, Aeolus had been famous for his hospitality and aid to passing seamen – Emile again. Even the nightly dinners were as described in Homer: 'They are always feasting . . . and the courtyard echoes to the sounds of banqueting within.'

When one of the fishermen made a toast, they cheered: '*A Emile!*' But holding high my glass of pastis, a tiny cloud in the fiery night sky, I was able quietly to say, so that only Adèle heard: '*A Eole!*' – to Aeolus!

Fishermen may have lost the sail-handling skills of their fore-fathers, but still no one understands the seascape better, so I was pleased when Emile's best friend Jeannot invited us to join him the next day for a view of the mistral from his boat *Mare e Ventu*.

Most of Tizzano's fishermen were tinkering. Only *Mare e Ventu*, Corsican for 'Sea and Wind', went out in gales. Near the start of the pier, a man with a sombrero sorted his basket of lines; a scarred individual contemplated his blackened engine; further along, a handsome, broad-shouldered youngster readjusted the mooring ropes of his small, blue wooden vessel. On *Mare e Ventu*, towards the far end, no one was visible, but from within the hull came constant, impassioned whistling – the joyful movement from something classical. Presently the whistling stopped. Jeannot's weathered face emerged from what had to be the engine compart-ment, scrutinized us briefly and lit up. 'Hello, young ones! Isn't life beautiful?'

Soon, we, the whistling captain and his burly Portuguese mate, Antonio, were powering at high speed from Tizzano into the fairground of waves. With a Force 7 wind blowing, the sea heaped fiercely off Pointe de Lattoniccia. But *Mare e Ventu* did not slow down and Jeannot did not stop whistling, except for when he sang. 'He always loves music,' Antonio said. 'It keeps him calm.' All day we hared round picking up nets laid a few days before. The first came up empty, the second brought only five or so fish. The third was better, with a spider crab and spiny lobster or two, but the fourth had been attacked by dolphins, and all the nets were hard work. To me, the seemingly endless nets sliding in over the bow could not possibly be as empty as they all were, but Jeannot and Antonio had learnt to live with small rewards.

The nets lay on the seabed a mile or more apart at about 200-metre depths, the only indication of their presence being small, orange surface buoys that were practically invisible in the rough waves. Jeannot, though, would fire *Mare e Ventu* from one set to the next without hesitation – and without looking once at the GPS in the steering cabin. His direction-finding technique was as old as sailing in the Mediterranean. 'We pass those two rocks. Then on that headland is where Emile once built a cabin, and over there is where we've got a friend always sitting on her sofa. Our fish are opposite the sofa.' The apparently barren stretch of Corsican coast was, in Jeannot's eyes, a landscape full of identity, right down to the unseen sofas and friends. This was coastal pilotage as recorded in the most ancient sources. As early as 500 BC, the Phoenicians had sophisticated guides to the North African coast, where they'd set up watering and trading points every fifty miles, or a day's sail. Homer, too, includes many details of this type of navigation, the witch Circe preparing no less than four pages of instructions for Odysseus' coastal passage into the Straits of Messina – fantastic instructions, full of monsters and gods, but seaman-like advice all the same.

I noticed Jeannot gave about as much time to the VHF weather forecasts as to his GPS. 'First,' he said, 'Antonio and I go out in almost *any* weather. Secondly, we are used to keeping an eye on what's happening. You learn many signs. For example, when a cloud sits on the top of that mountain over there – we say it's when the old man puts on his hat – that warns there'll be strong west to north-west winds. Then to know if the sirocco's coming, you check for cattle coming down from their fields on Rocapina.' He paused for effect. 'Really. They come towards the sea for cooler air. You know, one day the big beach there was so dark with bodies we thought there must be an invasion of sunbathers. We motored over to see and what did we find? Not tourists, my young friends, but cows – hundreds of cows all over the beach!'

By the end of the day, Jeannot and Antonio had filled a basket with a variety of fish, several of them grotesque, even partly poisonous creatures. They wouldn't be staying out after dark. 'Not like the fishing on the Atlantic back home,' said Antonio. 'In Portugal, they often go out for many days at a time. It's hard. They catch more fish, but they don't see their families, while we're always home at night.' Antonio and Jeannot took only a day off a week and at home were as busy growing vegetables as at sea they were catching fish. So they worked hard, but to an unchangeable rhythm, the heartbeat of the old Mediterranean. And they had insurance – against bad seas and bad people, as Jeannot said: a talisman of goat's horns mounted over the steering cabin of *Mare e Ventu*.

By early the next day, the mistral had mellowed, and so for one last time we climbed into the dinghy and rowed up the creek.

Emile sat outside his caravan. The place looked less magical in harsh sunlight – the net fence ragged, the sofa overused and the flowers perhaps weeds. Emile, though, beamed at seeing us and was sad when we said we would set sail. A true Corsican to the last, he made sure we left with an armful of various vegetables and other gifts from the unlikely cornucopia of his caravan.

We sailed out of the anchorage without switching on the motor and in half an hour were clear of the coast. About two miles offshore, we recognized the angular silhouette of *Mare e Ventu*. Jeannot and Antonio were hauling in nets. As we drew closer, Jeannot's whistling became audible. Something light, yes, Charles Trenet. *'Ya d' la joie . . .'* Our boats came alongside: *Shamaal* silent, except for a flapping mainsail, *Mare e Ventu* chugging in neutral.

'*Salut*, young sailors!' Jeannot shouted.

'Same to you, old man! How's fishing?'

'Terrible – almost nothing.'

The wind began to pull us apart. Jeannot bent down for a second. 'Hey, take this!' The Corsican threw a plastic bag, caught by Adèle. Inside, three dorades and a small, live lobster. Wind and waves tugged again. *'Bon vent!'* we cried.

II

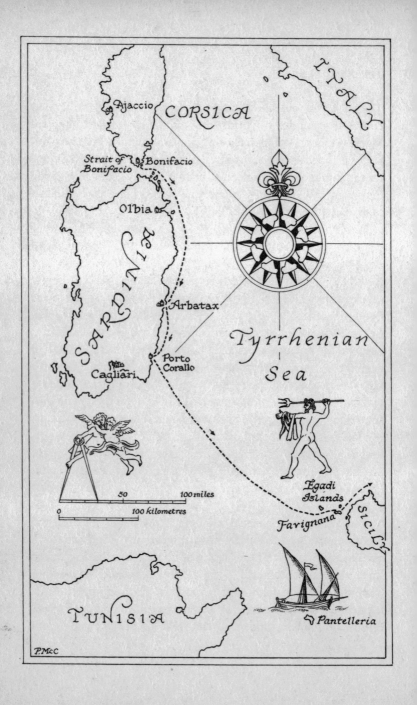

ITALY

CORSICA

Ajaccio

Strait of
Bonifacio

Bonifacio

Olbia

SARDINIA

Arbatax

Tyrrhenian

Sea

Porto
Corallo

Cagliari

50   100 miles

0   100 kilometres

Egadi
Islands

Favignana

SICILY

TUNISIA

Pantelleria

P.McC

The cradle of wind

The idea that all winds might issue from a single source is common around the world. Iroquois, Inuit, Japanese, Mayan, Maori, Chinese, Polynesians – all nourish myths of secret chambers, sacks and seers and priests that command the gales. Mediterranean winds were imprisoned in Aeolus' cave, but in Uganda they were believed to lie under the sacred hill Kahola, and in Malaysia at the peak of Batu Balok.

Bonifacio's claim was of purely local origin – there has never been any wider tradition that Aeolus or any other wind god lived there – but easy enough to understand given the setting. The strait between southern Corsica and northern Sardinia is barely seven miles wide, a stone mouth with a hundred ragged teeth. Bonifacio on the north side and the Sardinian resort of Porto Cervo on the south-east frame a high-rent tourist mall, summer home to the Italian Riviera and Hollywood sets. Mick Jagger had been there, Naomi Campbell was just leaving, Colonel Qaddafi's son was getting bad publicity . . . But the strait is as much a playground for the winds, a chicane, distorting normal wind into something more brutal and conjuring breeze from the stillest air. My sailing directions cautioned: 'The Strait of Bonifacio tends to funnel and increase the strength of winds so that a friendly Force 4 on the Corsican or Sardinian coast becomes a not-so-friendly Force 5–6 in the strait. If gales are predicted for the area it is best to run for cover.'

The harbour of Bonifacio, a fjord-like incision through the limestone of Corsica's southern tip, gives every impression of a mythological scene. The inlet is a full mile long, snaking under sheer cliffs and the citadel of the old town, but the slit opening from the sea remains invisible until the final approach. As it happened, *Shamaal* arrived off this secret haven in a deep calm. But the calm fell so suddenly – as if we'd run out of petrol uphill on a motorway – that the very lack of air seemed to be a signal. Just a quarter hour before we'd been clipping past Cap de Feno heeled under full sail, a frothy wake on our stern, a crisp set of waves at the bow. The last stretch was made to the thudding, unexpected accompaniment of the diesel.

Soon the skies were back to old tricks, with a westerly gale starting on the second of our four days' stay. There are established ways of estimating wind strength. Admiral Beaufort's venerable system and the varying pitch of whistling in steel rigging are only two. In Bonifacio, the indicators were endless. A beach umbrella bolting from its owners. Minidresses of the beautiful people refusing to stay down. Towels on balconies refusing to stay up. Palm trees in panicked motion. Postcard stands in a spin. Napkins, tablecloths, even whole tables taking flight along the quay. In other words, blowing hard: somewhere near the top of the scale. These were three days when not a boat left the fold and any new arrival, limping in from the strait like a straggler from a defeated army, provoked surprise and a hint of *schadenfreude*.

If the wind was not born in Bonifacio, then where? Mythologists have their explanation, scientists theirs – and the latter is no less fantastic. The natural philosopher will turn first to our life-giving star. Striking sideways and unevenly, the sun heats the Earth in bands – the equatorial regions on high flame, temperate latitudes at a simmer and the poles almost off the fire altogether – and it is in these discrepancies that wind and all weather is born. The word 'climate' comes from the Greek for zone of latitude, *klima*. Essentially, where the Earth heats most, hot tropical air rises, making a slow circle to the north and south. Nature, abhorring a vacuum, sends the heavy, sinking cold air of the barely heated poles into the space left behind. Limited to this pattern, the main winds of the world would blow constantly more or less north and south as long as the sun burned. But because the Earth spins from west to east, anything moving north or south, including air, finds itself bending to the sides. Through this Coriolis effect, the straight up-and-down pattern of winds mutates into a remarkably systematic set of belts. Westerlies blow along roughly latitudes 35 to 70, for example, where England and New Zealand lie; easterlies sweep the two poles; north-easterlies and south-easterlies rule the trade-wind latitudes; and in between – the equatorial doldrums – nothing much helpful blows at all.

That is the essence of world wind, but only the essence. Because land heats faster than sea, and one type of land heats faster than another, and neither land nor sea is spread remotely equally, this basic solar cookery becomes a varied affair. Nevertheless, as scientists guessed long before they really knew why, the wind is whipped up by the spinning of the sun, Earth and oceans. The Roman naturalist Pliny the Elder was on the right track 2,000 years ago when he wrote: 'the sun's rays scorch and strike everywhere on Earth in the middle of the universe and, broken, bounce back and take with them all that they have drunk. Steam falls from on high and again returns on high. Empty winds violently swoop down and go back with their plunder. . . . The Earth pours breath back to the sky as if it were a vacuum.' The medieval scholar Hildegard of Bingen believed the winds held all the elements together, each wind a wing of God working to keep the firmament, the fires and waters in the rightful place. Another medieval writer, Gervase of Tilbury, wrote that 'mountains and water cause winds', while William of Conches expounded the notion that four great ocean currents were responsible for whipping up the four cardinal winds.

Such theories at least grasped the global nature of wind and the vital role of water, which in one form or other distributes heat around the planet, so making Earth liveable. In fact, a good way to understand the great wind systems is as rivers of air rushing high around the world. Like a river of water, the rivers of the sky run neither straight nor smooth. The uneven riverbed, in this case littered with deep ocean pools, continents, deserts, forests and mountain chains, distorts the flow. So does the seasonal heating and cooling of land and sea as the sun moves slightly further north or south. The exchange of equatorial warm air and polar cool air is far from neat. Because two different masses of air do not easily mix, they begin to wrestle, creating turbulence much like the eddies formed when cold milk is poured into a cup of hot tea. As the eddy spins its way along the general stream, one part brings rain, another just cloud, another cold air and clear skies.

These eddies are what most people call weather. The dramas of the very high winds are almost as removed from the layman as the gales raging through space – the jet streams that wreathe Jupiter, the red dust swirling around Mars or the storms of unimaginable violence battering Saturn. It is the eddies that produce the wind in our sails. Move into a warm sector and the air will be rising. Barometric pressure drops and air is sucked into the sky, to be replaced by cooler air around the outside. This is wind. In a cold sector, the heavy air sinks, spreads like a spilled drink, greatest in pressure at the centre, and flows outward towards the lower pressure. More wind. A temporary eddy – formed today, dispersed the next – will produce lighter wind. An eddy that has time, say, while stuck in a convenient little corner like a bay or row of mountains, develops greater differences in pressure and so stronger winds.

So where in this merry-go-round does the Mediterranean fit? The clear heavens and winds over the deck of *Shamaal* seemed out of sync. Even weather maps, which chart the wind by showing where pressure is high and where it is low, often made no sense. Where one would have imagined a map covered in whirlpools of isobars and fronts, the one in Bonifacio's harbour office during the days of our enforced stay was all but blank. In other words, according to the meteorological authorities of France, there was no vacuum here to abhor – therefore no wind. The brass-cased barometer screwed to the main bulkhead in *Shamaal* also stared back without emotion. Barometers simply measure atmospheric pressure – a rapid rise or fall means one has entered one of those eddies. Yet so often our instrument was comatose. You tapped the glass to move the needle. It didn't budge. Tap again. No change. Outside, lunatic clouds gathered: flying saucers, broken plates, exploding balls. The palm trees danced, the water fizzed. Tap away. The gale came and went.

Some of the answer to this enigma lies in the unique geography of the inland sea. Just as the Atlantic tides are blocked from the Mediterranean, so, too, is much of the weather associated with the Atlantic and the European continent. Partly the Mediterranean is a fortress of peninsulas and mountain chains, partly one of the huge permanent system of high pressure and weak winds that inhabits an area centred roughly on the Azores. The net result is that in summer the weather is invariably hot and clear – for all intents, there is no weather at all. When outside weather does get through, it takes on a Mediterranean flavour. For example, an ordinary depression stuck in the Gulf of Genoa creates north-west winds in France, which are then transformed by the Rhône valley into the fierce mistral. Often – the tramontana and bora are two other examples – this is the pattern: a lesser wind is transformed by the corridors through which it enters the sea.

On a more localized scale, the variations become endless. Corsica may record simultaneously a Force 6 or 7 on the west coast, calm on the east coast and a gale in the Strait of Bonifacio – places only a few dozen miles apart. Strange as this sounds, the causes are simple. If a strong wind hits Corsica's west coast, the Strait of Bonifacio will funnel it into something worse, while the mountainous centre protects the east coast. Also, in summer a Mediterranean island will heat so rapidly it creates its own wind rushing from the sea. Therefore the already strong wind on the west coast of Corsica will receive a boost, while on the east coast the westerly wind and incoming sea breeze will collide, quite possibly cancelling each other out.

Likewise, the northern neck to the Strait of Messina creates strong winds in a north–south direction. The Strait of Gibraltar, principal gateway to the outside world, directs and strengthens winds either directly east, the levanter, or west, the poniente. And on a still smaller scale, there are almost countless such wind chambers, every mountain valley, cliff-bound island or narrow gulf a potential source. Greece's etesian, now usually called by its Turkish name, meltemi, may be one of the most regular seasonal winds in the Mediterranean, but even this varies immensely in strength and direction, depending on the tortuous layout of the Aegean.

Such was the uncharted world through which we sailed.

'Going out?'

'That's right.'

'Maybe you should wait another day.'

'It's meant to tail off tonight – haven't you seen the forecast up at the harbour office?'

'This is Bonifacio – *soyez prudents.*'

Our concerned neighbour on the quay was a neat man, good with knots and the like, his boat shiny clean. It was a shallow-bottomed motor boat he used for fishing, and I could have told him that *Shamaal* was a thousand times more seaworthy. But we were used to this kind of attention.

Invariably *Shamaal* would be one of the smallest boats, always lower in the water and shorter than her neighbours. The largest winch for hauling in sails was the size of the most diminutive on other yachts, the mast two-thirds the height. And, having only the tiniest sink and limited water supplies, Adèle and I were often to be seen ferrying buckets of dirty plates and pans to and from the public taps on the quay. Yet the same lack of comforts aboard translated into strength and seaworthiness the equal of many a larger vessel. The low cabin roof made a bunker against rain and sea. The small windows were stronger than large ones. The lack of space inside made it harder to fall down when the boat rolled in waves. Most importantly, the slender hull visible above water masked a thick rudder and giant keel below. Just over half of the vessel's weight had been plugged into that keel, a ratio of ballast to boat found on few craft. Built in the old English way, built to last, to take on the world, *Shamaal* was truly a survivor.

So we listened to our neighbour's solicitude with a light heart. Having climbed up to the edge of the old town early that morning, we were aware what sort of wind blew: enough to snatch the froth of a cappuccino from Adèle's lips. The sea in the strait had looked broken, lumpy and frozen still, as it always does from high up. Yet the French weather report was emphatic: things would calm down tonight. Making use of the strong wind behind us, we'd be able to reach Olbia, our first Sardinian port, around sundown. After our long tramping down the Corsican coast, it was time to make ground. I was already looking beyond Sardinia – to Sicily and the Aeolian Islands north of Sicily. Many sea miles lay ahead.

'We'll be fine,' I said. 'Our boat looks after us.' In the back of my mind I realized this was precisely the kind of comment people made before running into trouble, but we wouldn't turn back. The last mooring line was undone. We surrendered our precious slot in the marina and under a dozen pairs of curious eyes began slowly to chug towards the open sea. '*Soyez prudents*,' chorused our old neighbour. We cast one last look at the cosy safety of Bonifacio.

Letting go

Not all is doom in *The Odyssey*, even after the fiasco with the sack of winds. Odysseus finds the year spent on Circe's island (and in Circe's bed) so pleasant that his crew have to remind him the objective was to return to Ithaca. There are also periods of regular boredom, such as the six-day passage to the land of the giant Laestrygonians, when 'the heart was taken out of my men by the wearisome rowing'. However, most of the epic revolves around the theme of good fortune unexpectedly and suddenly turning sour, the opening of the sack of winds being a typical episode. The Greeks' arrival among the Laestrygonians is another. 'We found an excellent harbour,' Odysseus recounts, 'closed in on all sides by an unbroken ring of precipitous cliffs, with two jutting headlands facing each other at the mouth so as to leave only a narrow channel in between.' The harbour was so enclosed that the ships did not even need to tie up. Yet when the Laestrygonians attacked, that same haven became a trap and, unable to escape, most of the Greek fleet and its men were destroyed.

Cliff-bound Bonifacio has often been identified as Homer's model for the harbour of the Laestrygonians, but that wasn't the only reason this story came to mind as we headed into the straits. For the sea is the most fickle of surfaces and its dangers deceptive, often a surprise – in a word, Homeric. White foam patches give good warning of submerged rocks near a coast, but on windy days, when the sea is full of whitecaps, the telltale foam is lost in the false alarms. The rocks lie in wait. Rocks like those we passed fringing the Iles Lavezzi, two miles off Corsica, where a century and a half ago the French frigate *La Sémillante* foundered with the loss of all 773 aboard. At sea, small problems spin perversely from control. A yacht may run aground on a sandbank with little damage, only to remain stuck fast as the weather turns foul. A fierce, unexpected wind may turn what appeared to be the perfect anchorage into as much of a trap as the 'excellent harbour' of the Laestrygonians. A person may fall overboard and find, even in light winds, his boat sailing away faster than he can swim. People have drowned *next* to their boats simply because they had no way of climbing back up.

Behind the wheel of a car we take it for granted that a second's lapse of concentration may lead to annihilation, while on boats most things happen relatively slowly. (Losing a man overboard is an exception.) Then there are perils that no driver will know, and these are what fill sailing with mystique. Not dangers resulting from a mechanical or human error, but from outside elements: the waves, the tide and wind – above all, the wind. If the car is a symbol of human mastery, the storm at sea reveals our weakness. Most sailors, carefully picking the right seasons and weather windows, seldom need meet the fury of nature. But occasionally they do, and above all they always know that they *might*. It is like living under a volcano. There is also a mythical element to shipwrecks, for while car crashes, suicides, even fires leave some sort of relic, the drowned seaman and his vessel can vanish, literally be 'lost at sea'. Drowning is a lonely death. The passengers and crew from *La Sémillante* were unusual in having a nearby witness: a shepherd on one of the deserted Lavezzi islets. It happened, however, that he was a leper and through his deformed mouth barely able to recount the horror of what he had seen.

Late afternoon, we shot into the Tyrrhenian Sea. Behind, the last islets of the Strait of Bonifacio glittered white in the descending sun. Ahead, the headlands of east Sardinia paraded south like bathing elephants. 'Let's keep on?' Adèle had read my mind. Why stop for the night in Olbia, as intended, when going like this? Careering down wave fronts, squeezing through troughs and leaping southward, *Shamaal* definitely didn't want to stop. Adèle and I watched spellbound. 'Yes, let's keep on.' The wind began to veer from west to north. A following wind: Aeolus would abet our plan.

The physical exhilaration was only part of the reason to continue. There is a twisted satisfaction in giving the slip to one perfectly good port after another. Isola Caprera, Cala di Volpe, the anchorage behind Capo Figari and, soon, Olbia – in turn each of our safe havens fell behind. We felt as if we already knew these places. The guidebooks had every detail. The good restaurants, the smell in the harbour, the friendliness or not of the officials, the availability of showers, loos, washing machines, the prices (everything came down to prices) – each minute of a brief stay in port could be listed and budgeted in advance. Ahead lay only the night, waves and the deserted massif of one of the Mediterranean's most ironbound coasts.

The wind, as forecast that morning in Bonifacio, had eased off a good bit and, besides, it blew from astern, which always calms a boat. So I gave little thought at sunset to the thin line of cloud appearing on the north-west horizon. Adèle climbed down into the cabin and cranked the VHF for the evening Italian weather forecast. It would be reassuring to know what they said. From the dark cockpit, I could see one part of Adèle's face in the soft, red glow of the night light. To our right, the shore around Olbia sparkled. Ahead and to the left the sea moved invisibly. 'I think I've got it.' Adèle sounded mystified. 'But the way they do the forecast is weird – I'm not sure I took it down right. Maybe you should have a go.'

Each country's marine forecast has its quirks: Britain's is punctual, read by real people, but reptilian in its sangfroid; France's is unexpectedly chaotic and broadcast by a brutal computerized voice; Italy's, at least for the uninitiated, is plain bewildering. Evidently it is most complete, covering all the western Mediterranean, with wind, sea state, cloud and visibility predictions for four days ahead. But where in that maze were we? Read at dictation speed and consisting mostly of numbers – 'one', for example, meaning a calm sea, 'four' a rough sea – the result resembled an encrypted message. Once finished in Italian, a harp chord sounded and the entire broadcast was repeated in English, barely audible, the meaning no clearer and, oddly, several sections missing. Another harp chord and back to Italian. Add the mesmerizing sound of unfamiliar but evocative vocabulary and the simple message began to wrap itself into a riddle. *Est* and *ovest*, east and west, sound more similar amid radio static than they look. *Burrasca* can only mean violent winds – we didn't have to search through our weather vocabulary in the pilot book for that. *Moderato* and *forte* speak for themselves, but what about *debole*? A word association game played in the dark at sea on a small boat will never be the same as in the cosy nest of the car or home. My guesses were 'debilitate' and 'devil', but *debole* means weak. *Mosso, molto mosso?* These words kept recurring and with such Italian feeling, such rolling, singsong passion, but we didn't know they meant 'rough' and 'very rough'! My initial word association for *mosso* was foam. I had in mind one of those trendy coffees in London – 'I'll have one *caffè mosso* and one *molto mosso* to go, please.' Actually I'd been on the right track, but it was foam across the Tyrrhenian sea that was meant.

'All right, then, what did *you* hear?'

'North-east Force 4 tonight and tomorrow.' Adèle appeared surprisingly sure. 'And you?'

I hesitated. 'North-east Force 7 to 8 – gale.'

'Let's listen again?'

Adèle and I swapped places. The notepad on the chart table filled with numbers, wind directions, crossings-out and question marks.

'I'm sure they're saying *sette-otto*.'

'No, I heard *quattro*.'

We drove south, the wind increased and, in the cabin, the green light of the radio, our travelling oracle, shone unsteadily.

Shamaal plunged into the night, both sails reefed to a minimum, the boat seesawing through erratic waves at five knots. On deck, we moved in slow motion, using hands and knees to balance. Below, the stove swung on its gimbals, a stack of plates knocking rhythmically against the bulkhead. At the chart table I tried to envision the hidden landscape outside. The yellow border of land on the chart of east Sardinia looked friendly enough, but I guessed that dawn would reveal a wall of rocks and high cliffs. There was no longer doubt about the wind. Already it blew between Force 5 and 6, and the growing seas suggested we were in for much more. Olbia, one of the last places easy to enter, was now far behind, but I felt no regret, no wish to be tucked safely along a quay. Enough of tramping. Now was the time to feel the wider measure of the sea.

There is great, rare purity in this kind of travel. We did not even know where we would stop, or when, and we didn't much care. We were travelling not to arrive, but to keep moving. And that, however fleeting, is a kind of freedom that is impossible to achieve easily on land. Casually to abandon roads, phones, television, advertising, shops, bars, sewers, lifts, newspapers, buses, policemen, schools, politicians, laptops, pills, dentists . . . Well, everything – how long would it take? How far would you have to walk from your home in London or New York? How far would you have to drive, even if the car didn't tie you to all you were trying to escape? In a boat, a brief decision sufficed. The wilderness was all around us.

Movement for pleasure – the idea would have been incomprehensible to most people just two centuries ago, not to mention in the Homeric age. The very idea of a sea cruise (or even a swim) was practically unheard of, just as nobody climbed mountains for fun and only the few travelled on holiday. There is barely any record of sailing for the hell of it in the Mediterranean – Catallus' poems and a remarkable account of a regatta by Virgil are early exceptions – until the nineteenth century, and even then it remained rare. When the Bostonian Joshua Slocum became the first man to circumnavigate the world alone at the end of the nineteenth century, the fact he'd set out at all was remarkable enough. Yachting at the time was still the preserve of heirs and tycoons, while Slocum was just a career seaman who late in life decided to travel. Selling up in retirement and buying a yacht: today the idea is a cliché.

One of the earliest to catch the bug for unnecessary journeys was Percy Bysshe Shelley. Boats had no practical use for the Romantic poet, but they proved a form of escape, as they so often are, from his febrile life in Italy. In the dreadful summer of 1822, his wife Mary had had a miscarriage and a close friend's illegitimate daughter (the supposed father, Lord Byron, though it may have been Shelley) had died in the convent where she was being raised. Shelley also suffered from writer's block, heavy debts, nerves and foreboding that the eccentric English colony in Italy of which he and Byron were the centre was soon to break up. The idea of building two boats, the open-decked schooner *Don Juan* for himself and a larger vessel named *Bolivar* for the show-off Byron, promised salvation.

More than fifty years later, the adventurer Edward Trelawny would recall in his *Records of Shelley, Byron and the Author* how he found the young, otherworldly poet in 'ecstasy' with his new toy on the Bay of Spezia. 'Not more than 30 feet long', according to Trelawny, in other words a little longer than *Shamaal*, with two masts and two tonnes in ballast, *Don Juan* was a speedy craft. Overexcited, the poet and his pal Edward Williams began talking of the 'Mediterranean as a lake too confined and tranquil. . . . They longed to be on the broad Atlantic, scudding under bare poles.' So the stern and masts were extended to take still more sail and *Don Juan*, which had no covered deck, was transformed from a pocket racer into a thoroughly dangerous boat. Like 'a vessel of 50 tonnes,' Williams boasted.

Trelawny, while playing down his role in this madness, admitted his apprehension. Williams, despite experience in the Royal Navy, was not a natural seaman, while Shelley, whose time aboard was spent reading Plato or working on his unfinished poem *The Triumph of Life*, was 'uncommonly awkward'. Their only help, the lad Charles Vivian, knew what he was doing – but only did what he was told.

On 8 July 1822, when Shelley, Williams and the boy embarked the last time, a hot and oily calm enveloped Livorno. It was seven weeks since *Don Juan* had been delivered. A black streak to the south-west, the omen of an approaching squall, marked the sky. Fishermen were scurrying for shelter in their smacks as Shelley, dressed in a navy reefer jacket, white nankeen trousers and black leather boots, left under full sail. At 6.30 p.m. the squall struck, its fiercest period, according to Trelawny, lasting only twenty minutes, before breaking into gusty wind and lightning. Already, *Don Juan* had vanished.

How the boat sank has never been resolved. Some reports pointed to a collision, even that in a case of mistaken identity *Don Juan* had been run down by Genoese sailors hoping to board and rob Lord Byron's *Bolivar*. This was Trelawny's view. Count John Taaffe, an Irish literary dabbler known as the Laureate of Pisa, quoted an Italian captain with a different story: that *Don Juan* simply foundered under excessive canvas in the high winds. To an offer of rescue, 'a shrill voice, which is supposed to have been Shelley's, was distinctly heard to say "NO"'. When the Italians begged the English to reef their sails, 'one of the gentlemen (Williams it is believed) was seen to make an effort to lower the sails – his companion seized him by the arm as if in anger'.

The sea is poetic, but poets do not necessarily make good seamen.

Dawn illuminated foam-streaked seas and the oyster-shell silver of distant Sardinian cliffs. My off-watch ended as the sun came glaring, but I had hardly slept and could only wish Adèle luck as she left the cockpit for her own three hours of rest. 'Bed' was the sea berth opposite the chart table. You climbed in, lower legs wedged under the sink, and tied yourself down with a canvas cloth to stop rolling across the cabin. It was like sleeping through an earthquake.

Outside, the clear skies and early morning sun appeared cheerful, but the north-east wind whooped through the rigging. The anemometer held above my head recorded Force 7, a near gale. Waves rolled down from astern, watery boulders the size of *Shamaal*, either from due north or sneaking through from the east. Mostly they overtook straight under the rudder, lifting *Shamaal* end to end, and obscuring for a few seconds Capo Comino to our rear. Often, waves broke at the crests, the dark blue mass of water feathering into a curtain of green before shattering, white effervescence cascading down its face. Some broke against *Shamaal*'s quarter, showering the cockpit. First a strong thump that in the cabin sounded like a sledgehammer, then the hiss and bubble of escaping froth.

Sailing under nothing more than a small foresail we continued for the next two hours at four and a half knots. If napping while tied into a shaking bunk was difficult, then eating had become an ordeal. Adèle battled the paraffin cooker, but was sick three times before a cup of coffee could be made. Eventually she produced a potato salad that we ate with biscuits, every mouthful that stayed down a minor triumph. By midmorning, a full gale blew. We were down to the storm jib, which is the size of a towel, and by midday no sail at all – and still bounding south at three and a half knots on the flat, six knots down the waves. 'Force 8. Big seas, many breaking,' I wrote in the logbook. 'No sail. Taking occasional water over stern. Trying to avoid surfing – doing six knots on waves.'

To run before a gale in a boat steered by wind vane is something like an out-of-body experience – you are bystander and participant at the same time. Dry inside our oilskins and attached by lifelines to the boat, we appeared to be travelling in a magic cocoon through the storm. Yet the sea, so deep a blue you'd expect a dipped hand to return painted, rushed only centimetres under the gunwales. Sometimes the wider view, a good 360-degree turn, was breathtaking: everything jumping and heaving and rolling, and little *Shamaal*, her shade of blue so much more friendly, sliding straight through the middle. Rising and falling, we'd become part of the waves, and with no sail, yet still shooting forward, part of the wind – so much part of the wind that the voyage was almost beyond our control.

Leave a plank in a rough sea and, apart from up and down, it will hardly move. Give the plank a push at the right moment and it will join the wave, accelerating at remarkable speed: that is surfing. A sailing boat moving with the wind will not automatically catch waves in this manner but, when it does happen, the effect can be dangerous. In a rare worst case, the boat 'pitchpoles' – in other words, accelerates down the wave at such a steep angle that the bow digs into the trough and the stern is flipped over by the wave behind. The somersault is almost certain to wreck the mast and probably the cabin, so sinking the boat. Far more common is for the boat to scoot down the wave front, then sheer sideways to the wind in the trough, leaving the side of the hull exposed to the force of the following wave. This is broaching. A bad broach will knock the boat on to her side, or even roll her all the way over. If the waves are big enough, the forces may again break the rig or boat.

The main secret to managing high winds and waves – as Shelley perhaps understood, yet hated – is to reduce sail area and so speed. Reef sails, furl them: allow the wind to blow past. With skilful helming and the right boat (a long keel like *Shamaal*'s would help), it is possible to surf without broaching. A boat, in theory, could tear down one wave, keep a steady path, then catch the next like a Hawaiian surfer on a perpetual roll. But this strategy, demanding wave-by-wave concentration, was not for us. We slowed as best we could, took down the last sail, closed hatches, cockpit lockers – anything that would open and fill with water if we were to be knocked down – and clipped ourselves to lifelines. Then, with the wind vane steering, we sat back, spectators to the duel between the sea and *Shamaal*.

The unquiet grave

I was once a journalist in the region of California where deep, steep-sided irrigation canals crisscrossed the countryside and it was not uncommon for people to fall in and then, unable to climb out, drown. The corpse of the recently drowned is peculiarly disturbing, either puffy and bloated, or horrible in its softness and absence of wounds. There is also the suggestion in a drowned corpse of the waking dead – that the victim interred in water has returned to be buried again. This was the experience in June 1799 of Ferdinand, the Bourbon king, who found himself confronted by a man executed and sunk in the Bay of Naples several days before. Admiral Caracciolo was an old friend who'd betrayed Ferdinand during his brief overthrow by French-backed republicans. It was Lord Nelson, the Bourbons' British saviour, who ordered this rebel to be hanged from the yardarm of HMS *Minerva*, then dropped into the sea. How Caracciolo could have resurfaced is unclear, for more than his own weight in iron shot had been attached to his legs. But up he came, eyes bulging and, because of the weights, in a standing position, half out of the water and, so onlookers fancied, seemingly making for shore. Horrified, and already unstrung by events, Ferdinand ordered the corpse be towed to land for proper burial.

In the case of Shelley and Williams, it took ten days after the wreck of *Don Juan* before their remains were found, a further week and a half for the skeleton assumed to be that of Charles Vivian. Even the first corpses were almost unrecognizable when they washed up near Via Reggio. Shelley's body was intact, but his face and hands were gone. He was identified by the volume of Keats stuffed in a jacket pocket. Williams's body, Trelawny said, was 'much more mutilated . . . The flesh, sinews and muscles hung about in rags, like the shirt, exposing the ribs and bones.' He was identified by his leather boot.

Trelawny, the editor Leigh Hunt and Byron, watched by Italian soldiers and a handful of curious ladies, cremated Shelley and Williams in a furnace on the beach. Following Hellenic tradition, the fire was scented with frankincense and salt, the corpses soaked in wine and oil, a mixture that helped to fuel the blaze. The flames around Shelley were so intense that his 'corpse fell open and the heart was laid bare,' Trelawny wrote. Byron, who couldn't stand the scene, dove into the water to swim to the anchored *Bolivar*, just as he and Trelawny had swum earlier during Williams's cremation. Shelley's heart, gorged with blood during the act of suffocation, apparently refused to burn. 'The heart remained entire,' Trelawny said, '[yet] in snatching this relic from the fiery furnace, my hand was severely burnt.'

In my California days, the sight of police anywhere near the edge of a ditch or river was enough to make me suspect something amiss. The cops might have been there for any other reason, but their presence alone became ominous. Just as a single glove, a pram, key or open book found in an incongruous setting – say, on the verge by a road, or one's doorstep – can touch the nerves. These items may simply have fallen, but they suggest something has happened and are unwelcome, like oracles you never asked to hear.

Adèle was working on the chart below. I was on deck watching the waves, blue, black and white. Suddenly a flash of unnatural green: an inflatable dinghy, one of those flimsy rubber affairs for a child under ten, hurtling downwind roughly parallel with *Shamaal*. Five or six miles off Capo di Monte Santu in crazy seas, you didn't expect to see anything manmade – anything, except water, at all. Every few seconds the light object jumped several metres, paused, then skidded forward again, like a plastic bag on a windy road. In the brutal sea and innocent, lost toy, there was something deeply unsettling. When the wind began to bring us closer together, I gave in to my superstition and steered *Shamaal* clear. Very shortly, Adèle called up from the cabin. 'Did you hear that?'

'Hear what?' It was impossible to hear anything beyond wind and water.

She appeared at the hatch. 'Something on Channel 16 – somebody in distress, somebody screaming. I heard "*tragedia*" repeated several times.'

Everything else was forgotten, all our senses straining at the VHF. We stared and waited and listened. But there was silence.

The journey ended so abruptly that waking the next day in the safe port of Arbatax the whole episode seemed barely to have taken place. At the time of the distress call we'd been twenty-four hours and 100 miles from Bonifacio and set to continue. On all the east coast of Sardinia, there was no obvious place to shelter, not in that weather, and another day and night of running before the wind would have put us under the protection of the island's southern tip. Only Arbatax, a remote industrial and fishing port, seemed a possibility, but that, too, presented a problem: its entrance faced almost directly into the gale and waves. I'd called the coastguard for advice.

There is always a slight element of wonder when radio contact is established from sea to shore and on Sunday in sleepy Sardinia all the more. So when there was no answer to my initial calls I was not surprised. Arbatax lay only a couple miles south now and its moment would soon pass. But then a fourth call and contact. Yes, a coastguard officer said, we should try: the entrance was good, deep and wide – even in these seas. There was no time to debate. To reach Arbatax through the waves we had to begin a shallow-angled approach at once, or fly past the headland and continue south. Disconnecting the wind vane to steer by hand, we warmed the engine, held our breath and skated towards the surf.

Concentrate, I told myself. Flying towards rocks and the line of pounding waves felt wrong. Confused by the shoals and reverberations, the waves in the final 100 metres were steep and without rhythm. The wind in the mast and hull still sent us quickly over the ground and below water the propeller turned slowly in anticipation of the work it soon faced. Spray curtained the walls of Arbatax. Strangely, it was in these last minutes that we saw our only other boat of the day – a German yacht also making for the harbour. The vessel, much larger than *Shamaal*, may have been parallel with us for hours, but hidden from view by the seas. I was shocked to see how she lurched in the waves.

Rocks, breaking water, the tan beach and glimpses of that madly swaying German boat. We were in. The waves vanished suddenly, almost throwing Adèle and me off balance, but the wind blew unchecked. It blew so hard over the harbour wall that at full power *Shamaal*'s motor barely cleared us from the next set of inner walls. Exactly what would have happened in the

Greek myths, I thought: they make it through the gale, they negotiate the dangerous entrance, then *inside* the harbour are wrecked.

A necklace of car tyres and iron rings beckoned from the side of a quay built for ships. Not ideal, but if we could just get alongside without crashing into the wall or the other boats . . . I moved *Shamaal* crabwise, wind and propeller balanced against each other, a high-wire act that I wouldn't manage for long. A sailor, American it turned out, stood on the quay ready for our lines. Coil and heave – he got them. In the seconds it took to tie a few knots, *Shamaal* was made safe. 'That is some wind! Gusting to Force 9, I make it,' the American said. I tried to look nonchalant, but really I was glad I hadn't known that before.

Hallucinating mildly in our exhaustion, we moved numbly and silently through the routines of tidying sails, filling the logbook, mopping water. By the time we dropped into our bunks, we were already asleep. Where we were at this moment, at what time or even country I had forgotten and didn't care. Just that *Shamaal* was in harbour and Adèle and I could rest.

The following day the gale still blew. Spray rose rhythmically above the harbour wall. The huge straps of a cradle used to lift boats from the water flailed. Flags crackled and the few tourists about walked at angles. But *Shamaal*, waiting calmly at her mooring spot, appeared to have transferred magically from Corsica to this eerily depopulated Sardinian harbour. The sea leaves few traces and once the sails have been folded, the water dried off, the boat looks no different than before. Neither was there evidence of our experience. The fact that all night in harbour we'd slept restlessly, even waking suddenly in belief we were still at sea, seemed to reinforce the impression of a long dream. The waves, the surfing, the child's inflatable, the cry for help . . . 'What about that voice on the VHF?' Adèle asked. '*Tragedia* – I know I heard it.' I smiled and shook my head, the memory of that cry, like the memory of my fear at the sight of the green dinghy, pleasantly dimmed.

An hour later Adèle returned from an expedition into town and tossed a newspaper in my lap, *L'Unione Sarda*. On its front page was the headline: '*Morte in mare . . . Vacanze tragiche, vacanze di morte.*' One person disappeared, one dead of a heart attack and three more pulled from huge waves. 'Death from the rough seas,' the article below read, 'a terrible toll.'

Clearing the air

Had we been sailing in the nineteenth century, we might have avoided Sardinia altogether. The Admiralty sailing directions warned of malaria so 'pernicious' that in certain areas a foreigner had only to breathe the night air for 'certain death . . . as if he had swallowed some poisonous drug'. The locals sealed themselves indoors before sunset, only venturing into the dark with cloth held over their mouths. In June, most people fled the plains for high ground, while 'those who, from their circumstances, are obliged to remain, keep themselves well clad in thick woollens, to avert the ardent rays of the sun. Exertion and exposure to summer showers, are studiously avoided, and a spare diet adopted.' Sards, as poor, insular and obstreperous with interfering outsiders as Corsicans, were in no hurry to embrace humanity. 'It was too lost in the sea to play an important role,' Braudel remarked. 'Mountainous, excessively divided, a prisoner of its poverty, it was a self-contained world.' Even when the swamps were drained after World War II, the mosquitoes expelled and a few pockets, particularly the Aga Khan's Costa Smeralda around Porto Cervo, transformed into Mediterranean playgrounds, much of the island retained the spirit of those closed doors and masked mouths.

As it happened, the gale had already driven us past most of the island. A thirty-one-mile daytime sail took us from Arbatax to Porto Corallo, one of the only remaining harbours on the east coast. Everywhere, dry, yellowish mountains tumbled into the sea, with hardly a settlement beyond the occasional, distant cluster of white buildings. A substantial breakwater announced Porto Corallo, but the harbour itself looked as if a short time back it, too, must have been little more than an outpost. Now, great tourist works had begun in a 'Build and They Will Come' kind of way. Entering through the gap in the breakwater, we found a domino set of new, empty mooring pontoons. Beyond lay a bleak, dusty car park, then further on what appeared to be a newly constructed tourist village, almost complete bar the inhabitants. A fairground where the revolving horses outnumbered the people sputtered in the twilight.

Nosing in with no wind, we half thought the harbour might be abandoned – as if the Admiralty's fears of the *intemperie* were still current. Then a door in a builder's cabin by the car park swung open, releasing a group of men in white shirts. One came jogging towards us over the pontoons. Another vaulted into a dinghy and gunned across the water for *Shamaal*, with a last-second flick of the outboard motor to avert a collision. 'Welcome,' the man said in English. 'We are here for your help.' And, leaving me to ponder for a second the meaning of his words, he led us to a berth.

The port we discovered on waking was even barer than the night before. Only a few fishing boats across the water – their names, *Luigi*, *Christian*, *Marco*, apparently referring either to the owners or their sons – brought definition to the overexposed scene. One vessel, *Alessandro*, sported an elaborate painting on each side of the bow of the Virgin, supported by angels, being crowned queen of Heaven. But the fishing folk, their world as closed to outsiders as Sardinia once was itself, were also physically too far away to breathe life into our forlorn corner of the marina. A statue representing the anxious wife of the mariner, the eternal Penelope, stood near the fishing boats, her eyes raised, palms open, and I wondered if her supplication to the Lord of 'the heavens and the abyss, whom the wind and waves obey' would work for us, too.

The little weather vane at the top of *Shamaal*'s mast lay idle, pointing east not because there was any particular wind there, but to kill time, same as everything and everybody in Porto Corallo. The forecast over the radio was also inconclusive, mentioning southerlies, which were not good for crossing to Sicily, then 'variable winds' – in other words, impossible to predict. However, the barometer, after being jammed on 'fair weather' through the past week, had begun to waver, so perhaps something was afoot. At the harbour office, one of the unfortunates having to staff that cabin twenty-four hours a day looked surprised when I asked if he'd received any reports. 'The weather?' he said, gesturing through the door frame at the dazzling, hot rectangle of blue. 'There is your weather. It's good!' Adèle and I decided to take our chances.

That evening, as we saddled *Shamaal* for the trip and prepared to sleep a few hours before embarking, a flotilla of Italian yachts descended. First three mid-sized sailing vessels, then two shiny, just-from-the-showroom motor boats buzzed through the harbour entrance and, with the Italian genius for large gatherings, made straight for our pontoon.

No fewer than two dozen people of all ages spilt from these craft and with them the panoply of the Italian family outing. Pontoons drummed to the feet of running children, barbecue smoke idled in the rigging, a guitar appeared, bottles sprang open. In an hour or so the confusion of the initial invasion had mutated into three distinct parties. Twenty metres away the motor-boat family, or families, sat down to tables and chairs arranged along the quay as neatly as in any trattoria. The sailing families, for a reason we couldn't fathom, squatted directly in front of *Shamaal*, cooking, eating and sitting on the bare wood of the pontoon a few inches from our bow. In a boat between sat the odd group, two young, extravagantly handsome couples, making little noise, but distracting both woman and man to each side from their wholesome feasts.

Adèle and I slept fitfully, the after-smell of grilled fish, the commotion of the language and gurgle of wine invading our dreams. When the alarm woke us at one in the morning, only the sailing crowd remained. They were subdued and a little sentimental. One asked whether we'd been disturbed by the noise and tried to pour us wine. Another sang what sounded like a lullaby. But my mind was already outside the harbour. A southerly breeze tugged at the rescue flag on our man-overboard buoy. The night was deliciously black. When we motored gently away, our bow lights glowing red and green, the Italians stood to wave. Land soon vanished.

That first night a maroon half-moon floated over the horizon. In the morning our deck was tinged with fine, red sand from the Sahara 250 miles to the south and a sticky heat enveloped the boat, staining the woodwork dark: our first, small taste of the desert sirocco. As the wind became hot and slack, we, too, grew listless. Our appetites waned, books fell from the hand, and the sea had never seemed so empty. For the next three and a half days we tacked and close-reached across the Tyrrhenian Sea, the wind from the south and south-east alternately blocking and freeing our path. Our pencilled track on the small-scale chart could have been mistaken for the footprints of an inquisitive fly.

Tacking towards a point far beyond the horizon is to master the unknown: aim for long enough at two places and you will work your way towards a third. Much sailing is like this, a matter of logic, of shrinking huge distances into diagrams and imposing science on mystery. Once, I'd associated travel with drifting. On youthful backpacking trips, I enjoyed the sensation of waking without knowing where I would sleep the following night. A hostel maybe, or a newly made acquaintance's flat, a forest, a field, a city park and once a Romanian village graveyard – my house was where I happened to find myself at dusk. Only sailing had taught me to apply science. The sailor is not overly confident about his powers, but this is at least how he embarks, believing that science can and must be carved from the chaos.

These thoughts struck me the first dawn out from Sardinia when two wasps landed on the rigging. We were thirty-five miles from land. Did they know where they were going or were they lost? Science or drifting? A third possibility suggested itself the following day when in the afternoon Adèle made the alarming discovery that our instruments no longer agreed in which direction we were travelling. Our main direction finder was the compass, but the GPS, among its other functions, can also calculate bearings. It was while activating the GPS to check our position that Adèle noticed it told us we were travelling in a different direction to that given by the compass. The disparity between readings on the two instruments was at least twenty degrees, the difference, in other words, between arriving off western Sicily and missing the island altogether.

At first we assumed the steering compass was at fault, but when we checked against two small handheld compasses, their needles tallied with the main one. So perhaps the GPS was wrong, but never having known of this happening, or finding anything in the manual about such a thing, we could not begin to guess the cause. I knew very slow boat speed threw off a GPS but, at about three knots, we weren't going especially slowly. Another possibility was that a deviant magnetic source, some stowaway lodestone or iron lump, had lured the compass from its search for north. We knew every item stowed in *Shamaal* and would have ruled this out. But the strangeness of seeing our most reliable instruments – our pillars of science – go to pieces prompted a furious search. Paint containers, steel pots, engine spares, sail repair kits . . . we dismembered every corner of every locker and drawer within magnetic range of the steering compass. We found nothing.

Approaching midnight that second day, a wall of dark cloud crackling with lightning slid across the southern horizon, but I didn't care.

I was on watch while Adèle tried to sleep through the clammy night. The sea was smooth, the boat steering under wind vane, and it was impossible to feel anything other than lazy.

Often we listened to music on headphones to help stay awake during these watches, even if this increased the tendency to daydream. Adèle had a Walkman and occasionally she'd wake me with her whispered singing – comic at times, maddening at others, depending on which stage of my sleep had been interrupted. She was also a great stargazer and liked to give me excited accounts of the constellations when we changed watch. But for my part, there was nothing better during the graveyard shift than to flit through the airwaves of my shortwave radio.

How often in some unlikely place I'd tuned in to that radio! On a reporting assignment in the Arctic north of Russia, freezing in bed at Hotel Number Two, I'd nodded off to cricket commentary from the Caribbean. In empty Siberia, I'd listened to a discussion on overcrowding in Hong Kong. In Chechnya, the very information I'd transmitted to my news agency one hour earlier would sometimes return as a headline on the BBC World Service the next – a cycle beginning with unhappy events in some mountain village, then swinging through computers, satellites, telephone lines and radio masts back to the same mountain village . . .

Here, surrounded by stars and water, I preferred the scan button. French radio debating philosophy; mawkish Russian songs that made me nostalgic for Moscow; flashing, slithery tunes from somewhere in North Africa. A push on scan and away I sailed. Beep. Light propaganda on the Voice of America, heavier on the Voice of Russia. Beep. A fragment of Radio Four longwave, miraculously getting all this way only to tell me of some dreary English transport crisis. Beep. French *ballades* were my favourites. I sailed the globe with Charles Aznavour in 'Emmenez-moi au tour de la terre', followed Charles Trenet down 'National 7' to the south of France, and felt for Serge Gainsbourg's poor brute having to punch tickets of other travellers all day. If only he could be given a ticket of his own, a ticket anywhere – just being able to leave was the key. At least that was what I'd always thought, though surely, somehow, you had to return. As the refrain to one *ballade* said: '*partir, c'est un peu mourir. Partir, c'est un peu mourir . . .*' Only when I realized that the stars had blown out did I shake from my reverie.

The lightning was close now and the wind, veering towards west, was in a mood I didn't much like. As the cloud wall, several shades blacker than the black night, closed in, the stars in half the sky disappeared. Those westerlies were what we needed to reach Sicily and, with *Shamaal* finally flying in the right direction, I was loath to clip her wings. But a black wall can only be ignored for so long.

I didn't have to wake Adèle. After rolling placidly for two days, *Shamaal* suddenly began to jump and dodge. Lightning ripped down and rain, the first since we'd arrived in the Mediterranean, thudded in grape-sized blobs. Adèle rushed to disconnect the wind vane, only then, under the rainfall, remembering she hadn't a stitch on. While she took the tiller and stopped the boat, I clipped myself to the safety line and went to reef the sails. The foresail was simple: a pull on the roller wrapped as much of the triangle as you liked. The mainsail meant clambering around the mast. I put in the deepest reef, then slid back to the safety of the cockpit.

It took only a little longer for the full squall to hit. Tight-packed, triangular waves leapt like watery flames – nasty, damaging waves that kept up long after the worst of the wind had gone. We remained hove-to, pausing to let the chaos of fire, water and wind blow past, and only when the stars in our part of the sky reappeared did we continue. With the wind now blowing fresh out of the north, *Shamaal* didn't look back, and nor did we. Though we never discovered the cause of the problem, the compass and GPS, as if freed by the cleared atmosphere, once again agreed on the way. In the next hours we passed over Aceste Seamount, a mountain top lost 152 metres below the surface on the edge of a 1,000-metre drop. At dawn, we disturbed a thrashing, silvery school of tuna. The gaps on the chart were getting smaller. That the brisk northern wind gave way again to languid, sandy breezes from the south didn't matter: just before sundown we spotted the steep hump of Isola Marettimo, the first of the three Isole Egadi, off the coast of Sicily, rising like a carapace from the haze.

At sunset, Favignana, the largest island, remained invisible, in these light airs still nearly a night's sail away. But this time no cloud wall marched on the horizon and, with Adèle first on watch, I sank gratefully into my bunk. A little scanning for *ballades* on my radio, perhaps, and then sleep, the gentle kind that only comes in moving softly through the southern winds.

III

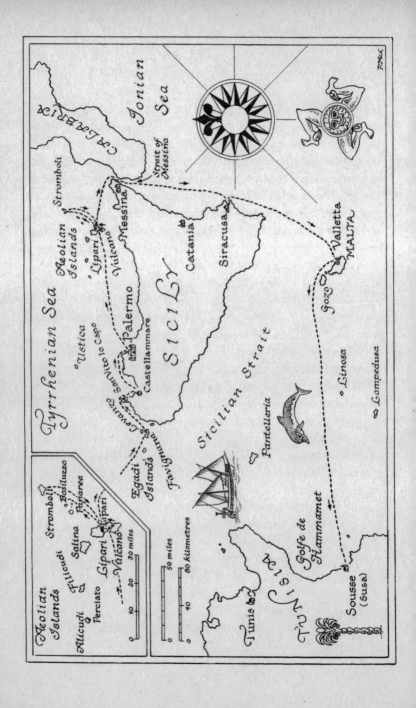

Ill winds

For the next couple of days, *Shamaal* lay to anchor in the snug harbour of Favignana. Wedged under the sheer and bare Montagna Grossa, the small town radiated an unexpected confidence. Handsome nineteenth-century buildings on the quay led to an elegant square where young and old paraded, pausing occasionally for lavish *gelati*. Tourism was the current source of this prosperity, but previously the island had been important as a centre for the processing and canning of tuna. There were still a few tuna fishermen here, tough, long-haired individuals who could be seen around the dock or, more easily, in the postcards depicting their traditional *mattanza*, or trapping of the tunny. Most of the tuna and, with them, the industry were gone, however, and the once impressive infrastructure for the fishing fleets lay in picturesque abandonment.

Otherwise, Isola Favignana was sparse and poor, the bleached hide of its main hill reminding us how much of the Mediterranean is not Europe. Already there'd been a hint of Africa in the sultry air and dust we experienced at sea, a murmur of the desert winds due later that autumn and following spring. Now, the presence of the southern continent was explicit: indeed, over the next days along the Sicilian coast, the ragged palms and searing light would give us the impression of having arrived in Tunisia for the winter earlier than planned. Ours was to be a roundabout route looping hundreds of miles around Sicily and Malta before stopping, but sailing direct we could have reached Tunis in just twenty-four hours.

Favignana also marked the start of a string of sites associated with Homer's stories. Of course, apart from the historical facts of the Greek–Trojan war and destruction of Troy, there is no absolute proof of anything which appears in *The Odyssey* or *The Iliad*. In his 1963 book *Ulysses Found*, Ernle Bradford made an interesting attempt to demonstrate the nautical feasibility of Odysseus' voyage, arguing the view that the places in Homer's tale are to be found right across the Mediterranean. Samuel Butler's 1922, iconoclastic version of this debate, *The Authoress of the Odyssey*, argued that Homer was a woman and the story based entirely around Sicily, while after an investigation in a replica galley Tim Severin decided that Odysseus never left Greek waters. The Sicilian archipelago will always have a strong case. Favignana, for example, has long been known as the 'Goat Island' where Odysseus and his men feasted after an arduous passage. Just across on Sicily proper there is a cave that Ernle Bradford identified as that of the Cyclops Polyphemus, and over on the eastern side lies the Strait of Messina, home to the monster Scylla and whirlpool Charybdis. To the north lie the Aeolian (Lipari) Islands where, again according to tradition, the wind god himself resided. It was there, among those gusty, volcanic sanctuaries, that I hoped at least to pick up the shifting trail of the old king.

The hedonistic throb of Favignana, on the other hand, seemed neither Tunisian nor Homeric, the goats having been transformed into skimpily covered young Italians and the thick stands of pine that covered the island only a century earlier into rock. Still, not so much unlike Odysseus, we, too, filled our bellies, victualled our ship and, after a good rest, departed once more, taking an eastward course past the land of the Cyclops and around the corner of Sicily.

On paper, this was a simple passage, a thirty-mile trip around the headland of San Vito, but the wind waged an exhausting campaign, shifting wherever we shifted, turning when we turned. Gradually those thirty straight-as-an-arrow miles became a crooked fifty-five, the easy day sail slid into the night, our goal of Capo San Vito retreating almost as fast as we advanced.

The coast had at first appeared in a sympathetic light, thick trays of white cloud balancing on the mountain tops like the mortar-board hats of professors. As promised on the chart, the shoreline was broken into manageable pieces, a distinct hill here, a cliff there, a stone tower, an industrial chimney – every one of these landmarks a jewel to the navigator. I had only to take bearings on this hill or that tower to fix our position on the sea. An hour later I might repeat the exercise and match it against our boat's speed and direction. Yet we became lost.

I never saw where I first slipped. Possibly I mismatched objects on land with those on the chart. Perhaps I got lazy and, instead of finding three reference points for bearings, settled for two. I might have become confused at the time I had to change charts: they did not overlap and between them ran a north–south sliver of unsurveyed water. One slip was enough. Ordinarily I might have unmasked the original mistake at the next fix, but the quantity of towers and hills made it possible to cook any evidence required. So, if something seemed odd, I could tell myself I'd misread the compass or that the building on the hillside, despite my doubts, really must be the landmark I wanted it to be on the chart. It was a case of one small error neatly confirmed by a half-dozen others. And as night fell and the coast vanished, I had to admit to losing the trail.

We still knew we were rounding north-western Sicily, that the lighthouse on Capo San Vito continued to glow ahead, even that we could resort to the GPS. Yet we were lost in that we'd blithely sailed into one kind of sea that morning and, without meaning to, entered quite another. Tired and chastened, we reached San Vito at 3 a.m.

Most of San Vito is a brash resort crowded with Italian tourists, but the adjacent harbour was muted and sullen. A row of long-unpainted fishermen's cottages, piled nets and rubbish lined the waterfront. Mongrel dogs tottered in the shade of anaemic vegetation. Dazed stray cats, ribs rippling through mangy hides, stretched in the sun. Flies sprinkled themselves everywhere.

Like many Italian harbours, San Vito was under the control of *ormeggiatori*. These range from professional hands serving visiting boats, to fellows who have discovered that sailors in need of water and shelter can be made to pay almost anything in return for the right to a tap and an iron ring on a wall. The *ormeggiatori* we found looked like the former, but behaved like the latter. After showing us fetid shower quarters and a source of non-drinkable water, a comically high fee was demanded and we were asked how long we would stay. Adèle and I answered simultaneously.

A short retreat took us to the anchorage in the broad bay outside. It would mean a session at the oars each time we wanted to go ashore, but there we could float free on six metres of water where the sand bed danced in the light. Perhaps, away from buildings and beach, we might also be cooler. The absence of wind in San Vito was so total it seemed as if the plug had been pulled on the atmosphere and the air drained away. On *Shamaal*, I sat under a pavilion of draped cloth in the cockpit. Ashore, the air became so still and hot that even breathing was difficult. The beach sand scalded bare feet and, in the streets beyond, half-naked tourists mingled like exhausted runners at the end of a marathon. At the ancient church where we attended Mass late one afternoon there was shade, but tears of sweat ran down the cheeks of the priest, enclosed as he was in layers of ecclesiastical garb. A story came to mind of a medieval Provençal archbishop who, by carrying sea breezes in a glove, was able to breathe life into a windless and barren mountain valley. But I'd have liked to see him try that trick in San Vito.

I'd heard it said that during a sirocco the oppressive heat was enough to drive up crime rates in Naples and Palermo. Also that in Sicily more than three days of sirocco might even be claimed as an excuse for a crime of passion. However implausible this seemed at first, these sweltering days made me think again. A small boat sounds like a breeding ground for arguments, but there is more sense of space than non-sailors would think and, everything being relative, a five-metre trip up to the bow from the cockpit can be as good as a temper-cooling walk round the block. Yet the heat, thirty-four degrees Celsius on each windless, late August day, was already so insistent, viscous and inescapable that it just might, I thought, drive a man to the edge. If a sirocco blew, with that fine mesh of sand, that extra degree of hot damp, would he go over?

'Sirocco' is only a general name for the desert winds that blow from all across North Africa and the Near East – the leveche of southern Spain, the chili in Algeria and the ghibli of Tunisia and Libya. In Egypt and the Levant, the local name is khamsin, meaning 'fifty' in Arabic, for the fifty-day period that the wind tends to blow. In the south of the Mediterranean, the sirocco is bad enough, an abrasive, hot blast from depressions travelling east through the countries of North Africa. It will heat the air, muddy the sky and dress streets, houses and people in red. Sand carries far into the Atlantic and, on occasion, lends a yellowish tinge to snow in the Alps. In Andalucia, the south wind will parch a wheat field before it ripens, making the grain fall to the ground during harvesting. Spanish farmers combated this by reaping in the freshness of the night, while Virgil was said to have protected his lands around Vesuvius with a trumpet that tooted automatically whenever the south wind blew.

But it is further north, after the sirocco has picked up Mediterranean sea moisture, that it becomes most noxious. The air takes on what Thomas Mann described in *Death in Venice* as a 'repulsive condition' – an unbearably clammy, maddening state that saps energy and ruins the nerves. An eighteenth-century English traveller visiting Naples told how six days of a sirocco had 'blown away all our gaiety and spirits; if it continues much longer, I do not know what may be the consequences'. A Parisian nobleman noted only days earlier for boundless verve was threatening to hang himself out of ennui and 'the natives do not suffer less than strangers ... A Neapolitan lover avoids his mistress with the utmost care in the time of the *sirocc*, and the indolence it inspires is almost sufficient to extinguish every passion.'

Even in the fifth century BC, Hippocrates, the traditional father of western medicine, was warning against the evils of the south wind. In his book *Airs, Waters and Places*, Hippocrates wrote that people living where there were warm southerly winds and mild winters had heads 'of a humid and pituitous constitution, and their bellies subject to frequent disorders, owing to the phlegm running down from the head; the forms of their bodies, for the most part, are rather flabby'. Women in such areas were subject to excessive menstruation, infants to convulsions and asthma, and men to 'attacks of dysentery, diarrhoea, hepalius, chronic fevers in winter, of epinyctis, frequently, and of haemorrhoids about the anus'.

Unfortunately, cities with cold winters and an absence of southerlies saw little improvement. The men were likely to be slender and well formed, and the population generally long-lived but, while the women menstruated only in small amounts, this would be painful. Men might have 'sound and hard' heads, but they suffered from overeating, ruptures, bowel problems and nosebleeds. 'Attacks of epilepsy,' Hippocrates cautioned, 'are rare but severe.' For the unfortunates living in cities where west winds were common, there was worse news: people there were simply 'pale and enfeebled and partly subject to all the aforesaid diseases'.

It was only about cities facing east that Hippocrates, born on the Aegean island of Kos, could be wholly positive. These enjoy good water and moderate temperatures, the people have good complexions, 'clear voices and in temper and intellect are superior to those which are exposed to the north' – a marked enthusiasm which made me wonder whether in the wise man's analysis there had not been an element of favouritism.

It so happens that the ancient capital and harbour of Kos, already an important place when Hippocrates was teaching, faces north-east – about as eastward as the slender, fish-shaped island will allow. Doubtless the site was chosen because it sheltered boats from the Aegean's lively meltemi, but as a more universal principle this easterly bias is hard to sustain. When the eighteenth-century French writer Voltaire helped to resurrect interest in the medicinal aspects of wind 2,000 years later, he wrote from his

London exile that it was precisely the east wind that was causing suicides and a 'black melancholy' throughout the land. 'Men who are strong enough to preserve their health in this accursed wind at least lose their good humour. Everyone wears a grim expression and is inclined to make desperate decisions. It was literally in an east wind that Charles I was beheaded and James II deposed.'

At sea, these issues become irrelevant. On land, the prevailing wind seems heartless, part of the landscape into which one is born. Men feel helpless. 'Anybody is as their land and air is,' Gertrude Stein said. If it is a wind that drives them mad, they go mad; if happy, then happy. If it is the type that brings haemorrhoids, then these, too, cannot be avoided. But the mariner is able to strike deals.

Consider the sirocco. Farmers and travellers on land cowered in the sand and heat, but to sailors who'd come to Africa with the dominant northerlies the hot southerlies of spring and autumn were a ticket home. 'Get under sail with a young south wind or an old north wind,' as an Aegean proverb put it. So although Voltaire's easterly brought nothing good on land, to me the east wind breathed life into our voyage, sweeping *Shamaal* down the English Channel en route to the Mediterranean. At sea, there are no permanently ill winds. They are made for travel: one to take you away and, because no wind stays the same, another eventually to bring you back.

Sergei Ostrovsky, a London friend, escaped from his City job for three days, joining us in San Vito for the hop to our next stop, Castellammare del Golfo. Having a build and metabolism better suited to Russian winters than the Sicilian summer, Sergei was no better at dealing with the rays than I. Only Adèle could thrive in this heat, feline in her ability to soak up sun. And so while Adèle ran about, Sergei and I slumped in the shade of the cockpit awning, swam and roamed the beach in search of freshwater showers. With three aboard, *Shamaal* – not to mention the rubber dinghy – suddenly looked very small.

After a day in San Vito, we made use of unexpected zephyrs from the west to depart. Gliding slowly under full sail, the short passage to Castellammare stretched to several memorably gentle hours, Sergei marvelling all the way at the ivory cliffs and azure waters that framed our temporary home. Adèle and I were delighted to see our old friend. The last time we'd been together was the day we'd started our journey from Essex. Sergei had been among the well-wishers on the dock, his brother Arkady playing a Russian song on the guitar as we cast off.

We found Castellammare in late afternoon, perfectly in time, as the epicurean Sergei pointed out, to find yet more showers and organize an agreeable dinner. The harbour, somehow by-passed by tourism, nestled between a cascade of old streets and stone houses, a fort and an enormous breakwater of modern construction. Because there were no *ormeggiatori*, we were at liberty to anchor anywhere along the quay, deserted except for a few fishing boats, urchins and lovers. In town, the narrow streets were empty and airless, as somnolent as those of San Vito and Favignana had been animated. But the moment the sun fell behind the mountains, Castellammare revived. Shutters opened, cafés filled, fishermen attended their nets, teenagers their scooters, women the shops, and a yawning policeman the traffic.

We ate on deck that night, cooling ourselves with fresh beer harvested by the indefatigable Adèle. Across from *Shamaal*, the town glowed like a lantern. From the fortress floated the voice of a female opera singer. How clearly her voice came over the battlements and across 600 metres of harbour. Next morning, when we rose early to see off Sergei, was hotter, and Adèle and I spent the day in search of breeze, flitting like wraiths through the old town. Even Adèle couldn't shake this one.

On embarking for Palermo the following dawn, something threateningly murky about the water in Castellammare worried me – we might not retrieve our stern anchor, snagged for ever on a jettisoned washing machine, a sunken boat or any of the other junk accumulating in deep, dark harbours. In the event, the anchor reappeared without trouble, the only snagging involving my hand and a discarded line of fishing hooks that had become wrapped around the anchor rope. The little blood did no harm and maybe, as a sacrifice of sorts, even pleased the gods, for no sooner had we exited the harbour defences than the first real wind in days kicked up fresh from the north-west. Once more, *Shamaal* cantered past headlands and cliffs, spray thumping and spattering over the deck. Palermo was not long in coming.

Several miles out and already the Sicilian capital could be seen sprawling between the high ground to each side – craggy, tree-speckled hills that had looked down on a city since the arrival of Phoenician settlers in the eighth century BC. Closer in, Palermo's huddled mass of life and history began to separate into recognizable parts – mellow golden domes, dishevelled apartment buildings, a flourish of gardens. Then we were close enough to see the bottom of the sea and to smell the city: an acrid whiff of chemicals and commerce from the docks, mixing, not unpleasantly, with the deep, eternally grateful perfume of recently watered gardens.

It was in Palermo, with its fierce reputation, that I hoped to ask about the link between the sirocco and crime. So, aided by Maria, a lively English-speaking student recruited in a cake shop on Via Vittorio Emanuele, I set off in search of the authorities.

'Actually, what you heard really might be true,' Maria said as we threaded the alleys in a detour through the old town. 'People here are already a bit crazy, you know, and when the sun hits forty degrees, almost no one can lead a normal life. But I don't know what the police would say.'

We had entered the intestines of Palermo, a rambling network of tiny streets and yards. In many European countries, such alleys would have been gentrified and flower-potted by now. The cobbles would shine, the doors double-lock. Previously unfavoured back streets would be chi-chi artists' retreats and the wider places full of boutiques. But in Palermo the poor quarter remained poor, stinking, tattered and furtive. Chainstore commercialism had not penetrated the warren and, in an echo of the Oriental bazaar, every trade had its own area. Mattress sellers in this street, furniture makers over there, mechanics here, food merchants along the way . . . Drying laundry flapped overhead, but few people were to be seen. Sometimes an old man or a group of wild-looking children appeared, then disappeared. In the silent, stagnant and clannish atmosphere, I could very easily imagine someone committing a crime and getting away with it. 'You crazy, too,' Maria laughed.

After a false start with an astonished street cop, we decided to go to the top and soon found ourselves at a headquarters of the *carabinieri*. Too many films had made me expect an earthy place, thick with cigarette smoke, flies and the clatter of old typewriters. In fact, Italy's *carabinieri* are one of the best turned-out police forces in the world, and the station was a swanky, glass-fronted establishment that could have doubled as offices of a management consultancy. At the main gate we were asked to wait, and a few minutes later two officers, their white leather cross belts, red trouser stripes and peaked caps gleaming in the sun, approached.

The older of the two men was pure Sicilian, oily, plump and dark as a ripe, brown olive. The other, slender, blue-eyed and fair-skinned, came from the north of Italy and had only recently begun to work in Palermo. From the start it was clear the pair had different agendas: the Sicilian revelling in the lurid details and his colleague stressing, through Maria, that little untoward ever happened in Palermo at all. So, was it true the sirocco could drive someone to crime?

'You bet,' the Sicilian enthused. 'We're always more busy at the time of the sirocco and also at peak heat in the summer.' This was when the sane went mad and the mad became madder, committing crimes and confessing crimes, regardless of whether they had taken place or not. The greater the heat, the more ambitious the confessions – bank robberies, family poisonings, assassinations . . . 'You get people coming in to claim they've just killed the American president, or that they *are* the American president,' the Sicilian said to faintly disapproving looks from his pale companion. Then there were the suicides. Like several hot, persistent winds around the world, the sirocco has been linked to rising suicide rates. Even the northerner agreed with this one. 'Yes, plenty of people kill themselves during the sirocco. The cliffs are full with them,' he said, and the two men laughed – police gallows humour.

I quickly followed up. What about the old custom of forgiving certain crimes of passion? The Sicilian policeman smiled, shaking his head. The northerner, I was pleased to see, looked indignant.

The Aeolian Triangle

On my chart, the Aeolian Islands, or Isole Eolie, were clear enough: seven mustard daubs on a white sea – Alicudi, Filicudi, Salina, Panarea, Stromboli, Vulcano and, in the middle, Lipari. But there is nothing to prove one of these is Homer's 'floating island of Aeolia' and, as with most other locations in *The Odyssey*, strong rivals exist. In this case the problem is even greater than usual, for one of the few details Homer provided was that of the island's buoyancy. Who could fix such a kingdom to a chart?

Preparing our departure from Palermo, the skies seemed to urge us on. The first batch of September gales blew through the Mediterranean and a new sense of volatility crept into the air. In harbour, calm alternated with brutal gusts. I saw them arrive at the far side, stirring up water and stripping washing lines before hurtling on to *Shamaal*, and hurrying out of the harbour altogether. Over the VHF – blocked by the surrounding harbour unless I tilted the mast and antenna while Adèle sat below scribbling – the forecasts changed at each reading. North-west, south-west, Force 3, Force 6 – no one was sure. Fitting enough, I thought, for a journey that would take us to the centre of the so-called 'Aeolian Triangle'.

This area, cornered on the Strait of Messina, the Aeolians and the remote island of Ustica to Palermo's north, is famous for its unpredictable and violent winds and, although the 'Triangle' title may be modish, the idea is solid, based on observation by experienced modern sailors. In the mid nineteenth century, Admiral William Smyth, Mediterranean authority of his day, also noticed unusually perturbed air around the Aeolians. 'Whether from the heat of the water by volcanic springs, the steam of Vulcanella, the incessant hot injections from Stromboli, or all of them added to the general atmosphere, it is certain that there are more frequent atmospherical changes among this group than in the neighbourhood.' Unaccountable – unless in the caves of those fire-spitting mountains sat the wind god himself.

In the end we left Palermo a little sadly. We'd made friends with Umberto, who looked after the yacht club, actually just a builder's cabin, and insisted we pay nothing. Also with the boy fishing from the quay and with our neighbours, a Dutch writer and sculptress on a boat rather larger than *Shamaal*. Palermo, even the rough area around the harbour (an area we would later see referred to in newspaper accounts as home of a child-killing Mafioso), was unexpectedly congenial. Behind us loomed the warehouses and gantries of the commercial docks. Sirens wailed to announce changes of shift and, every now and then, a cloud of bitter smoke would drift north over the yacht club. Rubbish lay in piles. But there were also young lovers singing and playing guitar on the harbour wall. Classical ruins could be seen across the water and nearby there was an outdoor theatre in the evenings, the actors carrying microphones, the audience perched on motorbikes, benches, each other's shoulders, even trees. When we finally pulled out, there was quite a little group to wave us farewell.

The wind stumbled and spun on the hills ringing the Bay of Palermo, and *Shamaal* struggled to tack to the open sea. Just off the harbour waited the Onassis family's regal former motor yacht

Christina O, and across the bay a yellow fire-fighting plane made lazy swoops for water. Finally we reached the outer edge of the bay, some four miles from harbour. Here, quite suddenly, the wind freshened and steadied. The sea whitened. Liberated, *Shamaal* took off through the waves.

An hour offshore, two large fishing boats bounced past, not 100 metres from our starboard side, in the other direction for land. A troubled-looking yacht, sails badly set, her deck a spaghetti of ropes, followed. No doubt they, too, had heard the latest forecast: gales in almost every part of the western Mediterranean and for us, in the central Tyrrhenian, thunderstorms and westerlies of Force 6. Adèle and I thought of turning back, but the wind, now almost from behind and blowing directly for the Aeolians eighty miles away, piped us on.

Running downwind, we were able to lower and furl the mainsail and continue under foresail alone. An oddity of sails is that less can be more, the chief aim being to find out what balances the boat, and so coax the hull through the water at greater speed. In basic terms, the wind on the mainsail will make the stern swing from the wind, while the foresail does the opposite, and managing that tussle is the essence of balancing a boat. But when the wind is from behind, this push-you-pull-me effect may only be a distraction, the boat yawing as the two sails compete. Halving our sail area by taking down the mainsail and running under that energy-filled triangle of the jib alone actually made *Shamaal* straighter – and faster. The wind vane was often the best teacher in these matters. Too much of the wrong sail and a wind vane won't steer properly, sneaking up into the wind or tailing off the other way. Get the sails right and the wind vane will guide the boat through waves and gusts without a murmur.

The sea became rough as dark fell and I went below for my first sleep. Water sluiced past the cabin as *Shamaal* shot forward at five knots. A permanent gurgle, like a tap left open, ran along the underwater hull next to my head. Sometimes *Shamaal* collided so hard with a wave I could swear something must break. 'Is everything OK?' I'd call up from my bunk through the hatch. 'Oh, yes, everything is very good indeed,' Adèle would reply cheerfully. The sound of the sea was far more frightening in the cabin than on deck. 'Are you clipped on?' I'd ask. 'Yes!' 'Life jacket on?' 'Yes!' Then, perhaps, I'd be able to sleep.

On such a small boat there is almost nowhere to fall other than into the sea, and I'd worry about Adèle. Sitting deep in the cockpit is safe. But often we had to half-stand to adjust ropes, or clamber on to the stern, crossing a metal rail and holding the rigging, to fine-tune the wind vane. One slip would be enough. Asleep, or even awake, I'd almost certainly hear nothing if she fell while I was below. At five knots the boat would be a half a mile away in six minutes: in the dark and rough sea, a person would vanish from sight much earlier. One slip.

I thought of Virgil's description of Palinurus going overboard, how steering alone at night he falls asleep and tumbles over the rail. 'Down fell Palinurus, calling again and again on his comrades, but they did not hear. The god then rose on his wings and flew off into the airy breezes, while the ships sped on their way none the worse, sailing safely on.' That's what would happen. Eventually the wind would change, the wind vane would become confused, the sails would shake, the motion would change – eventually, even in the cabin, I would wake, aware that I was alone. Just as after Palinurus' fall, Father Aeneas came to 'sense that he was adrift without a helmsman. In mid-ocean in the dead of night he took control of the ship himself, and grieving to the heart at the loss of his friend, he cried out: "You trusted too much, Palinurus, to a clear sky and a calm sea, and your body will lie naked on an unknown shore."' Whenever I rose from sleep, the sight of Adèle, mysterious and sylphlike in the dark, and so undaunted by the immensity of the sea, made me terribly glad.

We'd covered close on forty miles when we came to the thunderstorm. Blurry flashes became long, clean streaks lighting canyons, peaks and escarpments of cloud. All night, we tracked the storm's progress: 'Maybe, if we are very quiet and keep our heads down, we'll just be able to creep past,' Adèle said, and so we did. The system kept moving east with us, but always to the north. *Shamaal*, so small and low, escaped the storm god's notice.

The sun rose when we were sixty miles or so out of Palermo, immediately revealing the steep outline of the first Aeolian island, Alicudi. In an hour came Filicudi, then three more, each of them soaring and almost as insubstantial as the pink and white thunderstorm clouds now impaled on their peaks.

In search of Aeolus

Anchored on the east side of Vulcano, we watched tiny clouds of smoke puff from holes in the side of the active crater – inspiration, surely, for the traditional image of Aeolus spearing the hillside to release trapped winds. Antlike figures of tourists clambered over the peak, one or two of them perhaps wondering whether the whole mountain might not unexpectedly blow. Bathing later in Vulcano's sulphurous mud pool just behind the beach I, too, queried just how far below the surface the lava gathered. In the crumbling, straw-coloured rock to the sides of the pool, you could sit directly over the volcanic vents and feel the heat surge through your shorts. In the sea, too, there were places where the water bubbled warm. The thin mud in the pool was as hot as a bath and painted bathers' skin a chalky grey. With its bubbles, steam, soupy texture and scattering of about twenty fleshy Italians, the pool as a whole looked like nothing other than a huge cauldron at a cannibals' feast.

Out on the anchorage, the winds let loose in the afternoon, gusting hard enough to send crews rushing to check that their anchors held firm. One boat came away altogether, drifting dumbly out to sea. Her crew were on shore at the time, and she was only saved after being commandeered by sailors from another boat.

We were less lucky. A shout from Adèle woke me from slumber, but by the time I shot from the escape hatch the side of a large American yacht was almost upon us. I remonstrated, but the Americans, who had also been in their cabin, unaware that their boat was loose, were too late and too slow to avert the collision. For a minute or so our anchor held two boats: *Shamaal* and the formerly adrift, now entangled Americans. We'd taken the blow straight on the bow, the strongest point, and the bow roller, which is a steel brace for the anchor chain, had lightly pierced the fibreglass side of our new acquaintance. Our damage consisted of broken sealing, small cracks in the edge of the deck and chafe on our anchor rope. Damn it, I thought: not to strike a rock or another boat, but to be struck *by* another boat – almost another of these floating islands . . . 'We really do apologize,' the American man said: 'when it's all over we'll come over and buy you a beer.' Apologies and the offer were accepted, but the Americans, maybe nervous after watching us make repairs that afternoon, went without beer and stole away during the night.

The following day, we sailed through fickle airs to the main island, Lipari, and found a berth in the small marina at the corner of the main bay. Like Vulcano, Lipari rose sheer from the sea, but the sides of its mountains, long undisturbed by any eruptions, were gentle and green. It was here, more than 2,000 years ago, that Aeolus worshippers had centred their cult. The origins of the myth are typically confused, but the first-century BC historian Diodorus Siculus wrote that the Aeolians were an immigrant tribe whose first ruler here was named Liparos, hence Lipari. Their second ruler was Aeolus, known as a just and pious leader, kind to visitors and an authority on the use of sails. He had a reputation for being able to forecast the weather by observing fire, possibly the origin of the myth of his power over the winds. More baroque details we now associate with Aeolus – incest between his twelve children, a cave to imprison the winds and his immortality – came separately, first in Greek, then Roman myth. Finally, the boundary between man and god blurred for ever.

As for floating Aeolia, some say Homer invented the whole thing, others that he was referring to the way Mediterranean islands appear to rise above the horizon on hazy days. Lipari's claim has a problem in that it is one of seven neighbouring islands, not including crumbs such as Strombolicchio and Basiluzzo, while Homer referred to an island very much on its own. I wondered whether Homer had not based his idea on one of the volcanic islands that occasionally burst from the sea in this area, a phenomenon that would easily suggest buoyant land. To take a modern example, what now appears on charts as Graham's Shoal just south of Sicily was briefly Graham's Island in 1831, appearing overnight in a subaqua volcanic eruption, then sinking soon after – and threatening, according to the geologists, to reappear in the near future.

To their credit, though, the people of the islands have resisted exploiting their past. A handful of statues refer to the myth. Lipari's archaeological museum displays a few relics left by ancient worshippers. There was one gift shop named Il Templo di Eolo, with a sign showing an overweight wind god whipping up a gale. But there was no Aeolus Tour, no Aeolus Experience, and nor was there any line in Aeolian sacks, suitcases or handbags. In fact, there is no clear agreement on whether to call the archipelago the Liparis or the Aeolians. Inquiries as to the site of the cave where Aeolus might be spending his eternal rest drew a blank, a laudable show of restraint.

Because of the unpredictable weather, we dared make only a fleeting visit to Stromboli, about twenty-two miles to the north-east of Lipari. The island is almost conical, a perfect chimney for the clouds of ash and lava that spit daily from the top. Ancient mariners knew it as a natural lighthouse, its orange crest visible at night for many miles. Stromboli also makes an excellent candidate as the site of Homer's Wandering Rocks, where 'the very birds cannot fly by in safety' and sailors 'end as flotsam on the sea, timbers and corpses tossed in confusion by the waves or licked up by tempestuous and destroying flames'. But there is no harbour on Stromboli, nor much shelter, so we had to make do leaving *Shamaal* anchored off a black-sand beach while we rowed ashore for the afternoon.

Pulling the dinghy safely beyond any waves, we found ourselves near a squat fisherman, all shoulders and calves, his hair and beard shaggy, his face turned leathery by wind and sun. He made a startling sight. Where Emile in Corsica had hinted at Aeolus, this man was the clone. Between the fisherman and a little basalt carving of Aeolus we'd bought back on Lipari there was not a detail of difference. Stranger yet, further along the beach between more bright-painted fishing boats was another – an Aeolus as tousled, rough-skinned and windswept as the first. A search along the seafront flushed out two more. The wild-man look was in on Stromboli.

Strolling, with half an eye out for caverns, we skirted the shore, then turned to the otherworldly interior of the island. Constant eruptions had created a jagged, crusty landscape, softened by improbable quantities of flowers and vegetation. Cacti rose tall as trees and light-green grass glowed against the backdrop of black rock. In the village, prickly pear, cane, palms and shiploads of white, pink and red flowers choked the alleyways and walled gardens. We never discovered any cave, but did stumble on a villa, handsome and sad-looking, all shuttered up, its big gate bound in chains and cobweb. Set in ceramic by the gate: a wind rose showing the eight corners of the sky.

On return to our dinghy, I couldn't resist approaching the hairiest, most unkempt and leathery of the Aeolus types and asking the obvious question. The fisherman did not look surprised. 'Where is Aeolus? Sleeping today, but he will wake tomorrow.'

At dusk, we motored slowly around the island, eventually pausing about half a mile offshore under the flanks of the volcano. We were not alone. Eruption watching is an important business for the Aeolian Islands, and we found ourselves joined by several other sailing boats and two small, crowded ferries. The night deepened, feeding the mood of expectation. Total silence except for the gentle churning of engines and splash of the sea. Then it came: a gush of red fire from the top of the mountain. Tie your shoelaces and you'd have missed it, but Stromboli had performed. Almost as bright was the broadside of camera flashes coming from the ferry and, more weirdly, from the summit of the volcano, by now crawling with guided tours.

A noisy, boat-rattling wind swooped through Lipari harbour the next morning, ending any hopes of our catching up on sleep lost during the sail back from Stromboli. Evidently, Aeolus was up. The boats in Lipari's cramped little harbour were packed tight, and now they rubbed and pushed against each other like corralled cattle. Flagpoles around the quays hummed, masts swayed and dust devils danced through the trees. As usual, the only clouds over the Tyrrhenian were the odd, smiling cumulus amid tufts of high cirrus.

At about midday, when the harbour was at its busiest, a ragged old man cycled down the quay, in one hand a plastic bag of freshly caught whitebait, in the other a sheet of paper. We'd seen numerous locals tour the quay with wares, one offering cakes, another wine, another fruit and veg. Their prices were exorbitant and, although it was a mile's hike to the shops, Adèle and I had never been tempted to pay. This fellow, though, was new and, strangely, it wasn't the bag of fish he was trying to peddle, but the piece of paper – the day's weather report.

I was intrigued. Didn't he know that every boat had a radio and that by now we'd all received our own forecasts? His was undoubtedly just a copy of the brief synopsis pinned daily to the wall of the coastguard office up in town – plagiarized and by now barely useful. Not surprisingly, no one paid the slightest notice, and the old man was left alone to stalk the dock, pausing only as he drew level with *Shamaal*. It was at this moment that Adèle appeared from stage right with her film camera and began attempting an interview. Despite his somewhat manic attempts to court attention, the old man did not look especially pleased, and the exchange in Italian, broken on one side, spluttering on the other, soon degenerated.

'What's that?'

'The weather.'

'Is it for us?'

'Yes – you give me something, too.'

'You mean pay? How much?'

'Do you want the weather or not?'

'OK, but how much do you want for it?'

Instead of answering, the old man grumbled, waved the weather report, pretended to get on and off his bicycle, and issued what seemed to be curses at Adèle. Before I could move to placate him, he had finally remounted his bike and departed, hair, clothes and the piece of paper snapping in the wind.

In Europe, Aeolus is the oldest of his type, but gods, wizards and priestesses with power to deal out the weather and wind have been around ever since. As late as the first part of the nineteenth century, Sir Walter Scott met a hag in the Orkneys who 'subsists by selling winds. Each captain of a merchantman, between jest and earnest, gives the old woman six pence, and she boils her kettle to procure a favourable gale.' That phrase 'between jest and earnest' summed up my feelings. Between jest and earnest, I thought, we should have been careful with the man on the bicycle.

The common thread linking all these myths is that jailing the winds may not be such a glamorous task and that the jailers themselves are not always so attractive. A creepy tale by the eighteenth-century French writer Montesquieu relates how the son of Aeolus sells sacks of wind around the world before attempting to swindle a wealthy people of their gold. He is described alternately as whining, angry and abusive, a good example of why we are wary of soothsayers and their ilk, however loudly we claim not to believe in their powers.

In the ancient texts, Aeolus himself appears full of contradictions. He is generous and mean, powerful and subservient, godlike and racked by human concerns. Although known as king of the winds, he is more of a caretaker, usually releasing storms on the instructions of the Olympians, while his most famous act, the sewing up of the contrary winds for Odysseus, ends in disaster. There is a note of panic in his voice when Odysseus shows up on Aeolia that second time. 'Get off this island instantly!' Aeolus says. 'It is not right for me to entertain and equip a man detested by the blessed gods.'

The only immediate sign of retribution from our wind salesman was the loss of my *caffè freddo* in a table-cloth-lifting gust in Lipari that afternoon. Shops fought to keep postcard stands upright, and down at the unprotected waterfront there was mayhem as several large yachts began to slam against the stone wall. I never knew for sure which wind was responsible. In the alleyways of Lipari, no one could tell: the wind followed the walls. In one street, an old woman and I found ourselves looking skywards in amazement at a few raindrops. In the next street, the sun blazed. Back in harbour, the locals were as confused. Tramontana, one said, meaning the northerly descending from Italy, rather than the version from the Pyrenees. No, libeccio, a south-westerly, said the other. Northerly or south-westerly – couldn't they tell? I laughed and pointed out the flags. Look at that Italian tricolour: didn't it blow stiffly out of the north? Of course, it was a tramontana. The libeccio promoter shook his head, gesturing wearily to the other side of the harbour. There the flag blew equally stiffly: out of the south-west.

Scylla and Charybdis

We left Lipari at three in the morning, groggy on account of poor sleep amid the crashing and squeaking of boats in the harbour. As forecast, the wind had simmered right down and now blew firmly from the west – zephyros to take us into the Strait of Messina. The pre-dawn polka dots of stars, island lights and anchored boats revived me. The Aeolian Islands were an enchanted place, scattered bits of earth and sea, half-forgotten, half on fire, half-submerged, a bit mad, a bit inbred. But I was glad to be moving.

Dawn returned all the land stolen by night, the Aeolians, Sicily, even the ghostly outline of mainland Italy materializing in the grey light. The sea, black and quiet an hour before, sparkled and danced, and *Shamaal* sliced through the light swell. Then – not a noise to expect in calm water – a small knock against the hull. And another. A piece of driftwood? An oil drum? Wreckage? Fifteen miles from land, in deep water, *Shamaal* had hit a rock.

As soon as we began to look we saw them everywhere: pieces of whitish pumice, from pebble to fist size, scattered thick over the sea in a long, wide streak – an entire floating reef. We turned around and short-tacked through the stones, scooping them up with a hat. Hundreds upon hundreds of pieces of floating pumice. One bore the tiny chip of blue paint it had extracted from *Shamaal*'s hull. Where had they come from: the quarries on Lipari, the throat of Stromboli? At least one mystery had been resolved: surely this was how Homer, listening to the strange tales of returning sailors, had got his idea for the buoyant island.

The reason for that 3 a.m. departure was to time our arrival in the Strait of Messina, one of the few places in the Mediterranean (the Strait of Gibraltar and southern Tunisian coasts are others) where tides affect navigation. The first sliver of a new moon hung in the sky and that meant spring tides, or maximum gravitational pull, so we'd want to enter the strait when the current was going our way. According to figures cribbed from a neighbour's almanac in Lipari, our rendezvous with the Strait of Messina would have to be made by two in the afternoon or the seaway would close.

The reason there is normally little tide around the Mediterranean is simply that the sea is almost enclosed, protected from the ocean's twice-daily dip and bulge under the pull of the moon and sun. There are high and low waters on each coast, but so modest as to pass almost without notice. Even in the Strait of Messina, the maximum rise and fall of sea level is about thirty centimetres – impressive for the Mediterranean, yet small fry on the Atlantic coast, where depths commonly change by five metres and more. What the Strait of Messina does with this meagre flow is another matter.

Tides are essentially a moving bulge of water. A channel or strait will often mould this bulge into a long, seesawing slope, meaning in the English Channel, for example, that high tide around Plymouth coincides with low tide at the other end, some 300 miles away, in Dover. About six hours later, the slope having reversed direction, high tide will be in Dover, low tide in Plymouth, and so on. The Messina channel is peculiar in that it connects two seas, the Tyrrhenian to the north and Ionian to the south, which through being separated by Italy move to entirely different rhythms. This lack of synchronization means it may be high water on the Ionian side of the strait, while just three miles away in the Tyrrhenian it is low water. So, even if the underlying tidal flow is unremarkable, it becomes concentrated into an unusually steep slope. Gushing north or south, the seas then gather and squeeze through the bottleneck of the strait: at its narrowest, the gap is just two miles. Underwater changes are as extreme, with depths of as little as seventy-two metres in the tightest part of the strait, compared to 1,000 metres only ten miles to the south. Tipping a jug of water through a funnel would give an idea of what follows.

The meeting of two seas produces another dramatic effect. The Tyrrhenian is warmer and less salty than the Ionian, and the differences in water density are enough to create a circular pattern of currents, one running south along the surface and another north about thirty metres below. These swirling rivers of water, one denser than the other, are what create the whirlpools and eddies for which the Strait of Messina is famous. Charybdis, so vividly described by Homer, is a real whirlpool, identifiable by its circle of smooth, oily water in an otherwise ruffled sea.

Then the wild card in this already complex place is, of course, the wind. The high ground to each side of the strait channels and accelerates breezes as much as the subaqua topography funnels the sea. Anything other than northerlies or southerlies – in other words, blowing either straight down the corridor or straight up – is rare. These winds, often markedly stronger than those blowing just beyond the neck of the strait, can by themselves alter the strength and duration of the currents. They are famous for descending in sudden squalls, and a particularly strong wind against fast-flowing seas will raise Cain. Between this almost mythological combination of land, water and wind some thoroughly nasty seas, if not monsters, are born.

Our first view was a disappointment. We had arrived on time – the tidal current, if we'd understood correctly, would be with us – but there was nothing to see. All morning I'd talked up the strait to Adèle: a decade earlier, I'd tried to swim across with a friend, and memories of the misadventure flooded back. Now I felt like the film character bringing police to the murder scene only to find the body gone. No maelstrom, none of the tidal eddies, the *bastardi* and *refoli* we'd read about in the pilot book, much less any sign of Scylla or Charybdis. Capo Peloro was featureless and scrappy, the Italian boot looked in need of a polish. Our fair westerly was gone and, in fitful breezes, the water was smooth. Only the traffic was impressive. Gnat-like hydrofoil ferries buzzed perilously close, fishing boats did their best to move into our path and a warship slunk into the Ionian. A pilot boat guided a huge cargo vessel towards Reggio, a mouse leading an elephant. Then Adèle said: 'Look!'

Before I could answer, *Shamaal* was away. Everything happened that fast. The wind shot from the north, the current launched us south, and the calm sea broke into a field of small waves. With every minute south, the seas rose and the wind increased. *Shamaal* bucked past Torre Faro and Charybdis, hurtled on towards Punta Pezzo and, within an hour, had left astern the harbour of Messina. The water-speed log read three and a half knots. The GPS, which calculates movement across the planet, or ground speed, read seven and a half. In other words, we were riding at three and a half knots through a sea itself going four knots over the ground, a tidal performance worthy of many a wild English headland.

Imagine the ancient mariner coming upon these waters for the first time, an experience as unexpected and incongruous in the supposedly tideless Mediterranean as the discovery of floating rocks off Lipari. The sight and sound of breaking water near land signals the terrible possibility of reefs and, as he was driven by wind and current towards this maelstrom, the early seaman might well have expected to perish. He might say, as Odysseus did: 'I saw a cloud of spume ahead and a raging surf, and heard the thunder of breakers. My men were so terrified that the oars all dropped from their grasp and fell with a splash on to the sea.' Homer's Mediterranean never seems more credible than from the deck of a small boat.

Scylla was a nymph turned by Circe into a revolting beast, 'the creature with the dreadful bark', with twelve feet, six heads and triple rows of teeth. She ate six of Odysseus' companions as they sailed past while trying to avoid Charybdis. Today Scylla (Scilla) is the name of a village on the east shore of the Strait of Messina, but there may formerly have been a real whirlpool and some claim still to hear Scylla's yelp in the waves under the bluff. Charybdis is no myth. Admiral Smyth wrote in 1824 of seeing a seventy-four-gun warship 'whirled around on its surface', and that was half a century after an earthquake had much reduced the whirlpool's potency by altering the seabed underneath. Even today in high winds Charybdis and the other eddies are said to pose a danger to small craft. Much like Odysseus' anxious crew, we strained to catch a glimpse as we shot past. There she was, right between us and the fishing boats hauled on the beach: a glazed circle of water staring from the sea like a myopic eye.

At sundown we left behind Calabria, now black and capped in the diamonds of village lights. The north wind freshened and, before starting night watches, we took down the mainsail to run once more under foresail alone.

Lightning on the left, according to Pliny, is lucky, but this night it began on our right, exposing for a second at a time the malevolent bulk of Mount Etna and the towering clouds of a squall. A thunderstorm squall, which can be likened to a downward eruption, is a system that shoots the roaring high winds of the upper skies to the ground, the plummeting cool air then forcing warm sea air up in an eruption of its own. Maybe the ancients knew more than we think because similar advice – to leave a squall to port – is handed to sailors trying to bypass the awesome power of its gusts.

Some of Homer's best descriptions of sailing involve squalls. Unlike a proper storm, which may cover hundreds of miles, a squall is normally so localized that it can be watched coming and going. A sailor faced with cumulonimbus clouds may be excused for feeling he has been singled out. If the squall passes, even close, he is saved; if it strikes, he could feel, as said in war films, that it had his name on it. Homer's account of the squall that kills the last of Odysseus' comrades near the Strait of Messina is far from overdone. First Zeus sends a cloud to darken the sea, meaning it is a black squall, not the 'white' version known to strike in the Mediterranean with almost no warning at all. The wind swoops from the west with such force that the rigging breaks, probably because the sail has not been reefed. The mast falls, killing the helmsman, which would almost certainly make the boat broach sideways to the waves, and a lightning bolt makes a direct hit.

'The whole ship reeled from the blow of his bolt and was filled with the smell of sulphur. My men were flung overboard and round the black hull they floated like seagulls on the waves. There was no homecoming for them: the god saw to that.' It is a lifelike account. Running before the wind in the sudden waves for which the Mediterranean is equally known, the worst thing that could happen is that the helmsman loses control. The lightning bolt would at the least terrify the sailors and as the boat broaches, perhaps capsizes, only Odysseus has the presence of mind to hang on. The rest drown.

If *Shamaal* had been a horse-drawn carriage, hooves flying, wheels blurred, I would have undoubtedly stood to use the whip. As it was, we let out a little more foresail and set the wind vane to steer to the south-west. Come on *Shamaal*, get out from under that fiery sky! It was a skewed race but, when the unlucky streaks moved to our left, I knew we'd escaped.

Heading south

Siracusa was the grandest harbour we'd entered in a long time. Not grand as in busy, like Palermo, or chic, as in Bonifacio, but old-time elegant: all crenellations, balconies on stately buildings, big quays and soft, golden rock. The huge columns of what had been the temple of Athena ran like ribs through the flanks of the cathedral on Piazza Pancali – history literally piled on history. 'The most beautiful of all cities,' wrote the Roman orator Cicero in the first century BC. 'It is both strong by its natural situation and striking to behold, from whatever side it is approached, whether by land or sea.'

In the marina we found several other boats also on their way south and one or two we'd seen elsewhere before. There are circuits that yachtsmen follow around the Mediterranean little different to the trade routes or war routes of thousands of years before. Siracusa, a safe harbour a day's sail from the bottom corner of Sicily, was an important stop. We were also into the second week of September and, although the Mediterranean sailing season can extend right through October, the winds were flexing their muscles and everyone was starting to think about where to shelter. For us, that meant Tunisia, via Malta. Many others would stay in Malta and a few somewhere in Sicily. Siracusa had an end-of-party feel.

Moored alongside were two young Maltese, and one evening we found ourselves guests in their cockpit, along with two Germans. Not having been aboard larger boats for a long while, we were amazed at the difference in their lives. One could walk around the cabin, cook lasagne in an oven, lie down in the cockpit and read by any number of electric lights. The Germans' boat, a few berths away, represented another level altogether – with sails that appeared and disappeared at the push of a button, television and the kind of shower one might expect from a hotel. The two Maltese looked across at *Shamaal* in no less surprise. 'You're a romantic,' I was told when I said we normally used oil lamps.

A spanking libeccio started the next morning, blew hard all day from the south-west and stopped dead at sundown. The following day the performance was repeated. In the libeccio we were all equal: seaweed hurled from the water carpeted the pontoon walkways, but with a particular yen for the sides of the huge English motor boat being so busily polished. Waves piled up against the outer side of the marina and, soon, everyone was doubling lines to keep their boats safely tethered. Keeping people together was harder. Walking back to *Shamaal* with a wheel-barrow full of food and supplies I was almost blown into the water. Klaus, the German boat owner, said his girlfriend had become seasick simply sitting in harbour.

After a couple of days spent wandering through the Greek

ruins and treating ourselves to a final bout of Italian *gelati*, we left Siracusa. Several other boats set off at the same time, including the homeward-bound Maltese. We liked them. They were full of advice about their windy island and the lasagne had been good. I saw Stewart spend half a day up the top of the huge mast on the Germans' luxury boat. The fancy reefing system, in which the mainsail was wound electronically around a roller inside the mast, meant no pulling on ropes or struggling with canvas. One didn't even have to leave the cockpit. But it was a technology not always matched to the unpredictable violence of the wind, and the Germans had run into trouble. Klaus was lucky to have found someone as generous as Stewart to winch to the top of that mast. But I wondered what would break next – the boat or his girlfriend. The last I heard, they were sailing north, deep into the Tyrrhenian where there was now a gale blowing every week.

The rest of us did what millions of birds were now doing and headed south.

The Maltese took a head start and, by the time we'd raised sails and tacked to sea, they were gone from the horizon. The forecast was for north-westerlies, which meant raising Malta on the fastest and most efficient point of sailing, a broad reach. But what we got was south-south-east, a headwind, and, instead of smugly sitting back with a book, we found ourselves tacking all afternoon just to clear the coast.

At last, Capo Passero, the southern corner of Sicily. The beams from its two lighthouses guttered like candles in a draughty room – flash, dark, flash, dark – and then we were round the point and into the Sicily–Malta Channel. The sea, now rarely more than eighty to ninety metres deep all the way to Malta, almost immediately became rougher. These shallows form the submerged remains of what in prehistoric times was the toe on Italy's longer and less elegant leg, Malta and Gozo being warts. Similar shallows at the western corner of Sicily are evidence of the island's former connection to Africa. Between, though, and to every side, lie abyssal pools, so, although we would sometimes sail over no more than forty-five metres of sea, just ten miles to the east depths reached 3,000 metres. Here was topography guaranteed to create seas in its own image: broken, rough and quick to change.

Tearing west at six knots under reefed main and foresail, we left Sicily behind long before midnight. With water flowing constantly along the deck, we reefed the sails a little more, but there was nothing to stop the occasional flooding. *Shamaal* dipped and bucked as she struck waves full-on. Bathtubs of water broke over the foredeck, split around the cabin and sloshed to the stern, overwhelming the small scuppers, before shooting back into the sea. For the first time in the Mediterranean we wore not only full oilskin suits, but boots and hats as well.

It was also the first time in a long while – perhaps since the Golfe du Lion – that we'd met so much shipping. The Malta Channel is on the main east–west artery of the Mediterranean, the route from Gibraltar to Suez and the bypass to the Strait of Messina. Maybe the big ships, visible only from their navigation lamps (two whites for vessels over fifty metres, three reds or red-white-red in a stack for the real behemoths), were responsible for some of the awkward waves. We had several close encounters, always crossing behind when we could, for these leviathans moved many times faster than *Shamaal* and in the dark their speed was easier than ever to underestimate.

All night the wind stirred the sea, the sky and *Shamaal*. We reefed back, halving the mainsail and gradually cutting away at the jib. All the same, we kept flying at more than six knots. Soon, we'd left the worst of the shipping astern. A half-moon rose red then white, lighting a sea dressed in foam and phosphorescence. When the moon left, the stars gained in size and intensity, burning holes in the sky. At 0550, I wrote in the logbook: 'course – 220 degrees; miles run – 55.2; position – 36 degrees, 10 minutes North/14 degrees, 50 minutes East; wind – NW 6–7; remarks – Sea and wind up. Dawn. Further reef in foresail. Taking on solid water at 6.5 knots.'

Midmorning, we hot-footed into Valletta through the wake of a British naval flotilla steaming east.

At the main entrance, the port divided: Marsamxett to one side, Grand Harbour the other, and the star-shaped fortress of Saint Elmo between. What names! The first recalled the island's eastern roots, the second the days of great naval fleets and the third the Christian warriors who ruled as the Knights of Malta. All the momentous history of Malta was in those three names. Deep inside Marsamxett, the harbour and its appellations continued to bifurcate – Sliema Creek, Lazzaretto Creek, Pieta, Manoel Island, Hay Wharf . . . We pressed on to Msida marina. A fleet of sailing dinghies flew out on a regatta. A patrol vessel from the rather down-at-heel Maltese navy prowled. Curious, ancient-looking little Maltese fishing boats puttered out to sea. And in every direction the masts of yachts from all over the world swayed gently in the wind.

Plumb between Europe and Africa, east Mediterranean and west, Malta was intended by nature to be a pit stop. From the Phoenicians 3,000 years ago to the Knights Templar and the British Empire, the parched rocks have been little other than fortress, depot and harbour for other people. The historical overcrowding has left some incongruities. The island's illustrious and endlessly celebrated knights were of course not Maltese at all, the enigmatic Semitic language means that one of the most fervent Roman Catholic populations in Europe prays to Allah, and antique yellow English buses drive on the left through desolate landscapes of stone and brush.

However, to load *Shamaal* with supplies and prepare our last journey before winter, there was no better place. Odysseus may have been shipwrecked here, Saint Paul certainly was and, in both cases, the reception was friendly, for Malta takes its position in the sea seriously. The Royal Navy also used to dock in Malta and its departure had left Grand Harbour and its adjoining marinas overendowed with nautical know-how. For our more modest purposes, the string of chandleries along the front of Lazzaretto Creek was quite enough.

After months of voyaging, *Shamaal* needed a little care. There were two worsening leaks in the bow – not large or even visible holes, just tiny gaps around bolts that water from waves managed to force through. The hull was scratched and knocked. Rope ends needed work. The wind vane was slightly bent. The floor in the cabin, a wooden platform stretched over the bilge, suffered from cracks and rot. One of the two twelve-volt batteries was dead and the electronic log (measuring distance and speed) had gone berserk . . .

Somehow, Adèle managed always to look fresh. Her clothes were mysteriously unwrinkled, she wore a flower in her hair and never went ashore without jewellery. I, though, needed maintenance. In four months, my hair had turned wild, my face brown and newly lined. The cuts gathered in wrestling with the engine, rigging and all the other bits on boats that fight back had mellowed into scars. But my clothes were not going to mend. I was down to one of everything, the rest now missing pieces of varying size – a collar here, an elbow there. At sea I still wore my rags, even if just to make Adèle laugh, but soon the rules of land were going to have to apply.

Between Malta and the Tunisian port of El Kantaoui, there were still 200 miles of open water to go. There, we'd rent a cheap apartment and live as landlubbers for a while, escaping the worst of winter and readying *Shamaal* for relaunch in the spring. Mr Procter, of Malta's meteorological office, advised us to leave soon. The winds were at decent strength and mostly out of the east: a following breeze to send us to the Gulf of Hammamet. With autumn, Mr Procter was awaiting the arrival of the sirocco, even fouler than in spring because of the particular warmth of the sea moisture it would gather on the way. After, it would be the turn of the gregale, one of the most feared winds of all.

Blowing from the north-east, the gregale, or Greek wind,

meets no resistance until Malta, an unusually long fetch in the Mediterranean. So even if the gregale is below full strength (Force-10 storms are possible, but Force 5 is the average), the seas remain considerable. It was a gregale that drove Saint Paul from Crete to Malta in The Acts and another that so undiplomatically interrupted a summit between Mikhail Gorbachev and George Bush Sr on a ship anchored injudiciously off the island's east coast. Unfortunately for the Maltese, the gregale also exposes Valletta harbour's one great flaw: its entrance faces north-east. 'You can get waves that come in, rebound, regroup and create the strangest wave patterns,' Mr Procter said. 'Then there is real difficulty. Boats can't get in or out of the harbour.' Even the massively moored ships of the Royal Navy used to be discomforted by the gregale. In fact, there were only a few corners of the harbour complex that could be considered totally safe. Most yachts have to be hauled out on to dry land, and every year some are left in too long and are lost.

Mr Procter, whom we'd met while attending to business at Luqa airport, base of the meteorological office, told us how forecasting had been transformed since the days 'when we used more or less to stick our head out the window'. Even today, though, it was possible to be caught out by the awkward behaviour of Mediterranean skies. The Sahara, the mountains, the large islands and the sea all concoct their own winds, and the collected result resisted easy prediction. For example, a warning sign of the gregale is a low-pressure system south of Tunisia and moving north-east. But whether a gregale or the opposite – south-west winds – will occur only becomes clear after one knows which side of tiny Malta the depression will go. I asked if he'd taken any of the blame for failing to keep Gorbachev and Bush out of the famous summit storm. The weatherman chuckled. 'They'd decided to use their own forecasters.'

On a chilly evening after a hurried supper, we took Mr Procter's advice and headed to sea. After a week in Valletta, the darkness outside harbour was shocking. No more streetlights or cars or golden windows – just black waves and Malta already seeming far away. It was past midnight when we rounded Gozo, where we turned downwind and, for the next two days, barely touched the sails again. Due west, the compass said, though in spirit every minute took us deeper south.

In the morning we were passed by a high-flying flock of large birds. Ducks, we thought. They were taking their young to Africa for the winter. Millions of birds of every description were making the same journey and, in the spring, they'd all fly back north again. What path had they taken? Perhaps all the way down over Italy, then across Sicily, ready for the big hop over the sea. It would be one of the quickest routes with the least sea time. The best way had to be through Spain and past Gibraltar. The big birds could use hot, daytime thermals to lift them over the strait. But there were a lot of hunters in Spain, just as there were in Malta, in Italy, too, and Greece. We'd seen them a few years back while travelling in the Peloponnese during autumn: posses of hefty men dressed like soldiers popping their way through bandolier after bandolier before sitting down in cafés to tell loud jokes. Most of the birds they killed were very small, and it took a good dog to find their corpses in the rough Maniot maquis.

Then there were the trappers. In *The Story of San Michele*, Axel Munthe described the annual capture of birds on Capri, where he'd made his home. No one knew why but, once blinded with a red-hot needle, a bird sang incessantly. These decoys were then tied around nets to lure their comrades:

They came in thousands: woodpigeons, thrushes, turtle-doves, waders, quails, golden orioles, skylarks, nightingales, wagtails, chaffinches, swallows, warblers, redbreasts and many other tiny artists on their way to give concerts to the silent forests and fields in the north. A couple of hours later they fluttered helplessly in the nets the cunning of man had stretched all over the island. . . . In the evening they were packed by hundreds in small wooden boxes without food and water and despatched by steamers to Marseilles to be eaten with delight in the smart restaurants of Paris.

Doctor Munthe was so distressed he bought one hillside and made it a sanctuary, but all across Europe and North Africa the hunting of those 'tiny artists' continues.

Yes, they'd do better to stay out on the sea with their seafaring cousins, the shearwaters and shags, the cormorants and storm petrels. We could all follow each other – we were headed the same way.

On edge of the third night, an unspoken excitement: only thirty-five miles left and with the wind at Force 4 or 5, and steady from behind, we'd reach Tunisia in eight hours. If we found ourselves going too fast and outrunning dawn, we'd stop a few miles offshore, heave-to and wait like travellers at the side of the road. We didn't want to make landfall in the dark – and, besides, I had my own reasons to pause.

It had been a long time since I was last in North Africa. Then it had been to see my father, who used to go down to Morocco a couple of times a year by car from France, through Spain. His 'migration', he called it. Just out of school, I'd fly from England to see him in Rabat, where he lived at the Hotel Terminus, a clean, nondescript place in the city centre, the kind of hotel you could easily pass without noticing. Grave Moroccan businessmen and the odd Spanish tour group were the main guests, but my father was resident, Hotel Terminus the address on his chequebook.

He and I had been travelling for years then. From Spain, where I'd been born, to England, then briefly in my early teens to a boat and wherever the boat happened to be, and to island hopping of a different sort – journeying through short-term-let apartments and hotel rooms in increasingly unpredictable places. Provence, Biarritz, Megeve, New Mexico, North Carolina . . . A family of two, we travelled light, my father keeping only what could be picked up or easily moved: a car (which might be left unused for months in France), a small suitcase of clothes (one silk tie for emergencies), golf clubs and books. Based for most of the year at a British school or university, my own material needs were equally few.

The origins of this tour – a career change, family upheaval or simply the desire not to be tied down – gradually became unimportant, and movement turned into an end in itself, Morocco the latest idea. Even when we reached a place with the avowed intention of staying, house hunting made the perfect alibi for further travel. If Biarritz was no good, how about Santa Fe? How about Aix? Each time, my father (looking for perfection) was disappointed and so we continued, the exchange of air tickets, apartment keys and estate agents routine. Somewhere back in England in a warehouse, all the belongings we'd shed, our 'Stuff', gathered dust like a time capsule.

My father's odyssey closed unexpectedly in Florida after a decade but, by the time he took up fixed abode, my own travels had long since hit their stride. Growing up, I'd not always enjoyed those footloose days; as an adult I saw things differently. Just recently, I'd bought a small flat in London, thinking, after a few years working around the United States and Russia, that the moment had finally come to settle. Everyone else my age seemed to manage. But I was finding that travel burns bridges as fast as they are built and that stopping, let alone turning back, can be hard. Certainly Adèle, a migrant herself, had done nothing to slow me. And here we were, a few dozen miles off North Africa on our own boat, with *our* Stuff left behind in an attic.

IV

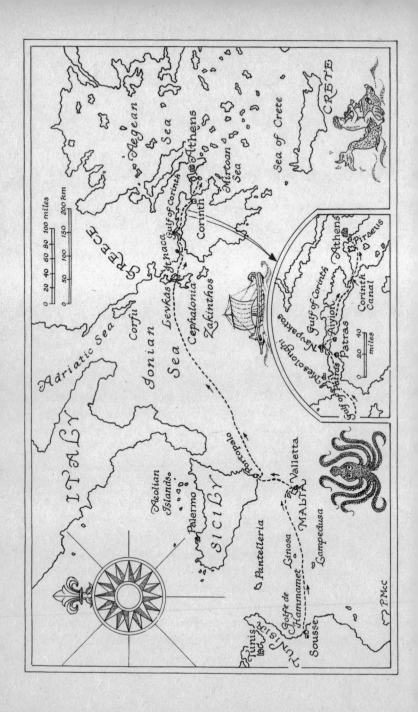

Ships of the desert

The coast along the Gulf of Hammamet is shallow, creeping from the sea into the olive plantations of Tunisia's Sahel. El Kantaoui, one of a handful of purpose-built yacht harbours in the country, lies in the middle, and it was here that *Shamaal* would sit out the winter.

With its cobbles, white arches and balconies, El Kantaoui is supposed to resemble an ideal Arab village, but Tunisians were mostly there to serve drinks and food, or parade in djellabas and sell jasmine. The exceptions were members of Tunisia's ruling class – slow-moving men with bejewelled wives who liked to graze in the restaurants and amble through the boatyard, itself the concern of the son of the interior minister. Before going ashore, we spent two days moored in the swankiest corner of the harbour, flanked by big foreign yachts and a tourist 'pirate ship', while we unloaded gear on to the quay. The pile, apparently so much bigger than the interior of the boat, amazed us as much as it did tourists walking by. Sails went into red bags, ropes were stripped and coiled, the water tank pumped clean, the engine re-oiled, the deck given a protective coat of wax. Unburdened, *Shamaal* rose a good centimetre or two higher out of the water, as if to say thanks. But even after so many preliminaries, the moment of surrendering *Shamaal* to the boatyard crane came as a shock. Following almost five months of constant movement, we were grounded, and *Shamaal* was on dry land.

We rented four whitewashed, blue-shuttered rooms in Sousse, a town a short distance along the coast. Because we were planning to stay almost six months, we'd wanted a furnished apartment in the Arab quarter, away from tourist streets, where the prices would be lower and the atmosphere improved. Our estate agent, whom we found asleep in the sunshine outside his office, said he had the perfect place – the only hitch being that he would have to renege on a previous deal to let the same flat to a group of students. 'They won't be bothered,' he exclaimed with a smile. *'Je n'ai donné que ma parole!'* – 'I only gave my word!'

The apartment was on the third floor, its balcony overlooking the sea and the Omar Al Khatab mosque. The minaret's loudspeakers were about level with our bedroom window and each dawn we woke to the muezzin, his amplified voice oddly resembling the howl of an electric guitar. This was a bare, spacious flat and, after the boat, the high ceilings and tiled floors at first seemed unmanageably big. Having to change rooms, close doors and find light switches proved a novelty. The solidity of the floors and walls was unnerving, and for more than a week after arriving in Tunisia I found myself giving the occasional involuntary stagger – my rubbery legs compensating for the fact that the platform below me no longer moved.

When the first big sirocco blew that October, Adèle and I were suddenly back at sea. Whirlwinds sucked litter from the streets. Dust devils spun between apartment buildings. Birds catapulted past the minaret. The sky turned yellow and the wind drowned even the muezzin. We scrambled to each window closing shutters. All down the street people were doing the same. Everyone had identical light-blue shutters, and in the gusts they banged and slammed. The crisp, cheerful noise of breaking glass echoed around the neighbourhood. Quick, get those shutters latched! When we'd finished, Adèle and I laughed: it had been just like reefing in a squall.

Slowly the lure of warmth, light and a life uncomplicated by the consumerism and ambition of Europe took hold. Sheep around the olive trees in our street, cockerels keeping the imam company at dawn, orange and lemon juice sellers everywhere, cat fights and the morning ritual of throwing open the blue shutters – these unimportant colours and sounds filled our days.

Tunisians, like the Moroccans I remembered from my father's migration days, had perfected the art of killing time, of sitting around and showing no frustration. Many times I tried to ask about the wind, or simply the next day's weather, and each time – unless it was a fisherman – was met with amazement. 'What will the wind be? How could I know? It's not up to us.' The main national newspaper, *La Presse*, published a weather map that was almost laughably crude, just two or three badly drawn suns and clouds scattered approximately over a hand-crafted chart of Tunisia. The evening television forecast was slightly better, but never showed maps of isobars or any detail beyond what was happening in the major areas of the country. 'Here,' one of the boatyard workers told me, 'it is always sunny except for when it rains.' But when did it rain? 'When God grants it.' In Algeria that November, the mosques had been full of people praying for rain. It rained, and in Algiers 200 people died in flooding.

In winter, the lower number of foreign visitors highlighted just how little outside of the tourism industry there was for locals to do. In our neighbourhood, the women appeared to be employed permanently in cleaning their flats or cooking, and the men in occupying cafés. Turning one of our rooms into a makeshift office, I spent the time researching what I could of the Mediter-ranean, taking notes and writing a little. Adèle, meanwhile, read her way through the shelves of Sousse's one good Francophone bookshop. While I buried myself in my papers, she also embarked on occasional trips – to the oasis town of Tozeur, the holy city of Kairouan, the chi-chi resort of Sidi Bou Said, the scraps of what was once Carthage and, for three days, a village wedding in Tataouine. Other than the capital Tunis and Sousse, I saw little of the country, and each time I looked forward doubly to her return, both for her presence and the adventures she might recount.

At New Year's, though, I put down my pen, joining Adèle and a gang of six London friends for a trip into the Sahara. The Londoners brought with them a mountain of luggage and no less a quantity of metropolitan gossip, making me realize, with mixed feelings, how estranged from our previous lives Adèle and I had become. When our bus rattled inland, it was the first time I had left the seashore in many months.

At Douz, a market town on the edge of the Grand Erg Oriental, we transferred to a huge jeep, bumping and sliding for hours down desert roads identified as such only by the ruts of previous vehicles. We might turn left at a bush, right at a pink-faded Coke can on a stick, but to the unhesitating driver these were the equivalent of neon-lit highway signs. At a patch of dunes and scrub we finally stopped. Our guides for the next week, three small, dark men in turbans, were waiting, and with them the nine camels that would carry our baggage and supplies. The jeep, followed by several nervous pairs of eyes, disappeared back towards Douz, the camels groaned and the guides, barefoot and fleet, started to walk.

For five days we did little else. Walking in the desert is akin to sailing. You move slowly and surely (even if sailing is somewhat more erratic), and the riches of a landscape that initially appears monotonous are gradually revealed. You have time to notice and absorb details. Any ripple, change of colour or temperature in the sand and air becomes significant. You begin to feel comfortable in this alien environment, yet are unlikely to want to hang about longer than necessary. You keep moving.

Erg in Berber means 'sea of sand'. Camels, carrying the traveller's home and goods, are called ships of the desert and, as their plate-sized hooves glide over silky sand, they do appear to float. Sand itself shares many of the characteristics of salt water. Saharan sand is fine as powdered mustard (and not dissimilar in colour), the grains the size of a full stop. Nudge a pile of Saharan sand and you set off a miniature avalanche. A handful refuses to stay long in the hand. Paddle about, or even walk all day barefoot, and the most tender skin survives unharmed – refreshed, even. It is, in other words, about as close as a solid substance can be to water. Desert sand, like rain and spray on a boat, invades the eyes, nostrils, ears, clothing, bags, books, food and drink. Sand is useful. The guides showed us how to use sand to clean dishes, rubbing until the surface gleamed and the last dry grains fell away. Also for cooking: a layer of sand over the hot coals of a brushwood fire creates a remarkably efficient oven. Yet to be stranded without camels in the middle of the desert would be to know the terror of the man overboard, fated to watch his ship sail away.

Daily routine on a trek is also close to that of a coastal passage: early rising, simple food, all-day travel and the late afternoon search for shelter, an anchorage in one case, a convenient clump of bushes in the other. Navigation, though, is more akin to that in the open sea. Trekking east towards the Libyan border, Sayid, one of the guides, explained the Bedouin's methods. The sun showed east, west and south, Polaris at night showed north. Then, like islands far offshore, there were the landmarks, just a handful of crags and small hills in the emptiness, but each of them vital. 'Each place has a name, but the nomads never carry maps or compasses; nor do they measure distances,' Sayid recounted. 'They have the knowledge in their head from childhood. It takes maybe three years to know your way around this part of the desert.' The Bedouin's other guide was the wind. Here, the principal wind was the behari, which blows from the south-east, bringing moisture from the Mediterranean and precious winter rain. Sayid also spoke of the ghibli, a variant of the sirocco. Winds, as on ships centuries ago, were used as a sort of compass reference, while in poor visibility they were often the only way for the traveller to keep going straight.

In such an extreme environment, the wind has extravagant effects. One wind will deliver rain, coaxing shoots of green from nothing; the next buries that miracle under new mountains of sand. 'The wind may be invisible, but it decides a lot of what happens in the desert,' Sayid remarked. I thought of Antoine de Saint-Exupéry's plane crash in Libya when, with little more to drink than the juice of a single orange, he and his engineer Prévot seemed sure to die of dehydration. Yet they survived, and all because the wind during that period, a rare and unusually humid north-easterly, slowed the rate of evaporation and so their dehydration. It was a close thing. The day they were rescued by Bedouin, the breeze switched to the west, a desert wind, wrote de Saint-Exupéry, that 'dries up a man in nineteen hours'.

In spring, storms displace millions of tonnes of sand, transforming the landscape. Where there was scrub and hard ground before the storm, there'll be only the tufts of drowned bushes after. Where there was already sand, fantastic ranges of dunes form – huge ocean waves frozen against the sky long after the tempest has passed. Many of the sandy places we crossed that week had been bare and rocky only two or three years before. The northward push of the desert was as unstoppable as the sea's erosion of an exposed chalk-cliff coast. All day we could see the southerly breeze driving thin streams of sand north, like vapour. Sometimes miniature whirlwinds spun over the sand – the waltzing jinn of the desert.

The worst of any Saharan wind remains the simoom, Arab for 'poisoner'. In a simoom, sand and dust darken the sun. Vegetation, camels and men can be engulfed. Herodotus told the legend of a Persian army that perished in the desert when such a wind 'drove the sand over them in heaps as they were taking their midday meal, so that they disappeared for ever'. Later, he described how a tribe named the Psylli found their water supplies dried up by the hot south wind. A tribal council decided unanimously to declare war on the wind. 'They marched out to the desert, where the wind blew and buried them in sand. The whole tribe was wiped out, and the Nasomones occupied their former domain.'

This war, futile as ever, continues. Each day the wind pushes the Sahara northward, and the fertile coastal plains on which Tunisia's food supply depends are slowly buckling before the pressure. Around Douz and all along the border between the Sahara and the plains, trellises of woven palm branches stand in defence, sand piled high on the windward side and, often, starting to gather on the other. Like groynes on a shingle beach or sandbags on the banks of a swollen river, these simple barriers do a remarkable job, yet their foe is infinitely greater and more patient. How many of these barriers, I thought, must already have joined the warriors of the Psylli and Persia in their shifting tombs.

Sayid had made his peace. For him, a sandstorm was an occupational hazard and not one to be fought. In drastic conditions, he said, the herder's tactics would be not dissimilar to that of a hard-pressed yachtsman: stop, batten the hatches and let the weather blow past. 'We shelter next to the camels, wrap ourselves in our turbans and wait.' After the storm, the camel driver looks up to an unrecognizable world. No tracks, no familiar line of rocks, no bushes, only petrified waves of sand – an image of the storm at its height. Anyone but the most experienced desert traveller would be lost.

In an expanse of scrubland between two areas of huge, curling dunes, we came across the grave of a nomad. An oval pile of stones was all that marked the spot. There was no headstone, no epitaph and, one day, shrouded by the jinn, there'd be no stones.

Foreigners

A couple of times a week, Adèle and I would go from Sousse to El Kantaoui to work on *Shamaal*. I looked forward to these days. The boatyard was primitive in terms of equipment, but the paint- and oil-stained ground made me feel at home. The workshop, blaring radio, clatter of tools and the dozen different-shaped boats propped along the concrete stand: it all seemed so familiar. I've always liked the atmosphere in boatyards. In Britain, they are places where you still find shipwrights – skilled craftsmen working with their hands to make beautiful but useful things. Even if the shipwright does not use such words to describe his knowledge, he must understand nothing less than nature, physics, history and art if he's to do his job well. The boatyard also becomes a haven in any harbour from the glare of barely used plastic yachts that fill up the quays and pontoons. Up among the sheds and decommissioned craft you will find people sawing, drilling, hammering, painting, gluing, varnishing, splicing, welding. The scene is the perfect antidote to the sterile and pampered atmosphere often found on the water. At good boatyards, the workers will not resent an owner repairing his boat on their turf. They make excellent teachers: their knowledge is too precious to hoard and, for the boat owner willing to ask, then listen, there is the whole science of creation to discover.

Other lessons can be learnt from the boats themselves, for these tend to be as individual as the owners, reflecting not only their wealth or lack thereof, but also taste, philosophy and something of their likely fate. A number of huge, handsome sailing yachts were kept in the harbour at El Kantaoui; so, too, a few small gypsy vessels like our own and almost everything between. In the yard itself, the boats varied depending on the work being carried out. There were old-fashioned sailboats, the odd speedboat belonging to well-off locals and small, wooden fishing smacks hauled for repainting and repairs.

Because we were staying for so long, *Shamaal* had been propped up near the back of the yard, almost, but not quite, among the wrecks. Of these, there were half a dozen – not all full wrecks, but on their way, boats taken out of the water one winter, just like *Shamaal*, full of hope, full of plans, and never sailed again. Others could be seen still afloat in the marina, tied up, ready to leave, but unlikely to do so.

I supposed money problems, divorce or death had interrupted some of these voyages. Or a winter's reflection that persuaded the owner the sea was not for him after all. A voyage might be postponed – *wait and see* – without the owner having to admit that the decision had been taken to abandon the vessel. These dream graveyards are found all over the world. Gibraltar, as a kind of highway junction between northern Europe, the Mediterranean and the transatlantic routes, is famous. Some sailors, having been halfway around the world, will run out of time, funds or desire, and sell up. Others, after only the first leg from northern Europe, discover they are seasick, afraid and tired. Even the idea of returning by sea to England is too much, so they also sell up. Gibraltar is renowned for bargains. Tunisia is another such place. Here, the idea of suspending or calling off that ambitious voyage would sound simple. The rates for keeping a boat are some of the lowest in the Mediterranean, the weather is clement, the boatyard people sufficiently honest. But the sea won't let go of its victims so easily. The fleeing owner is unlikely to be able to sell his boat in Tunisia. He might take her to Malta or Italy, but that means a voyage. A year or two passes. By the third, the boat, roasted under the African sun and pummelled in sandstorms, is deteriorating. She may need work even before reaching Malta, not to mention being sold. Another year or two passes . . . Giving up in an organized way – a fighting retreat, one might say – would pose no problems, but that is rarely the way dreams end.

Right alongside *Shamaal* was the saddest of ruins, a steel craft of thirty-odd feet named *Ursula*. With a long keel, cutter rig and ratlines to climb the wooden mast, she had obviously been built with long-distance voyaging in mind, but a decade must have passed since anyone had been aboard. Rust-caked holes gaped in the hull, the sides buckled and every piece of wood had been bleached a greyish white. Otherwise, she was as the day she'd been lifted out of the water, a freeze-frame of the moment before the crisis. The anchor was lashed to a railing, fenders were still attached, a winch handle lay undisturbed. Even the mooring lines last used to tie her to the dock remained in place. Some of that gear, like the anchor, could be cannibalized, but whether out of honesty or superstition, the fishermen, yachtsmen and boatyard crew of El Kantaoui never went near. Only a raucous, extended family of stray cats – black – were at home on *Ursula*. A dozen kittens were born there during our stay.

'I've never forgotten this remark by a sailor, told in resigned and laconic tones,' wrote Isabelle Eberhardt in her journal of North Africa, *Prisoner of Dunes*, at the turn of the twentieth century. '"At sea, there're nothing but fools and paupers." Certainly the paupers he referred to are the actual sailors, submitting to constant danger and the hardest of lives. As for the "fools", they are the visionaries and vagrants, the unicorn hunters, those who, like us, "stand the hazard of the die" – emigrants and aspirants.'

The fishermen of El Kantaoui going out each night in their bright-painted cockleshells for a few dinars were the paupers. We, abandoning the security of land in hope of understanding the sea, the fools. European yachtsmen wintered in Tunisia because it was cheap and because the sun shone longer than they had ever believed possible. But also, for some, because here, more than anywhere in Europe or the North, one could enjoy the lightness and edginess of being foreign – a vagrant and unicorn chaser. One could, as we had, rent an apartment and make a few friends. Yet there was no risk of things becoming cosy, of thinking that removing *Shamaal* from the water put our travels on hold. No, Tunisia was a port of call, a place where in arriving the seeds of our departure were already sown.

I knew the risks. *The Odyssey* is a story, among other things, about the seduction and pitfalls of endless travel. There are warnings, too, in Paul Bowles's *The Sheltering Sky*, where Kit and Port, as so many travellers, are overtaken by events. Similarly, in the extraordinary fate of those European sailors 300 or so years ago who 'turned Turk' when they were captured by the pirates of North Africa's Barbary Coast. These men, mostly English and Dutch, were sometimes able to negotiate exotic and luxurious new lives in return for serving their Arab masters. A French chronicler in Algiers, the chief stronghold of the Barbary pirates, noted in 1606: 'the great profit that the English bring to the country . . . has made them cherished by the janissaries above all other nations. They carry their swords at their sides; they run drunk through the town; they sleep with the wives of Moors; in brief every kind of debauchery and unchecked license is permitted them.' Except – and this was the big proviso – the licence ever to return home. So these, too, in a way, were travellers.

The Mediterranean, sea of innumerable landfalls, always tempts you further. Byron and Shelley in Italy, Graves in Mallorca, Bowles, Kerouac and all those crazy Americans in Tangier – the Mediterranean is a classic place of self-exile and wandering, and North Africa, in its absolute reversal of everything northern, perhaps most of all. In de Maupassant, one of that long list of French writers lured to the Maghreb region (Flaubert, Dumas, Gide . . .), there is the voice of every restless northerner before or since. As he wrote in *Sur l'Eau*:

How I would like to live like a brute, in a bright, hot country, in a golden country, with no crude and harsh greenness. I would live in a vast, square house, like a huge box shining in the sun. From the terrace the sea can be seen, where those white sails, like pointed wings, of Greek or Muslim boats are passing by. . . . I would have brought to my door a white or black horse, supple as a gazelle. . . . In the calm of the evening I would go, in a mad race, towards the wide horizon which the setting sun tints with rose. Everything becomes rose-coloured there, at dusk, the burnt mountains, the sand, the clothes of the Arabs, the dromedaries, the horses and the tents.

I'd not always understood my father's yearly trips south, but now, living myself 'like a brute, in a bright, hot country', I thought perhaps that I did.

Spring brought the sirocco. Dust turned the sky a hazy yellow-brown and whirlwinds filled the air with street litter. Grit spread through our flat, mounting in small heaps on the balcony. On *Shamaal* things were worse. The boatyard was adjacent to a beach and, in high winds, its coarse grains mingled with rust-tinted Saharan sand, penetrating every locker and compartment of the boat. Sometimes it took a broom to clear the deck.

For tourist businesses in the town, the end of winter and start of preparations for the new tourist season brought a different set of worries. The attacks in New York and Washington the previous year had persuaded many Americans and Europeans against travelling to Muslim countries. Already, we knew Americans who wouldn't bring their boats to Tunisia. This seemed more the pity because, of all North Africa, Tunisia had made the greatest effort to open up to visiting yachts. Morocco's harbour facilities were only just beginning to develop. Algeria's 570-mile coastline was out-of-bounds. Libya was also off-limits. Egypt and Syria had almost no yachting facilities. Israel and Lebanon were not for everyone. A red line runs through the middle of the Mediterranean.

In the yard, workers moved without pause from boat to boat, scraping hulls, painting and hauling batteries. This was the crucial period before the summer heat, but a chaotic one, the skies filled with sandstorms, squalls and all the detritus of depressions sweeping back-to-back down the North African deserts and coasts. These were weeks when the windowpane makers worked overtime, when wearing of shawls, scarves, burnooses, djellabas and any other loose-fitting traditional garb required concentration. On the roads, overladen mopeds barely made way upwind, while motorized rickshaws struggled to keep wheels on the ground, their passengers cowering under coats and sunglasses. At the boatyard, it was not unknown for a fresh paint job, carefully executed in clement conditions, to be peppered an hour later with sand. Before making exceptionally sticky and rather slow-drying repairs of my own to *Shamaal*'s keel and bow (minor scrapes and knocks from the previous year), I would first spend an hour sweeping, even shovelling, surrounding sand and dousing the ground in water. Not yet at sea and already the wind had us on the run.

Absentee boat owners reappeared now to unlock their red-coated yachts and prepare for the season ahead. Grave Germans tinkering with electronics, garrulous Frenchmen propping up the coffee bar, quiet Norwegians hosing and re-hosing their boats. We made friends in the loose way travellers make friends: exchanging information picked up along the way about islands, anchorages, currents; joking about Tunisian work practices in the harbour; marvelling, or pretending to marvel, at each other's yachts. There is a great sense of shared purpose among cruising people – they are in the same boat, so to speak – tempered by the knowledge that they will all soon head separate ways. Friends, therefore, but rarely close friends, for otherwise one might never depart.

By the end of March, *Shamaal* was in order. Painted, oiled, varnished, re-glued, re-screwed, bolted and plugged – our little fortress stood in defiance. She was launched on 2 April between gales. I hoped Adèle and I were as ready. After so long on land, the sea looked awfully wide.

The Greek wind

Weather forecasters publish predictions for five days on the Internet, often in the form of isobaric charts. Swirling pressure gradients and knobbly fronts over the map of Europe always look reassuringly detailed, but the forecasters are the first to admit that, beyond the first twenty-four hours, nothing is sure. After forty-eight hours, there may be as little as fifty per cent reliability. Up around seventy-two hours and into the fourth and fifth days, the squiggly patterns enter the realm of guesswork.

That is on average. In the days leading to our sailing for Malta, the forecasts went awry within twenty-four hours – and badly. A predicted easterly Force 3 became a north-westerly Force 5; clear skies meant dense cloud; and talk of occasional showers brought blue skies and a gale. The gales swept through like unannounced trains.

Twice we made our goodbyes only to have to go through a new set of hellos the next day, the weather or updated weather forecast once again drastically changed. The customs officer responsible for signing us out of Tunisia became stressed and seriously suggested we leave in a gale: the paperwork was done! Then I became stressed. We had a meeting arranged with my father in Malta in four days: he arriving by plane, we by *Shamaal*. A week earlier there seemed to have been so much time to get the boat ready and complete the two-day crossing. We'd planned carefully, but time runs fast when you need it most, and now with the clock wheeling it was only luck, not planning, that would decide. '*Il faut jamais prendre un rendez-vous sur la mer,*' chided one of the old fishermen in the yard. Cantankerous old know-it-all, I thought. But he was right.

So finally to throw ourselves one morning to the mercy of the sea felt good. We departed at 4 a.m. (the unsociable hour a revenge on the customs officer), course ninety degrees. We'd leave Ile Kuriat lighthouse and shoals to starboard and from there abandon land for the 200-mile or so crossing to Malta. According to the final forecasts, we had a three-day window of west winds – perfect for sailing east – before once more the weather turned.

Africa fell astern at dawn, *Shamaal* on the broadest, easiest of reaches, almost downwind, at five knots through slight waves. Overhead, a flock of long, white birds beat vigorously in the same direction. The great spring migration had begun, for them to some misty lake or wood of landlocked central Europe, for us a winding path through the eastern Mediterranean to Greece.

Apart from a few hours' shakedown outside the harbour, we'd not been sailing for half a year and my senses felt raw. Returning to *Shamaal* was not like getting back on a bicycle after six months, but rather like rediscovering a country, albeit a country compressed into the space of a large cupboard. I must remember its laws, its customs and language. So while Adèle slept off the early start, I sat alone on deck and listened to the boat and the sea.

Midafternoon on the first day, when we'd made fifty-two miles, or a quarter of the passage, a whale surfaced twenty metres to starboard. I was in the cabin when I heard Adèle cry out. The soapy, charcoal-grey creature, big as the boat, was swimming nonchalantly, directly into our path; if Adèle hadn't yanked the tiller to one side, then it seemed we would have been bound to collide. The whale seemed not to care, altering neither speed nor course. Two lazy arches of the back and it went clear. After, it kept parallel a while at some distance on our port side, then, with a final arch, slipped under the surface and vanished. I thought at once of the whale we'd encountered on the way to Corsica the previous summer. From the mysterious blue abyss of the Corsican sea such a visit had seemed miraculous, an honour, but this time I felt only disquiet and could hardly say why. Perhaps because the water was opaque and shallow, only sixty metres deep. In such an unlikely place, the giant creature emerged almost as an obstacle like an uncharted rock, a reminder, at least, of the alien world upon which we were trespassing.

As it happened, the meeting with the whale coincided with a change in wind. I'd noticed the sea change first, a humpbacked swell from the south rolling up against the slight waves. The wind followed: a southerly breeze pushing aside the gentle airs of the west. Couldn't last, I thought. The forecast had been sure: light west winds, becoming north-west. Nothing about south winds. Nothing about strong winds either. But the wind kept on from the south and grew fresh. We were still headed for Malta, but on a closer reach under reduced sails. The gentle stroll was over. Water knocked heavily against the windward side of the hull, the far gunwale dipped under and Adèle and I retreated into oilskins – the Mediterranean in early April is surprisingly frigid.

Sailing fast through a building sea, we found ourselves among hundreds upon hundreds of jellyfish, walnut-sized blobs with tiny gas-filled sails protruding above the surface. Leaning over the side, I scooped one up in my straw hat for inspection, surprised as I did this by the speed at which the water passed. These were *Velella velella*, or by-the-wind sailors, and they, too, were travelling between sea and sky, but their presence brought little comfort.

Their journey would end wherever the wind blew, for they had sails, but no rudder, and their passiveness only highlighted our perverse determination.

Force 5 became Force 6, the sea gathered and I looked into the sky, trying to imagine ways in which the weather maps might still be proved right. Low, grey cloud to the west might signal a warm front. That could still mean the south wind was temporary. It might veer to south-west or west, then later north-west, just as had been announced – perfect for reaching Malta. By sundown, though, the grey cloud of my supposed warm front had vanished, the south wind blew harder than ever and the sky, littered in ripped cirrus, was bloody. We began to prepare for heavy conditions, tightening the hatches, putting away any last loose belongings and readying food for the hours when it might be too difficult to cook.

That first night we crossed the halfway point to Malta, but the wind had crept to south-south-east, putting *Shamaal* on an ever more constricted course. 'Waves bigger,' I scrawled in the log-book on a lurching chart table around midnight. 'Some breaking against bow. Spray over whole deck. Rigging howling.' On watch that night I braced myself in the cockpit as *Shamaal*, steered by wind vane, went mogul-bashing against the wind. The motion put me in a kind of trance, as if all were out of my control and, like the *Velella velella*, we now simply sped towards a destination chosen by others. Smash went *Shamaal*, smash, smash, smash. The bow split wave after wave, spray falling, thudding and slapping over the deck. These were plankton-rich waters, and the deck, constantly soaked, began to glow. Behind, the rudder ignited a thick ribbon of cold, pale fire.

Such a night, the phosphorescent sea all around, was too overwhelming for me to be able to consider Malta more than a navigational abstraction. How unimaginable that soon we would see spring flowers; that I would take my first swim of the year, diving from rocks into clear pools; and, after six months in a Muslim country, hear the voice of the muezzin replaced by bells.

That Adèle and I would soon meet my father seemed least imaginable of all. His flight around a quarter of the world would be complete in the hours it took us to travel seventy miles. Yet both trajectories, one long and swooping, one short and jolting, had been calibrated to end at the same place – a speck of rock in the watery crossroads of east and west Mediterranean – and, more trickily, at the same time.

The sideways force of the waves pushed us off course so that we never saw the lighthouse on the tiny Italian island of Lampedusa. We sailed fast and, by dawn, had weathered the even smaller outcrop of Linosa. Waves heaped against the knuckle-shaped island where red and green and yellow fishing craft lay high on the beach. I could see the figures of two people on a clifftop path and for a moment watched them wistfully. Then Linosa fell astern and we were alone with the sea again.

The journey was entering new territory. Our first rendezvous with the sweet west wind had been missed and we found ourselves in an unfamiliar crowd. If the wind remained so, fresh and out of the south-south-east, our luminous little ship would reach Malta in twenty-four hours. I again imagined the pathways lit with flowers and the diving pools between sea-worn rocks. I imagined greeting my father at the airport and what a time we'd all have. But these were forecasts, their reliability suspect, and, instead of flowers and pools, the only image to stick was that of the whale, like a warning, under the bows of *Shamaal*.

Every hour the wind strengthened and backed: south-east, east, east-north-east, each click of the wind rose forcing us to a tighter point of sail, and *Shamaal* heeling harder all the time. Malta could no longer be reached direct. Adèle tried filming, recording the rhythmic lurching of the boat through black-and-white seas, but was soon driven back by the spray. We began to tack, aiming first at one side of Malta, then the next. But the waves were steeper now and the deck awash. Each time we rose over one wave, the prow buried itself in the trough of the next – like sailing into an endless succession of walls. And when the second night fell, the wind blew from east-north-east, that is, directly from Malta, at near gale force. Just thirty miles from Gozo and the nearest safe harbour, the gregale – the same wind Proctor warned us about – had stopped us dead.

Water dripped from my oilskins and face as I hunched over the chart table, legs braced against the opposite bunk, and tried to conjure a way out. An obvious solution was to wheel the boat around and run. Running took the sting out of a storm. It was the prime defensive measure – exactly what Saint Paul's ship did when struck by the 'tempestuous' gregale near Crete some 2,000 years ago. The opposite, to head upwind against the waves, was impossible. The boat, particularly such a small boat as ours, would take a beating and go nowhere. Running made sense, but to where? We surely couldn't go back all the way to Tunisia. Between, there was only the fishing port in Lampedusa. The idea of retreat galled me. On the small-scale chart, the pencil line of our journey jogged from Tunisia to within two centimetres of Gozo, three from Malta. A few centimetres between us and the rendezvous with my father.

'I told you so!' the old Tunisian fisherman would say. Don't crow, I'd mutter back. We had almost made it, after all, and there *had* to be options. We could run to Lampedusa, wait for the weather to improve, then get back. Or maybe the gale would last only a few hours, a blip in our journey. Malta was so very close . . . My finger traced over the chart. Malta, Lampedusa, Malta, Lampedusa. Run or not? If only there were a fresh weather forecast: the idea had not completely lost its magic. Years of conditioning, of faith in technology, of believing there are answers, are not easily overcome.

I called into the VHF. No reply. I called again several times. To the coastguard, to the harbour authorities, the lighthouse over the western tip of Gozo, to anyone I could think of . . . No reply. I switched off the radio. The pale, green light on the receiver faded. We were alone.

Things became strangely simple. The gale might last an hour, a day, a week: we didn't know. We didn't know whether we'd make it for my father's arrival. We didn't really know whether running to Lampedusa was safe – a port, after all, is only of use when you are tucked up inside. Look what happened to Saint Paul's ship when it reached Malta: wrecking in the 'violence of the waves'. Out here, we didn't *know* anything. There was no forecast, no deus ex machina, no book of answers. As the old Tunisian said: '*Il faut jamais prendre un rendez-vous sur la mer.*' One made appointments on land, shuffled, cancelled and fiddled with them. There was 'time management'. But not at sea. There are no paths or footprints on the sea, no future or past – only the present.

Setting the tiny mainsail and storm jib against each other, then lashing the tiller, we stalled *Shamaal*, her nose at an angle of about forty-five degrees to the wind, the waves slipping harmlessly underneath. Hove-to, we bobbed up and down the side of waves like a bottle. Waves fizzed. The noise in the rigging was horrifying, literally: the unnatural, spooky, violent noise of taut steel cables sawing the wind. We were tired, cold and a little sick. Five hours of darkness lay ahead. But we had learnt a lesson. Taking turns to sleep and to huddle in the cockpit on watch for ships, Adèle and I let the present blow past.

By dawn we had drifted to within fifteen miles of Gozo and I hoped to see its outline, but there was only the sea – the jumping, spewing sea, a sea of rich, white foam at wave tops; thin, streaked foam down the sides; and spindrift like smoke.

Shivering, soaked, tired and deafened by the noise of the waves pounding *Shamaal*, there was little need to talk. Adèle and I simply got through the day, taking three hours of watch, then collapsing under a damp sleeping bag for the three hours off. Most waves *Shamaal* took well, lifting, heeling and coming upright again like a boxer ducking a blow. Some waves, though, had almost vertical faces, and *Shamaal* reeled, tilting heavily in the trough before the big keel yanked her back up, water now flowing in torrents around deck. There were moments on looking out that I gasped. Sailors have long talked of mountainous waves, but the hyperbole is unnecessary. A three-metre wave ranks as rough, a fourteen-metre wave phenomenal – nothing to do with mountains, but enough to break apart a minor ship. The gregale forms large waves by Mediterranean standards. So what we faced, in land terms, were sizeable mounds, waves of four and five metres. Hundreds or thousands of them in all directions, all linked, all moving, some breaking at the top, the shattered water racing down the face like scree. *Shamaal* was caught in a landslide and we were clinging on.

Our expensive waterproofs struggled to keep up. Spray invaded sleeves, collars, hoods, zips, seams. Inside the boat, everything one touched became wet – bedding, charts, the floor, the sides. At first we used towels to mop up the floor and seats, but then these, too, became wet and, once wet, nothing dried. We became cold. Blowing from high-pressure systems over the Balkans (hence the Greek name), the gregale is a chill wind. Often it is associated with the bora, the Adriatic northerly so violent that handholds have had to be erected in the streets of Trieste. A thuggish pair.

So two layers of clothing became three and four. Two small blankets came into service – even sodden, they provided insulation. At last, I found Adèle in two hats, a hood, two pairs of gloves, oilskins, two pairs of socks, boots and two blankets. The entire ensemble, compressed into one soaking red ball, left only her blue eyes uncovered. Eventually, she became badly seasick. This was hardly surprising, given our picking a storm for our maiden voyage of the year, not to mention the fact that almost every sailor, including the greatest, has suffered at some time. But Adèle was too proud to admit her misery, and the first I knew was when she shot from the cabin, pushed past and collapsed over the railing. One is rarely sick just once. On she went, again and again until I feared she might disappear altogether. But she endured.

★

On the second day of the gale, a small, dark bird appeared. At once it caught my attention, not just because it was the first living thing I'd seen beyond *Shamaal* since Linosa, but also for the odd flight pattern, a sort of darting and stabbing between the waves. The tricks of an acrobat, I wondered, a storm petrel maybe? Or something else – the desperate, failing attempts of a stranded bird to stay in the air? I'd never know. The spray and motion of the boat made the bird hard to follow. I paused once to wipe my stinging eyes and, when I looked up, the bird was gone.

The incident loomed large in a day when all existence seemed to consist of water – of waves, wash, foam, whitecaps, spray, splash, pools, rivulets and streams. *Shamaal* heeled so hard a few times that the sea spilled right above the cabin windows, swirling green and white beyond the oval frames. Leaks sprang in places we had carefully fixed and places we never knew could leak, sometimes a single drop, sometimes a trickle. As water invaded, paint pots in the bow storage section lost their labels; books became wet bricks; the sensor on a spare life jacket reacted to the growing pool in its locker and inflated; packets of biscuits turned to mush. Dirty water rose from under the engine into the main cabin. We started to pump. Adèle, now recovering, tried to make us tea and spilled boiling water over her arm – harmlessly, given the thick collection of layers.

Our second visitor came during my watch that night: a ship. This was the first vessel we'd seen since Tunisia three days earlier. The navigation lights appeared distant, but I knew they couldn't really be more than a couple of miles away. I counted five lights: a white, a green and white, and a red and green. Numbly, I deciphered the code: a fishing vessel, a trawler, and pointing our way, yes, from the direction of Malta, goddamn, and heading straight towards us. The initial surprise of this intrusion turned to mesmerized interest, then alarm. The lights became crisp, their layout giving an idea of the ship's structure, a strangely broad and high outline, maybe of a factory boat of some sort.

No need to shake myself to stay awake any more, nor to rub my drenched gloves to keep warm. Adrenalin and gnawing fear took care of that.

'Quick, Adèle!' She piled from her bunk. 'The big torch. Quick!' To be run down in a gale, I thought: this could hardly be happening – but it was. *Shamaal* was unmanoeuvrable in these seas, immobilized, and the mystery ship closed fast.

Remain calm. First shine the torch – it was one we always kept in reserve for this kind of moment – and, if that didn't work, light a white flare. I played the torch against our deep-reefed mainsail, the bright beam shining against soaked and straining canvas. From a distance, tiny *Shamaal* must have looked like little more than another flashing wave. The lights grew brighter and bigger every second. My fingers closed on the flare, pushed off the cap, then relaxed . . . The ship was turning. That awful symmetry of lights signalling collision became lopsided. Slowly the whole arrangement swung about. Now we had only the starboard side of the ship. She crossed our stern, with about fifty metres to spare. Soon after, someone switched on the working lights, a blazing white glare from the stern decks, and, still glowing, the ship disappeared over the horizon.

I was too tired and too wrapped in my own world to bother trying to raise them on the radio – it wasn't switched on – so I would never know why they'd aimed so at us. Maybe by mistake. Maybe out of concern: it would have made a strange sight, this small boat hove-to, protected only by the beam of a torch.

About two hours later, the wind eased. By then, we'd stopped thinking about an end to the gale. In fact, in a strange, exhausted way, we'd just begun to consider this existence normal. But the wind dropped to Force 5. There was no trick. The waves became round, *Shamaal* settled down, and in short order we'd untied the tiller, set the wind vane and begun to tack towards land. We hardly dared speak of our relief, but after thirty-six hours hove-to we were again on our way. The wind kept easing, the sun rose and shortly the blue, high ground of Gozo floated into view.

Hour by hour the day softened. Adèle cooked a huge breakfast. The sun shone enough for us to hang a few clothes on the rails. The wind dropped to Force 2 and we turned on the engine, motoring slowly along Malta's scraggy north coast. The Red Ensign, tattered at the edges and crusty with salt, hung limply. *Shamaal*'s motor chugged drowsily. Once more we discussed the spring flowers we'd see, the rock pool I'd dive into, the times we'd have with my father. He'd land tomorrow. We'd buy a good whiskey to celebrate.

Late afternoon, we passed Saint Paul's Bay, where the apostle's ship is said to have grounded at the end of its headlong run from Crete. By evening, we could see the domes and battlements of Valletta. The sun was setting as we moored against the wall by the *Black Pearl* in Msida marina. The man on the neighbouring boat helped us with our lines. 'From Tunisia, you say? So you were *out there* last night? We were seasick tied up here in port!' Wearing a mishmash of the last dry clothes aboard, Adèle and I stepped up on to the dock.

A chance conversation with a Tunisian taxi driver came to mind. He'd been almost the last Tunisian I met – the one taking me from our flat to *Shamaal* for the final time. He'd asked whether I believed in God. This was just as the taxi arrived at the harbour. Why yes, I'd said. 'That's good, but at sea there are many people who believe in God, who pray to him, who swear to thank him for ever . . . and forget all this the moment their feet touch dry land.' When I touched dry land, the stone quay seemed to tip beneath my foot.

Our mattresses, clothing, books and some of the equipment took days to dry even when left on deck under the sun. We recovered more quickly, thanks in part to the gift my father made us of a room at the hotel where he stayed. It was a happy reunion. All that week, though, as we toured about Malta and Gozo, I knew what was on my father's mind. His son and daughter-in-law were meant to be established by now, earning proper salaries, showing responsibility – certainly not running around at sea. The bedraggled state in which he'd found us had only reinforced these parental fears. Of course, I imagined that in his heart he knew very well what we were doing: any traveller recognizes his kind and he could hardly fail to. But the hotel became a sort of advertisement for the life we were missing. Certainly, without my father, we never would have spent a night there, never lounged in the double bed, never zapped through satellite TV or wasted countless gallons of water in the shiny bathroom. But there was no turning us now. When my father left after a week, even Adèle and I were surprised by how much we looked forward to checking out and getting back to *Shamaal*.

For a few more days we hung around Valletta, gathering supplies and catching up with our Maltese friends from Siracusa and the Dutch writer and sculptress from Palermo, who by luck were also berthed in the harbour. Perched in a bar overlooking the boats, all the talk was of plans for the summer, of islands, bays and creeks. The Dutch wanted to sail to the Black Sea. The Maltese hadn't much time and would settle for Sicily. We, too, were bound for Sicily, but only as a stepping stone to Greece – the broad Ionian, the gulfs of Patras and Corinth, Athens and its Tower of Winds, the kaleidoscope of the Cyclades . . . No, there was no chance of turning us now.

A winter crossing in spring

Malta is best seen at a short distance. The view from the harbour is perfect, and our last sight on leaving Valletta was of the eggshell cathedral and crenellations glowing in the western sun. If only we could somehow have stayed there, suspended between forts and churches, always about to leave or arrive. Up close, Malta had proved to be composed almost entirely of monuments, most of them squat and overadorned, like ugly jewellery. Between the monuments were traffic and dust. So while *Shamaal* nudged her way between the breakwaters and headed north, I savoured the dying moment. In the low rays, gold sparkled about the citadel from which the Knights of Malta once catapulted the heads of slain Ottoman assailants. Across the water, from where the Turks floated crucified Christian defenders, bristled Fort Tigne. Someone prepared to swim from the rocks – a gentle, final sight. Not half an hour later, Malta sank into the dusk. We were at sea, and already the waves punched *Shamaal*.

We'd had an awkward experience while on the island. There'd been the three of us – Adèle, my father and me – visiting one of those oddly grandiose yet provincial small towns. It was Sunday and in the main square they had a flea market, good for antiques and books of dubious origin, 'I LOVE MALTA' T-shirts, straw hats and other usual fare. Then between the hats and books we'd come across a man selling songbirds – goldfinches, greenfinches, warblers and a few more exotic-looking creatures – trapped during migration. The idea to buy as many as we could and set them free came to all of us more or less simultaneously. Common sense made us hesitate, but not long. It was too easy.

Soon enough, we'd carried eight of the captives to a patch of rough ground behind a church. A tiny drum roll might have been apt. Instead, feeling slightly shifty, we looked around, looked at each other and unclasped the cage doors. One bird immediately hopped to the opening and flew off, then a second, but an unnerving stillness followed. Something was wrong: six birds remained, a bundle of bright feathers and silent vocal cords, and each refusing to fly. Standing up on that hill we could only look from the cowering birds to each other and back to the birds, then hope, only there was nothing to hope for. A clipped wing is a clipped wing, and neither our innocent failure to notice this nor the fact that feathers eventually grow back could save the experiment from failure. We got them out in the end and set the empty cages down on the ground, but it had become a squalid affair. A hop, a chaotic fluttering of shorn wings and, one by one, our birds made away, all giving up in about the same place just down the slope. Strange to see, six brightly coloured songbirds clinging to one shrivelled bush and none of them singing.

The incident returned to me throughout the crossing that night. I supposed that cats must have got the non-flyers by now, but the two that could fly, maybe they'd been able to rejoin their migration north. I hoped so. This was not the season for anyone or anything to be caged.

Crossing the big shipping lane in the centre of the Malta–Sicily strait it seemed that half the world was on the move. Red, green and white, the lights of huge ships slipped silently east and west. Crews of every cast, goods of every description raced to and fro, and through the middle of them our own fragile cargo.

Then, fifteen miles off south-east Sicily, a peculiarly high set of red and green lights. My eyes seemed to play tricks: no boat could be that high, yet a boat it seemed. Nearby another pair of red and green, this time much lower. I stared for minutes into space, my bearings confused. Where did the horizon meet the night? Where did one boat begin, the other end, and how far away were they from us? The high lights moved suddenly at speed around the lower lights, far faster than any usual boat. Between the small red and green spots, a thick beam of white pointed down like a proboscis. Of course: a helicopter hovering over a ship of some sort. Aircraft carry the same night lights as boats. Following what must have been a search of the area, the helicopter left to fly directly over us. For a few seconds, the proboscis sucked away all the darkness, leaving *Shamaal* in a pool of light and noise before the darkness poured back in again. The helicopter, now without its searchlight, clattered, then buzzed, then slid silently towards the Sicilian coast.

This was an experience we were to have several times over the coming days. For in addition to migrating birds and fish, we shared the seas that spring with record numbers of the world's escaping poor. From Africa, from Iraq, from Kurdish Turkey and from Albania, they took the frightening step beyond the cage door. Some would fly, others be put back, still others perish. The helicopters were looking for them, so, too, the sleek patrol boats and air force surveillance planes, but the seas were neither so small nor so bare that many couldn't slip the net. After all, each time *Shamaal* or any other boat came under scrutiny, some other place was being left unwatched. Their routes were no different to those of the birds. The perils of the sea were paramount – only Spanish newspapers bothered now to report when bodies of migrants washed up around Gibraltar – and therefore the shortest crossings, like that to Sicily, were the most popular. Sicily, poor, exhausted by its own history, but still the fulcrum of the Mediterranean, east and west, north and south: as long as birds and people crossed the sea, this would not change.

Just after dawn we came upon the low, sandy south-eastern corner of Sicily and nudged our way through the shallows to Portopalo. We hoped to re-supply and to catch a weather report before the long crossing to Greece. The harbour, consisting of a bay protected by two enormous breakwaters, was an oddly quiet place. The actual town of Portopalo was at some distance up a hill. Down here, a fleet of rust-striped fishing trawlers lay to moorings, but ours was the sole sailing boat. The fishing vessels appeared mostly unmanned. The quays, too, were deserted, and the single shoreside restaurant was shut tight. Only when we rowed through the boats in the rubber dinghy did we flush out any life: a man appearing then disappearing through a hatch; a boy in dirty jeans heaving on ropes the thickness of his arms; guard dogs all puffed up with responsibility. The few men loitering about the harbour sheds gave us long stares as we walked up to town. There are still places in the Mediterranean that, at certain times of year, give the impression of never having seen an outsider.

After a year of travel, the remoteness matched us well. The sea, once the conduit of information across the Mediterranean, had become an isolator. If we wanted to reach someone, we had to wait until we were on land. Then we needed a working phone booth or one of those hole-in-the-wall Internet cafés. If someone wanted *us*, things really became complicated. Probably a little string remained around our necks, but not enough to yank. Any post had first to go through the address of a London friend. She could forward it, but to where? I pictured the stacked envelopes in their London camp, an army stranded, never to see the fair lands its generals promised, and dying of inaction. When bureaucratic harbour officials demanded to know our next port, we ourselves could often only guess. Now, since leaving Tunisia, our VHF radio, the ship's most important link, had given up. No transmission, no reception: radio silence appeared to be final and, for a while, we'd be reduced to putting into ports even for weather and news.

Whether Portopalo was going to cooperate was another question. Once ashore, rows of broken fishing boats led to ramshackle greenhouses, to empty streets and finally to the town centre, where the church bore a weather vane in the shape of a swordfish. One establishment advertising Internet access had no computers. Another was closed. The search took us eventually to a small place housing the local coastguard. This, too, was shut, but a young, uniformed man smoking out of an upper floor window agreed to let us enter. After listening to our explanations given in poor, staccato Italian – *'piccola barca'/'meteo previsioni'/'radio no funcciona'*, etc. – he led us to a VHF set and pulled up two chairs. The Italian marine forecast takes a long time and, while I scribbled, the coastguard had time to quiz us about *Shamaal* and London, sounding as if he had never been on a boat, much less to another country. A crib sheet pinned to the wall to aid communications in English with passing ships reinforced the impression. 'What port do you come from? What cargo have you on bord?' The phrases became increasingly dramatic. 'When will you go away? No, you must go immediately away! At least, you must go away in one or two hours! You must go out twelve miles from the coast!'

The weather report was good: three days of northerly or westerly winds, and no gales. We'd leave the following day.

The harbour was half-empty early the next morning, many of the fishing boats having gone out overnight. About ten, as we were about to leave ourselves, the fleet began to return, crewmen standing tired and relaxed on the high, steel bows. *Mare Chiara* came racing in like all the others, a man jumping overboard into the trailing dinghy to take the lines from the bow and tie up to a mooring buoy only a short distance from *Shamaal*. One of the crew, muscular under a layer of fat, shouted across the water to us. Not understanding, we signalled back, a friendly, non-committal smile and shrug of the shoulders – the thing the English do so well when the intention is actually to avoid contact. He shouted again, this time holding a silver fish by the tail. We repeated our gesture, slightly startled by this breach of Portopalo's rules of silence. I guessed what would ensue. Taking advantage of a picturesque setting, the fishermen would try to sell us fresh fish that we didn't want and at absurd prices. They would act insulted when we said no, then we would say yes to something small just to get away. After, we'd justify the purchase to ourselves by saying it had happened in such an authentic way, knowing all the while we'd been fleeced. In other words, after a long night of work, this gang of cut-throats had stumbled upon a far easier prey than small, shy fish. All this flashed through my mind in parallel with a vivid sense of curiosity: just as we were about to leave, sleepy Portopalo was coming to life.

The battered dinghy barely held the four men from *Mare Chiara*. One steered, two sat in the bow and the last held a crate of fish on his lap. Once alongside *Shamaal*, they looked more than ever the boarding party from a corsair ship: heavy-set, unshaven men with battered teeth and knotted forearms. The crate – golden shrimp in one half, silver sardines or some other small fish in the other – was raised for inspection. We couldn't help smiling. 'How much?' asked Adèle, veteran of Tunisian marketplaces. The fishermen's faces, already shaded in fatigue,

darkened. 'No, no, no,' one replied. The crate was pushed towards us. There were words in Italian we could not understand.
Again the crate was offered. We looked back, incredulous, tried
to decline out of English politeness, saw that this only angered
the fishermen and quickly accepted. Big smiles filled the dinghy.
Rooted to our spot on *Shamaal*'s gunwale, we were still holding
the crate when the crew of *Mare Chiara* turned their dinghy
around, and still when they waved a final time before disappearing between the other boats on their way back to land.

All that day, sailing slowly towards the toe of the Italian boot,
we feasted, a dotted line of shrimp shells marking our wake.

Our Maltese friends had urged us to coast hop to Greece. 'You
want to watch out at this time of year. You think April is spring,
but to us April is winter. Even May is kind of winter.' Indeed,
sticking to the coast, a sailing boat could feasibly go from Sicily
to anywhere in Greece during summer months without a single
night at sea. The toe leads to the arch, the strange protuberance
at Crotone to the Italian heel, and finally a seventy-mile passage
across the Otranto Strait to Corfu, before the green islands of the
eastern Ionian and all the jigsaw puzzle of Greece. For many
centuries, this has been the path for oared galleys, nervous sailors
and anyone with time on his hands. But our priorities were
different. There were 290 nautical miles direct to the first Greek
port – possibly far more with unfavourable winds – and, when
the sun rolled up from that big, blue, bare space, we answered
its call.

Although we quickly lost sight of Sicily, the presence of land
remained strong. Behind lay the lowlands of Siracusa, invisible
even in the dazzle of electric storms, and to the north, dwarfed
by the horizon, the steep barrenness of Calabria. Only gradually
did the sensation of being fully disconnected from land take over.
First, the western Mediterranean planning chart ceded to its
crisp, unused eastern companion. Then one of those military
surveillance planes came, circling noisily and low enough so that

I could see the wing markings. When it turned back for Sicily, I knew we were finally off their screens. A new journey had begun.

The Ionian may be the deepest and broadest of the Mediterranean's internal seas – we wouldn't spot a ship until the Greek coast – but rarely were we alone. Bonitos jumping, dolphins cruising, loggerhead turtles soaking up the sun and great fleets of migrating birds flying north: all taking part in the whirligig of spring.

The flocks moved quickly and without hesitation, apparently from Libya towards Greece and Italy. At least, that was the direction of their flight. It has never been established exactly how birds navigate, but they appear to use celestial navigation, memorized landmarks and some form of magnetic pulse. It is in any case a near miraculous feat performed twice yearly and with great efficiency by millions of otherwise humble creatures. The insistent, one-chance-is-all-we've-got way they flew moved me. Obviously the sea for them spelled death and had to be crossed quickly, but it was the instinct to live, not fear of dying, that propelled them through this endless cycle of voyages. When two swallows perched on *Shamaal*'s mast for a rest, I thought at first that they might stay. We were, after all, going their way, but not a minute passed before they took off again, beating hard. That powerful urge to keep moving was something I thought I could understand.

It happened that, for the first time on any of our crossings, we had no fixed destination. There are three main islands off the centre of western Greece – Zákinthos, Cephalonia, Levkás – and it made little difference to us on which we landed. From all of them we could later reach Ithaca and, from Ithaca, Athens. The wind, despite those hopeful forecasts of following westerlies, was contrary, shifting from the north-east to south-east. With the wind vane set to keep us as close to the wind as possible, this meant that sometimes we sailed towards Levkás, sometimes to Zákinthos and, occasionally, as far north as Corfu. If the different winds cancelled each other over time, then Cephalonia fell into place. Winging eastward, a sense of lightness came over us both: if not better sailors, we were at least becoming better travellers. No longer the temptation to look for lanes and all the grids and codes that define life on land. No longer the stubborn vision of our boat moving across vast fixed spaces like a marble rolling over a floor. We moved, but so did everything above and below and around. Levkás, Zákinthos, Cephalonia . . . It didn't matter. Like the migrating birds, we knew only that we must push forward, if not in the right direction, then something close – whatever moved us fastest across the sea.

If our methods were unsophisticated, then so were the instruments we used. Like most of the fancier equipment on *Shamaal*, the electronic log was now fully out of commission, replaced by a mechanical device consisting of a dial like something from an early racing car and a small bronze propeller that trailed on a line behind the boat. The depth sounder had become erratic, so in anchorages we would often have to double-check with the old-fashioned lead-and-line, a weight at the end of twine knotted every metre. The autopilot, an electronic machine that guided the tiller during tedious hours of motoring, still worked, but this, too, would soon give up, to be poorly substituted by a lashing of shock cord. *Shamaal* was progressively shedding her most modern accoutrements. We'd almost forgotten the existence of the two remaining operable cabin lights, long replaced by the apricot-yellow glow of paraffin lamps. The little GPS was in one piece, but I wondered sometimes whether the sextant, which I was starting to master, wouldn't be called into service after all. We were no Luddites, but fixing electronics is difficult, replacing them expensive, and we were neither electricians nor rich. The satisfaction, even romance, of primitive alternatives – this would follow.

From dusk onward, the cloud built, slowly encircling our world and blotting out the stars. Only to the east was there bare sky. I wished we could go faster and escape, but the storm caught up and the last eastern light was snuffed out. Heavy, round, cold drops of rain fell, but the sea was smooth, as if the waves had been cowed, and *Shamaal* heeled, running fast in the gathering wind. What a night: unfit for small boats and even more so for the small birds. From the north-east blew that cold, bullying wind, not at all what they or we wanted. Lightning wove through the sky and thunder gunned from moonburnt clouds.

At dawn the sun rose bathed in ghastly red. Lightning flared white and distant rain showers fell in geometrically neat lines. Adèle and I sat together on deck, intrigued and wary. Miraculously few yachts are struck by lightning, even if an aluminium mast would seem to make an ideal conductor. In theory, a bolt could cannon down our mast, causing serious damage or injury. Our only defence was the steel cable we'd dangled from the base of the mast into the sea overnight. It was meant to earth the boat, but was a rarely tested DIY arrangement that in appearance, at least, seemed laughably inadequate. Now a new threat. Dark lumps formed at the base of a cloud wall to the south, three or four at a time, and from each lump, like a butterfly escaping its chrysalis, wound long, dreamy wisps that snaked and twisted towards the sea. Waterspouts – tornadoes, really.

Vague, useless fear: in a direct hit, *Shamaal* might well be destroyed, yet there was nothing, even less than against lightning, that could be done. From a distance the waterspouts appeared to move without malice or reason, truly like butterflies, corkscrewing from sky to sea. Some evaporated immediately on leaving their cloud. Others became distracted, describing a graceful, looping S on their way down. A few reached their goal, momentarily connecting heaven and earth. One brushed the sea's surface, a witch's bony finger that I could see make the water hiss and boil white.

When the squall zeroed in, rain fell so hard that the sea foamed. The wind swung through ninety degrees. Then, just as abruptly, the rain stopped and the wind died, and reappeared, some minutes later, as a light westerly breeze. Beyond the vaulted clouds of a cold front, the sky shone and, in twenty minutes, we were clear. The day was well advanced, but it felt like the beginning of time.

It was that afternoon that a small, greenish-brown bird, a warbler of some sort, came to stay. Many hundreds had passed overhead. A few perched awhile on deck, then, in the usual manner, left. One stayed. We called him Icarus. Like the others, he began near the bow, as far from us as possible, before discovering how wet it would be. Moving slowly astern, he investigated the dinghy rolled up and lashed on the foredeck. He hopped around the mast. He even left the boat and circled a few times before coming back. Quickly he gained confidence. He perched on the stern rail, then by the tiller, then in the cockpit. I found him on my bare foot one minute, in the cabin the next. Nestling in a corner between pilot books and the bulkhead over the chart table, he tucked his head under a wing and fell asleep.

Icarus stayed the rest of the day. At nightfall we were sure he'd leave – so many of his kind had flown over – but all he did was change position. Now above the chart table, later inside the cupboard behind the stove, up by the white flare near the main hatch and even in the place amidships where we kept Adèle's camera and other fragile gear. How long had he been flying? Where had he started? Africa was about 500 miles to the south. Surely he'd run into the thunderstorm – a lost bird crashing against the walls and columns of that dark fairy palace. We tried giving Icarus breadcrumbs. Also a little dish of water. But he only wanted sleep.

Adèle and I went through our watches that night in a state of elation. There were three of us on board now – three travellers – and all of us tiptoeing around the edge of the same vast hole. We imagined Icarus staying until Greece, only a day and a half away. We'd deliver him right to his summer home. Maybe he'd not want to leave at all. At dawn we crept excited, but ever so discreetly, to his cubbyhole. Icarus was still asleep. Five minutes later, Adèle checked again. He was dead.

His body was soft, but no longer warm, when we dropped him into the sea. Strangely enough, just at that moment we sailed past the corpse of another warbler. Adèle was distraught – inconsolable.

All morning I sat alone on deck watching the Ionian play in the sun.

Sixty miles west of Greece, two flies buzzed through the rigging, reminding us of land. A warm front covered the sky, sending winds strongly from the south-west. We had the mainsail down and scudded on a broad reach at five or six knots under jib alone. Waves rose from behind and slipped underneath without so much as a hiccup. A gale could blow and I didn't think *Shamaal* would care. We were racing for the finish line now.

Our first glimpse was a mountain, silvery and insubstantial. The clouds parted a little and another mountain emerged. The clouds closed and the original mountain vanished. The sky shifted, swimming, billowing and shrinking, and with each mutation the landscape beneath also changed.

About ten miles out and we could still not say for sure where we were. The GPS would have told us, but we didn't want to find out from satellites. Our dead reckoning put us on course for Cephalonia, the best of all landing places, but no sooner did we take bearings of some mountain top or island headland than the pattern altered. The lowlands that intersperse the high ground of Cephalonia rose and sank beneath the horizon. Mountains lined up to create the impression of new islands, and sometimes the sky came so low that the whole scene disappeared altogether. How many times we congratulated ourselves on our chart work, only to curse our overconfidence a minute later. For one moment it seemed we had gone so far off course that we were in fact approaching northern Levkás, a tricky place in strong winds. By and by the jumble of land, sea and cloud took final form and we found ourselves dead on course for north-west Cephalonia. After more than 300 miles of open sea, a perfect landfall was at hand.

Ithaca

Our first good view of Ithaca was from Cephalonia. Anchored in a deserted cove, we could look across the narrow channel to the dark woods of Mount Neriton, close to where Homer imagined Odysseus to have lived. There is disagreement about whether Homer's Ithaca and this island are the same. Odysseus' description of his homeland being the 'farthest out to sea' of a group of islands is an obvious discrepancy. Otherwise, Ithaca looked as I'd always imagined it: brooding, secretive and haughty.

Our anchorage, about a quarter of the way down the eastern side of Cephalonia, was a horseshoe inlet fringed by low cliffs and steep, thickly wooded hills. Nestling in the head of the cove, a meadow twinkled with spring flowers – marigolds and Venus' looking-glass, chicory and hawksbeard, sea lavenders, woundworts and crane's-bills. There were no houses or boats near, and the cove barely featured on our chart. During the day we lay in the tall grass under an olive tree, gathered flowers and drank wine. In the evening we lit a fire and cooked on the beach before rowing back through the dark to *Shamaal*. Only once did we have company: long-haired, bugle-horned, human-eyed goats that came through the meadow shaking their bells with only the purpose, it seemed, of standing awhile and looking silently into the sea. After three days we weighed anchor and sailed to Ithaca.

Just twelve miles separated us from the Ithacan capital, Vathi, on the far side of the island, but the journey took all day. A north breeze parried us all the way up the channel to the north of the island. No matter, we said: once around the tip of Ithaca, a straight run would take us quickly the rest of the way. Yet at the top of the island the wind became east, once more in our face. Only the southward leg along the east side of the island remained, and there, unlikely as it seemed, another headwind awaited. Three coasts, three contrary winds. A little less than halfway down the east coast we gave up, striking sail and motoring into an emerald cove for the night.

Islands distort and redirect wind, much as a boulder creates eddies in a river. That much is easy – a diagram can be drawn in seconds – but it is not even half the story. The heat of an island creates new winds, mountains arrest some, accelerate others, and all these must meet, mingle, die or dance. The pairing of two islands means the re-diverting of already diverted winds. Add a third and fourth island, then a mountainous mainland, a few peninsulas and gulfs . . . Chaos may be the only word for the resulting pattern. This is Greece. Already in the anchorage on Cephalonia there'd been the occasion when one breeze blew at *Shamaal*'s bow, an opposite one at the stern, less than eight metres apart. Watch the sky, sailors say, but here also the water, the flags and birds, that dragonfly, the dust over the rock, the swaying of grass.

We had just acquired a replacement VHF radio, a small walkie-talkie type, and each day there were weather reports, first in Greek, then English, though this was not a country for forecasts. Most signals died against the cliffs and hillsides, leaving only static in their place, and what we did hear was never right. Just words and numbers from a hat, or so it seemed. Yet still we listened, just as still we read myths about which little or nothing could be proved. The forecast we received while in the emerald cove was wrong again, but this time in our favour: we entered Vathi with the wind on our tail. About the first thing I noticed after tying up in the ancient harbour was a hand-drawn wind rose on the wall of an office: *tramontana, grego, apeliotis, sorokos, ostria, garbis, zefyros, maistros* . . . The roll call in scribbled Greek characters was the first of many versions I'd see in Greece. Eight names: after 4,000 or so years of watching these skies, they were still all anyone knew for sure.

To avoid a spell of strong winds, Adèle and I spent a couple days in Vathi watching the clouds weave between the high hills. The town is in a deep inlet locked within a far larger bay, and the mountains seem to slide across the exit once one has entered. Gusts swept down, turning the water in the harbour pale green and white, but *Shamaal* was well moored, tugging gently this way and that, the way one shifts feet while being forced to wait.

In the evenings young Ithacans lit firecrackers – marking a saint's day, then some football victory – and for a while the noise of explosions would drown the wind. This was also the time when the old men went to cafés to argue and young women paraded on scooters in the main square. From *Shamaal* we could people-watch with a Homeric twist, dividing the public into those who would have stayed loyal to Odysseus during his absence and those who would not (in the book, nearly everyone). Two evenings were enough for us to decide, probably quite unfairly, that the proportions had little changed.

On the third morning, the wind stopped. We did not wait for a favourable breeze.

Into the narrows

A sea of beaten, polished metal led to Mesolóngi. Not a bird or fish broke the flatness and the tiny, white triangles of other sailing boats appeared glued to the surface. For a while east of Ithaca we lay becalmed, stupefied by apathy and heat. From time to time the sails filled and we slid forward, but mostly we sat still. A British-flagged classic yacht, one of those long, expensive slivers of wood from the early twentieth century, swept past under motor. Then a merchant vessel, her low, black hull and white superstructure unexpectedly elegant in profile. Then a trawler, ludicrously tough-looking in such a calm setting. It was time to follow. Motoring now, sails furled, we entered the Gulf of Patras and headed for the mainland through the gathering dusk.

Mesolóngi lies in the most un-Hellenic of landscapes. The usual prodigious mountains are there, but inland and far off enough to lose their power. Here the coast is given to salt marshes, mud banks and narrow, dredged channels. Unlike most of Greece, where a boat can sail within a stone's throw of shore without danger, the land creeps stealthily seaward, concealed, yet shallow enough a couple of miles out for a man to stand. So even when night hid the last, blurry scraps of coast, we always knew it was there, and closer than was comfortable. Eight metres read the depth sounder, seven, six, five ... Byron was nearly shipwrecked here while attempting to reach Mesolóngi to join Greek independence fighters in the last days of 1823. The ship ran aground in a squall, but was then blown back into deeper water – minus most of the crew, who, in panic, had already jumped overboard. Eventually the hapless seamen were picked up and Byron, who seems to have enjoyed the farce, made it safely to Mesolóngi, little expecting to die three and a half months later from a fever.

An hour passed before we found the entrance to the passage through the marshes. Briefly a wind came up and we reached this way and that trying to match the puzzle of shore lights and markers to the symbols on the chart. A lighthouse appeared to be in the wrong place, a light that should have been green shone red and nothing seemed to make sense. Mesolóngi may have lacked the imposing natural fortifications of typical Greek harbours, but it could claim an altogether more subtle system of defence. We were almost upon the beacons we'd been searching for before we knew. The wind had died again and the shallows barely rippled as we motored through.

It was late and we were the only boat in that whole dark place. Three miles remained before Mesolóngi, the way marked by pairs of red and green lights, each spaced just within sight of the other to show the limits of safe water. On one side of this hidden channel the marsh stretched to a line of wooden houses on stilts. Porch lanterns illuminated ramshackle jetties and small craft. A few cars rolled along what had to be a causeway, their headlights so low on the horizon they may as well have been in the sea. On the other side of the channel, shacks and wooden bungalows with mosquito screens teetered at the edge of the mud bank, where dinghies lay tethered to creaking wooden landings. Reeds and untidy trees poked from the darkness. A mosquito, the first I'd heard that year, droned past.

As Mesolóngi port loomed through tall trees, I looked back. Every speck of light – the torch of a fisherman rowing a skiff, the new moon and stars, the glow of far-off habitations – was caught in the water. The navigation beacons reflected so strongly that the tall poles they sat on seemed to double in height, making the water appear endlessly deep. It had become impossible to judge accurately the limits of land, sea and sky, and we edged forward on faith alone. It was a shock, like waking from an afternoon sleep, but also a relief, to arrive in the brightly lit harbour. Few boats were in, and isolated pools of lamplight only exaggerated the darkness of the quays. We headed for the high wall opposite a rust-stained cargo ship named *Sofy*, and Adèle climbed up with the lines. Somewhere in the town where Byron spent his final hours, a bell tolled midnight. The last thing I saw through the forehatch before falling asleep was the bow of *Sofy*, weary with dents and miles.

At dawn we returned to the Gulf of Patras. Easterlies were forecast and we needed a head start on what would be a hard sail against the wind. Silky mist covered the marshes, but, otherwise, all exactly as before: the houses on stilts, the shacks, causeway and matchstick jetties. Daylight had brought little solidity to the ephemeral landscape of the night. A heavy, low barge passed in the other direction taking up most of the channel. An old man sculled between reeds in a flat-bottomed boat. A heron folded and unfolded its body like a collapsible ruler. And then we were out. Here were the two markers we'd had such trouble finding the previous evening. Here was the sea and there, just beginning to stir, the east wind. Hauling in the sails, we began to tack towards the narrows of Rhion.

In 1571, two and a half centuries before Byron came to fight Turkish rule in Greece, one of the greatest forces ever assembled against the Ottoman Empire had made its way up these same confined waters. More than 200 galleys and fifty or so other craft from Christian Europe rowed towards the Rhion Strait, a one-mile gap where the Gulf of Patras ends and the Gulf of Corinth begins. Waiting for them that October day was Ali Pasha, with a Turkish force of even greater size, bringing the total number of combatants to an estimated 100,000. The result was the battle of Lepanto, named after a town just beyond the strait and which is now called Návpaktos. Twenty thousand or so Turkish men were said to have been killed or captured – the prisoners included Ali Pasha – and fifty of their ships destroyed. Despite 8,000 dead of their own, the Christian alliance had secured a great victory. Miguel de Cervantes, one of the many wounded and the future author of *Don Quixote*, declared it the day 'Ottoman pride and haughtiness were broken'.

The scene of massed, close-quarter combat is almost impossible to imagine today, used as we are to violence of a more remote sort. Even the spectacle of hundreds of large, oared ships, vessels little changed since the time of Roman galleys, does not easily translate. A twelfth-century account of a Norman fleet rampaging through the Adriatic gives a taste. The approaching biremes, wrote Anna Comnenos, daughter of the Byzantine emperor Alexis, formed 'an uninterrupted wall with their oars, creating a deafening noise. Around these ships he had the transport vessels like a belt enclosing the combat fleet. Seen from a distance, if one had been watching from an observatory, one would have said the naval expedition advanced like a floating town. . . . The sight of Bohémond's barbaric fleet inspired terror. If the warriors of Kontostephanos recoiled in horror, I wouldn't dare blame them.'

Tacking into the narrowing gulf against rising winds, I had plenty of time to reflect on how such ships might have coped. Even with shortened sail and a modern boat we were hard pressed. This was not open-sea sailing, where hours of deviation from the desired course are easily made up later. Here, every tack counted – indeed, almost every metre. It was a laborious process that became harder the further we went: the narrower the gulf, the greater the contrary wind and current, and the less our ability to manoeuvre. While we herringboned back and forth across the gulf, several other sailing boats simply motored up the sides. There, the waves were smaller than in the middle and, although the yachts still faced some resistance, their path was straight and therefore many times swifter than our own. The first boat we scornfully dismissed: the cheat! An hour later came a second, needling along the coast and over the horizon before we'd advanced a couple of miles. Then a third. We began to wonder.

At times it does seem that this confounding sea was never meant for sailing. *The Odyssey* and *The Iliad* are filled with the ill consequences of relying on the wind. The peregrinations of Odysseus are an obvious example. Menelaus, we're also told, spent eight years stranded in Egypt waiting for a fair breeze, while Agamemnon had to sacrifice his beautiful daughter Iphigenia in order for the wind-bound Greek fleet to reach Troy. Not surprising, then, the strength of Mediterranean sailors' attachment to alternative sources of power – oars then, diesel or petrol today. Lepanto, fought almost entirely by oared galleys, took place three quarters of a century after Columbus had sailed across the Atlantic and half a century after Magellan's sailing expedition circumnavigated the globe. In other words, while Portuguese and Spanish caravels opened the oceans under canvas, the greatest navies of the Mediterranean were fighting with ships, tactics and seamanship reminiscent of the sea battles of the Greeks and Persians 2,000 years earlier.

The galley certainly had its drawbacks. With a single sail, the galley could use the wind, but the rig and shallow hull ruled out sailing in anything but the most straightforward conditions. For their part, oarsmen were expensive to maintain and relatively inefficient (large medieval galleys were capable of no more than twenty horsepower, about the same as an engine in a mid-sized modern yacht). They also had to be skilled. The typical trireme, for example, had three decks of overlapping oars, about 170 in total, while in the seventeenth century there were monsters with eight men to each giant oar. A glance at modern rowers training on any river will give an inkling of the coordination needed to manage such vessels.

At the battle of Actium, just north of the Gulf of Patras, Mark Antony discovered too late the mistake of sending inexperienced rowers against the well-crewed, nimble galleys of Octavius Caesar. Although the two fleets were of about equal size, Octavius' galleys were able to swarm around the poorly managed enemy vessels, in Plutarch's words, 'always three or four of Caesar's ships around one of Antonius' ships'. Curiously it was at the very same spot in 1538, almost 1,600 years after Octavius' routing of Antony and Cleopatra, that well-rowed galleys once again ran circles around more ponderous opponents. In this battle of Preveza, named after a village close to Actium Point, it was the Ottomans of Barbarossa with the better fleet and the Christian alliance that suffered.

An exception that day was the success of the sailing ship *Galleon of Venice*, which, despite being immobilized by lack of wind, managed to use cannons to repel swarms of Ottoman galleys. Here was a glimpse of the future, a time when weight of firepower from bulky sailing vessels, not the traditional agility of galleys and bravery of their crews in boarding the enemy, would count. The revolution was not to be completed overnight – Lepanto was still three decades off – but times were changing. While famous as a galley battle, Lepanto was the last major engagement of its kind. Modern navies needed floating castles able to wage and survive artillery battles and that meant sailing ships. To master the seas, Mediterranean powers were finally going to have to master the winds.

Our own battle was still on. We had resisted the temptation

to motor and were finally making ground. Patras was astern and the Rhion Strait was within reach. A few more tacks, a few more zigzag miles, and we'd be through. This, of course, was purely a private struggle. The engine long ago circumvented the wind, and I didn't have to watch the yachts sneaking up the gulf under motor to know how unnecessarily painful sail travel could be. But the fact that man had managed to abandon the contest did not mean to me that the contest was over.

We entered the strait, jabbing side to side and dodging ferries. The hulking legs of a bridge under construction at the very narrowest part added to the crowding. Work had clearly commenced only recently and our chart, printed too early, still showed the area free. Of course, the legs were easy to avoid – the gaps between were wide enough for big ships – yet their blackened, concrete sides seemed to will us to calamity. The sea became choppier, swirling angrily around the ramparts of the half-made bridge, colliding against the wake of ferries, then swarming around *Shamaal*. With an almost audible pop, we were through.

The gates of Athens

The medieval harbour of Návpaktos, the old Lepanto, is barely 100 metres across and almost round, with only the narrowest of openings in a high wall to connect with the sea. There were no other yachts there when we arrived, no boats at all, except for a dozen small fishing vessels in various states of disrepair. Looking far more Italian than Greek, the town spread upward, culminating in the ruins of a Venetian castle, now become a park – a soothing end for a place that once looked on so many of the dying and dead.

Bright, bustling Návpaktos was the kind of town where Adèle liked to disappear, coming back an hour or two later with some puzzling example of the local cuisine, a dashing item of clothing found on sale, an antique postcard, a haircut or quite simply an account of all that she had seen. On this occasion, while I stayed behind tinkering with the engine, she set out, returning in late afternoon with a set of scarlet worry beads and a huge ice cream, both of which by that time were welcome.

A day later, we left Návpaktos in an easy mood, the engine newly oiled, the worry beads clicking against the cabin bulwark. The breeze was from astern and, with only ninety miles left to Athens, a great stage of our voyage was drawing to a close. There'd be no open sea, only the Gulf of Corinth, the Corinth Canal and a short hop through the northern Aegean. Almost 3,000 sea miles since sailing out of the River Crouch in Essex and we were at the portals of the Greek capital.

Flanked by steep, green hills, the gulf had the aspect of an Alpine lake, a cosy atmosphere that heightened expectations of a simple ride. But at sundown the wind vanished and our Swiss idyll took a perverse, Mediterranean turn. Lightning and thunder dropped from thick, black skies, the bolts in white and shades of purple and green. Some struck close, the electric spark and whiplash boom barely separate. Silent forks of light flickered far beyond the horizon. 'No wind, only lightning, thunder and showers,' Adèle jotted in the logbook. 'Looking for shelter.'

The luxury of being in a gulf is that shelter is always close to hand – just five miles off at the town of Aiyion in our case. We were soon there, motoring through a fleet of fishing boats, mostly *lamperas* using powerful lanterns to lure octopus and other fish to the surface where they could be impaled on a trident or hooked. Once arrived at Aiyion, though, our troubles began. The town and dock were submerged in yellow streetlamps, scrambling our senses as we ranged up and down between darkness and light. The place seemed impenetrable. There was no red beacon around which we could orientate ourselves, as marked in the pilot book. The quay had been taken entirely by an ocean-going freighter and a large fishing vessel. The corner recommended by the pilot book for anchoring bristled with dangerous-looking poles, just visible in the glow of the town and flashes of lightning. We were about to concede defeat when a figure appeared on the deck of the fishing boat, calling us over to moor alongside.

Fifteen minutes later we found ourselves seated with Captain Spiros in his trawler's cosy saloon. Spiros's boat, named after himself, a common conceit among Greek fishermen, stood a good two metres higher in the water than *Shamaal*, seventy-six tonnes to our two and a half, and they lay next to each other like a whale and calf. Apart from Spiros there were eight men aboard, a mixture of handsome, young Egyptians and rather elderly, professorial-looking Greeks. Spiros was most extraordinary. Middle-aged, but massively built, he had hands, wrists, forearms and neck of gigantic strength. Nor did the rotunda under his T-shirt seem out of place – seeing a slim Spiros, you'd have said something was missing. His face, alternately kind, hardened, sad and full of memories, had only one working eye.

Like so many of his countrymen, Spiros had served in the merchant navy years back, hence his workable if poorly oiled English and happy memories of Hull, Harwich and pub food, though it was possible he was just being polite. Never had I met a fisherman so enamoured with the sea. I wondered: had it been difficult to adjust to the smaller scope of his new career? Not at all, Spiros said, because as a fishing captain he was free, and it was this freedom, not the length of a journey, that made the sea appear grand. He had no master, no permanent home port (Aiyion was one of many temporary stopping places) and fished only in ways that fitted the roving way of life. He likened the sea to 'a woman or a fire: never the same, never to be left alone'.

Spiros approved heartily of our voyage, tracing its progress across a small map of Europe, then asking when we planned to sail home. That caught us out a little. Adèle and I looked at each other, laughing, and, instead of trying to answer, turned the question on Spiros. 'You know what,' he replied, 'for me home is right here – this boat. It is my home and my love. I've no need to think of home, for I am already there.' The sweet Greek coffees were down to muddy dregs. It was midnight. We thanked Spiros and the crew. One by one, down ladders and through hatches, everybody dispersed, and for a few hours the loudest sound was the gentle push of *Shamaal* against the trawler's sides.

Daylight quickly uncovered the topographical mysteries of the harbour and inconsistencies in the pilot book. The freighter was gone now, leaving empty a huge quay. A pier we'd been unable to identify did exist, but was hidden, like the single red beacon, behind a mass of construction works. Aiyion itself spread untidily around the bay, an easy place to miss, intentionally or not.

Kapetan Spiros had returned from a brief dawn excursion and was unloading its catch to a waiting refrigerated truck. We motored up to bid farewell. The crew looked different in daytime – the Egyptians a shade older, the Greeks younger – and Captain Spiros was weary. One of the professors threw a large plastic bag. 'Catch!' Twelve squid and another dozen small fish landed heavily and slightly bloody in Adèle's arms. We were blessed. '*Efharisto, efharisto!*' we shouted. Thank you! *Shamaal* eased east and Aiyion, as if grateful to recover its anonymity, sank rapidly into the sea.

What remained of the gulf was a millpond of light winds, long calms and growing numbers of boats and ships making for the Corinth Canal. There was no terror or jubilation here, only mild distraction and monotony. Jellyfish like shuttlecocks bobbed up in thousands. A fireworks display fizzled above a small town in poor imitation of the lightning the previous night. A score of dolphins paraded, dipping and rising in unison as if on a carousel. Though still afloat, we were geographically almost in the centre of Greece, and the road on the south shore was just close enough for us to see the tired faces of drivers. The note of a siren slid up and down. We heard a plane for the first time in two weeks. A train rattled east. The fact of being on a boat was now almost incidental: we'd become part of the great commute to Athens along with half the rest of the country.

By the time we entered ancient, now dismal Corinth and from there the canal, the shine of sea miles, of Spiros, of shooting stars and freewheeling nights before the wind had gone. We became irritable and impatient. A boat without sea room and without wind is not a boat. It is a broken car, a poky caravan, an awkward sack of belongings, a financial liability. You cannot stand up; it is too hot to sit down. You are surrounded by water, but it is filthy. This is not what boats are for. We should have enjoyed the canal. We read the usual stuff. How the Greeks and Romans used to haul their ships over the isthmus. How Nero's 6,000 Jewish slaves began digging, but got nowhere, and how for almost two millennia everyone went back to hauling ships. Apparently the Greeks finally finished their ditch only in 1893. All this was lost on us. We argued. We turned our noses up at the murky water. We poked fun at the eroded, collapsing sides. We cursed the fat catamaran yacht tailgating us all 3.2 miles of the way as if this were a standard traffic jam, which, with two cargo vessels and eight yachts stuck in a one-lane water road, it was. Boats are not made for these places; nor were we.

All the more surprising then to erupt from that barrel into the foaming, sparkling, azure Aegean Sea. Here there was space. Land, too, plenty of it: the Peloponnese to the west, Athens to the east, and islands like silver lilies as far as we could see, but there was also wind, a gusty, unfettered wind and, because of that, space. Yachts imitated gulls and gulls the waves, everything white and dancing. Eastward, great ships come from far waited in black and red herds outside Piraeus. A day's sail, past Salamís and the lizard-dry hills to the north, and it was time for us, too, to pause. Ahead, the uncounted flat, white roofs of Athens huddled and glistened like broken quartz.

V

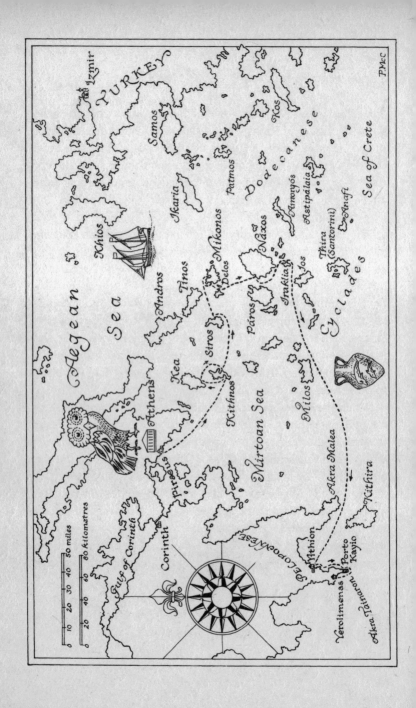

The Tower of Winds

Slender shadows fell from ruined columns and arches over the worn paving of the Roman agora. Out of a taverna on the corner of Aiolou Street came snatches of conversation, but otherwise there was silence. In the afternoon sunlight, the marble sides of the tower glowed gently. We'd wasted no time coming here after leaving *Shamaal* in harbour: in a city full of wonders, the Tower of Winds beckoned.

The surrounding neighbourhood of Plaka was inexplicably deserted. Wild fig trees sprouted from roofless houses, and restaurant touts stood in secretive alleyways with nothing to do. Few cars came this way and the only pre-season tourists flocked immediately to the Gate of Athena at the other end of the agora, or up the hill dominated by the Acropolis to our east. Seated back-to-back on a large stone – it turned out to be the marble foot of some long-dismembered colossus – Adèle and I realized that, apart from a dozing cat or two, we had the place to ourselves.

When the tower's creator, Andronikos, was at work back in the mid first century BC, the atmosphere would have been closer in spirit to the traffic-choked modern Athens we'd seen on our way in than this privileged island of calm. Then, the heart of the city was the Greek agora, a sort of super department store cum city hall barely 100 metres to the west. Later, under Roman rule, the city centre drifted to the new agora complex in the immediate surrounds of the tower. One has only to see the ruins of substantial temples, the marketplace, Hadrian's Library and even the *vespasianae*, or public toilets, to gauge how bustling a spot it must have been.

For a relatively small building – it is only twelve metres high – the tower boasted many marvels, making it not only a public attraction, but a focal point for astronomers, savants and, it is said, disciples of Aeolus as well. Apart from its most visible function of weathercock, the tower, still known to some as the Horologion, was a famous timekeeper. Sundials protruded from each of the eight façades and a clock, powered by water from a cistern, itself fed by a spring from the Acropolis, was built into the south wall. In addition to showing the hour, the clock, called a *clepsydra* (water thief), is thought to have included a rotating diagram of the night sky that tracked the rising and setting of the constellations. After the classical era, the Tower of Winds was turned into a baptistery for an adjacent church and, in the eighteenth century, a holy place, or *tekke*, for Ottoman dervishes before being definitively abandoned until the twentieth century.

It is remarkable how well the structure has ridden out the ages. Apart from the water clock, two demolished Corinthian porticoes and the missing bronze weathervane in the form of Triton, the tower is almost intact. Rising from a three-stepped platform, the big blocks making up the eight walls must look no less solid than when first heaved into place 2,100 years ago. The coned roof, decorated with red tiles running ribbon-like from pinnacle to rim, is also whole. The rays of the sundials, etched into the stone near the top, remain, though the gnomons casting the sun's shadow are modern. Adèle found a discreet reminder of that early Christian period: a small cross inside a circle carved into each side of the main door leading into the tower.

As Andronikos intended, though, it is to the representations of the winds, carved around the top of the tower, that the eye still turns. The eight figures are not unscathed: one lacks a face, another his feet and still another – perhaps most painful to a wind – wings. Yet incredibly, none has been obliterated and all are recognizable. Some are almost pristine. The frieze's success in depicting motion is immediately striking. Every figure is a fully outstretched winged giant, his head close on the heels of the wind around the corner. The eight walls each measure only 3.2 metres across, meaning that, from wherever one stands, there are always three façades and winds visible, each one from a slightly different angle: coming, in full view, and leaving. One almost expects the entire tower, with its playful, spinning-top-style roof, to rotate. Originally, this effect would probably have worked even better, for the Triton on top really did whirl (or, as one might have pretended, stayed still, while the frieze, like frames of film, did the spinning).

Despite the damage, there is little trouble in identifying the figures' characteristics today, although there is occasional disagreement over what those attributes mean. Moving anti-clockwise, as does the sequence on the tower, this is the cast:

North: Boreas. The personification of strong wind. His hair and tunic stream behind, and he clutches a cloak with his left hand. In his right, he carries a huge conch shell as if it were a bugle or loud-hailer. Glowering and thickly bearded, he appears to be checking the effects of one blast on the conch before blowing again.

North-west: Skiron. He, too, is bearded and bears a rather intense, stubborn expression. He is in the act of tipping a large, delicately carved urn and, as the name refers to the Scironian rocks near Corinth, the urn's contents have been taken to signify something, possibly charcoal, that would dry up rivers. Others claim the urn is filled with water and signifies showers. Statistically, this is not a common wind in Athens.

West: Zephyros. Young and effeminate, he flies on his side, rather than the more menacing frontal position, and carries a huge pile of flower petals. He is almost naked.

South-west: Lips. He is also barefoot, but wears a tunic and cloak. Like Zephyros, he is unbearded and youthful, but his legs and arms are stronger. He appears to be in a ship and grasps the prow – either holding the boat back or giving it a push forward. Andronikos' intentions here are debatable. Some say he portrays Lips negatively to show how south-westerlies prevent boats leaving Athens. Alternatively – and this seems more likely given the dominance of more northerly winds in the

Aegean – Lips might have been shown in the act of helping a boat *back* to Athens.

South: Notos. Despite serious damage to his face, Notos is unmistakably determined to empty his water urn. He represents the wet southern winds of winter.

South-east: Euros (elsewhere often called Apeliotes). Shown as a winter gale. His cloak, sandals and wings give every impression of great speed. His heavy-set and bearded face is brutish, and he carries nothing but the cloak in which he is wrapped.

East: Apeliotes (otherwise Euros). Another of the gentler types, the east wind flies in a friendly posture and carries a blanket brimming with grapes, lemons, apples, something like a melon and what Adèle persuaded me, however unlikely-sounding, might be a bunch of bananas.

North-east: Kaikias. A common strong wind, Kaikias is stocky, heavily bearded and none too friendly. Looking right out at the viewer, he tips small, round objects from a large vessel, either a tray of some sort or a shield. These objects are variously interpreted as hailstones, ruined olives or ordinary stones, but the meaning is the same: Kaikias shakes the world.

What fear the unclouded Mediterranean skies provoked – and not only fear, but also passion and hope! Look at the affection with which Apeliotes is portrayed. The blanket of fruits almost bursts. Or Zephyros. Sailors still refer to 'gentle zephyrs' for breezes that move a boat almost without effort. Homer said it was a west wind that cooled the souls of Greek heroes in the Elysian Fields. It is also Zephyros that blew Aphrodite on her scallop shell from the foaming sea. In Botticelli's famous painting, he is to the goddess's right, wearing only a loose cloak and clasping the nude Psyche in his left arm. Around him tumbles a galaxy of pink roses.

But the north and south winds were the heavyweights in this pantheon. North winds literally moulded Greek civilization. No Aegean harbour was valuable if it couldn't provide shelter from the meltemi, or etesian as it was known, blowing from the northern quadrant in summer. And when the Greeks set out to trade and colonize, they tended south to Africa, west to Sicily or northeast into the Black Sea, rather than due north into the dreary headwinds (today's bora) of the Adriatic.

South winds were embedded in the Greek mind for quite different reasons. In northern Europe, we associate the south wind with warmth and plenty, but to the Greek, as to any southern European, it was the 'breath of the wild ass', the desert blast that killed crops and made people mad. In Greek mythology's version of the biblical Flood, it was the *south* wind that sent the downpour, a detail on which the Old Testament is silent. And when Pliny talks of blood falling from the sky, he is almost certainly referring to that filthy, sandy rain the sirocco brings from the Sahara.

So the air to the ancient Greek teemed with characters and, in a sense, this is how it would appear to all future Mediterranean navigators, from the Romans to the British 2,000 years on. Long after the ancient gods were replaced, the old superstitions, or rather the sense of helplessness at their heart, would remain. In some parts there were legal interdictions on putting to sea during the winter months – in the Levant, for example, from Saint Dmitri's day (26 October), to Saint George's (5 May). The Coptic Christian calendar purported to show the exact dates and types of gales, 20 March being the date to expect a two-day easterly blow called the 'Big Sun' gale, 29 April bringing a forty-eight-hour easterly sand wind, and so on. The khamsin, Egypt's south-easterly version of the sirocco, is scheduled to blow from the day after Coptic Easter to Pentecost. These were the rules and anxieties of obsessed peoples – not, in Mediterranean eyes, that there would be any need to apologize, for, until the steam engine, it might fairly be said that fortunes really did turn on the wind.

Take the northerly gales that decimated the invasion fleets of Persian King Darius and then of his eldest son, Xerxes, so helping to save ancient Greece from subjugation. Or the calm that stopped a squadron of Genoese ships within shouting distance of Constantinople, which they were attempting to relieve from Mohammed II's great siege of 1453. (Six hours later, with the Genoese on the verge of being captured, the wind returned and, for a short while longer, Constantinople could stand!) The history of the Mediterranean is written in these small interventions of the wind. Consider the saga of Nelson's contest with the Napoleonic fleet in 1798. First, a summer mistral scattered the British and allowed the blockaded French to escape Toulon. Then, Nelson spent two and a half months searching for his foe, much of this time wallowing in calms. Finally, Nelson's ships boxed in and destroyed the French fleet in the Egyptian bay of Aboukir, but they did so after a gentle north-north-westerly breeze gifted them the crucial upwind advantage. How differently the day might have gone with a slight shift to the west or south-west, forcing the British to tack towards the waiting enemy guns . . . In the age of sail, men at sea and sometimes empires with them were, like Keats's gnats over the river:

> . . . borne aloft
> Or sinking as the light wind lives or dies.

Eventually, an attendant from the ticket booth ejected us from our seat on the marble foot, and while Adèle went exploring I spent the remains of the afternoon on the steps of the tower itself. As the sun circled, so did the shade and so did I, first under Boreas, then Kaikias. A little way in front a black cat lay curled on a fallen capital. On the other side of the tower, Zephyros and Lips basked in the heat. The wands of the sundials cast thin lines across pale stone and a breeze, Apeliotes, began to sift from the east through the poppies and grass.

I'd visited Athens twice before and seen, as one does, its

illustrious monuments, yet somehow missing each time this quiet corner and the modest little tower for which I suddenly felt a wave of affection. So compact and complete, there was real life in this building, a thousand times more so than elsewhere in the agora, or even a great deal of the Acropolis itself. The temples had been stripped of their gods, the agoras of their purpose. Even the latrines had become relics. The tower was different: it retained its vital active ingredient, the *wind*. It was like an antique watch, battered and, without Triton, missing its hands, but still ticking. The wind personifications remained relevant. The eightfold division of the horizon – calculated more than 1,000 years before the appearance in Europe of the compass – was spot on. Boreas really was at north, Notos at south, Zephyros at west and Apeliotes east. The tower worked. Yes, if only Triton could be replaced.

But what the tower could not signal was the end of our journey. We had indeed come to the centre of the ancient Mediterranean. And had I been an adherent of Aeolus' cult, or a man of science, I might have been satisfied. But a weather vane only tells where a wind is coming from, while, as a sailor, I was more interested in knowing where it blew. It was only by raising sail again that I could expect answers. We still had far to go. First the Cyclades and the capes of the Peloponnese. Then west, 1,500 nautical miles or so across the middle of the sea to Spain, to the Pillars of Hercules and the gateway to the Atlantic Ocean – the place, ultimately, where all Mediterranean journeys had to conclude . . .

The shadows lengthened. The breeze gathered. An orange tree popping with fruit began to stir. A palm waved gently, and through the ruins came the scent of cedar. Apeliotes – on the long haul west, it was just what we were going to need.

Bidding the black cat farewell, I rose and went to find Adèle.

Archipelago sailing

It is impossible to sail quickly through the Cyclades. Actually, with a good meltemi from astern a boat might sweep through the entire archipelago in not much over sixteen hours, but that is not the point. It is impossible because the islands and the sea impose their own rhythm. The distances may be tiny – maybe fifteen miles between islands, maybe just two – but the essentials of the journey are identical to those of any sea crossing: farewells, the no-man's land between, landfall and a new world. These are not the humdrum, high-speed crossings of tourist ferries. Each trip on a sailboat, placid or dangerous, dull or joyful, is unique, and everything, even leaving harbour, takes effort and time. Stepping off the ramp of a ferry, one might say: we're here. Step ashore from a small boat and you say: we made it.

So without much of a plan other than to go south and east, we crossed the Sea of Mirtoan in a steady, mile-eating breeze. At sundown we started our watches, three hours on, three off, as usual, but the warmth of the darkness and kindness of the sea made us reluctant to sleep. There'd be little night sailing once we entered the island labyrinth, and it was fun for a while to sit up together and share the gentle night.

Silently we threaded through constellations of lighthouses and ships. The mosquito-like buzz of ferries thinned and the glow of the mainland died. *Shamaal*'s tricolour navigation light at the top of the mast swayed tipsily, red, green and white, between the stars. We were alone again. I was not sorry to have left behind swarming Athens. Everyone there rushed and because everyone rushed everything took an age to do. We'd asked half a dozen acquaintances how they liked living in Athens, and they all replied with the same word: hell. How could they stand it? Again, the response had been identical: the sea. *Thalassa* – it was what made Athens and would save Athens.

About 1 a.m. the wind fell away, and *Shamaal* came to a halt.

A slight haze crept over the sea, and the moon shone back from under our keel. For a short while we floated there immobile in blissful quiet. I was off watch, but the change in motion had woken me. Adèle and I looked at each other through the hatch, reluctant on such a night to be the first to say the dread words: 'Suppose it's time to motor.' We needn't have worried. For a minute or so the thunder and vibration of the engine seemed sure to break the spell, but this was a night rich enough to absorb any disturbance. Imperceptibly the noise of the motor faded until we hardly noticed its presence, and once again there was nothing in the world other than stars, the moon and the velvety darkness between.

Somewhere south of Ákra Sounion, southern tip of the Attic coast, we pushed through huge fields of phosphorescence. Eerie, hand-sized patches of dull light floated just under the surface in all directions. I leant over the railing to get a better look, but the amorphous shape of the lights gave nothing away about the creatures behind them. Shining a torch into the water seemed to stir up more of the same.

Phosphorescence, meaning simply a heatless light, is a strange phenomenon, but not half as strange as some of the beings that create it. The most common bioluminescence occurs as tiny, light-emitting organisms streak through the water. Their wake appears as a shooting star, an intense ribbon of green and gold that burns off almost immediately. Some simply flare up as white dots against the dark sea. Any disturbance – a dolphin, the rudder of a boat or just a hand in the water – will ignite them. They can even be provoked on occasion by a night-time flushing of the boat's sea-water toilet. It is a surprising and beautiful thing to see diamonds and emeralds swirl about the porcelain bowl.

What we saw that night was less common, not so much points of light as pale flakes of irradiated snow. Almost certainly these were jellyfish, but just below and around the brighter flakes shone an almost constant, milky half-light the source of which we could not fathom. How little about these lights, Coleridge's 'death-fires' and 'witch's oils', anyone really knows. Even the reason for their show is a matter of debate. The common explanation is that the light is a reaction to fear, but why should anything trying to flee advertise itself so spectacularly? Perhaps the light blinds or confuses the predator. It may be a form of communication, the subaqua version of our navigational alphabet of flashes and fixed lights used on the surface of the sea. No one is entirely sure. There are species of fish whose mouths glow when they hunt, apparently as a lure – *lamperas* of the deep. There are phosphorescent creatures living in organized groups. They form tidy ribbons of light stretching hundreds of metres, sometimes several ribbons side by side, but also rotating, wheel-like formations and balls that rise to the surface and erupt in concentric rings. Many land people mistakenly assume that science has tamed, or at least made banal, the ancient mysteries of the sea. Yet we do not even know for certain how sharks navigate or why dolphins play. Every sea voyage, even a froghop between islands, remains one of discovery.

Motoring and sailing a little, we reached Kíthnos shortly after dawn. Silvery, steep and bare it looked, a mountain licked clean by the sun. We had now entered the Cyclades, the magical archipelago named for the ring – *kuklos*, meaning 'circle' – it forms around the once-sacred island of Delos. For the next weeks we would rarely have to sail at night. Navigation would be straightforward, a matter of pointing at mountains and ticking off bays, while shelter offered itself around islands as regularly as the numbers on a clock. No surprise that the early seafarers, having cut their teeth here, were so horrified by journeys into the emptier stretches of the watery world. And little wonder that wherever they looked they saw magic and gods. The Cyclades, like a giant Venice of island palazzos and sea canals, gave every appearance of a divinely ordered world.

Our first stop was a tiny natural harbour on the west side of Kíthnos. A whitewashed chapel stood on the stony hillock above the anchorage, just as above so many Greek anchorages, and with it a one-room cottage housing a goatherd. Apart from two modest and shut-up holiday bungalows, there was nothing for miles.

Adèle was gathering a post-night-sail breakfast – coffee with condensed milk, bread and ham, a slice of hard cheese – when the goatherd arrived. He was past middle age, dry as rope and rode a mule with the nonchalance of a cowboy. Seeing that we were the only boat in the anchorage and he the only person on land, we readied for the obligatory Greek salute of the right hand and greeting of 'Yasos', curtailed by real locals to a drawled 'yas', or even 'ya'. But the salute never came; not even the preliminary eye contact. Down from the rocks rode the goatherd, across the beach and up the crag on the other side towards the chapel, singing to himself and shouting at the goats, each as scraggy and tough as the bushes on which they had to survive. All this time he studiously ignored our presence, though we were anchored not thirty metres from his path along the beach. He stared blankly at the ground, at the nape of his mule's neck, and at the sky – anywhere but the small, blue boat across the water just to his left. It was a display of coldness most unusual in hospitable Greece, the symptom, I supposed, of a recluse's losing campaign to retain his isolation. There were no roads or major tourist settlements near, but a yacht, like the pirate raids that once terrorized every part of the Mediterranean, left no corner safe.

The southern tip of the neighbouring island of Kéa lay not more than a few hours distant and, after one night in the goat place, we sailed up. The new cove we found, called Órmos Polais, consisted of low, red-tinted cliffs to one side, a reef and an islet to the other, and a small beach. This time it was clear that we would neither disturb anyone nor be disturbed. The silence was so profound that after a while it gave way to noises we don't usually hear, of birds rustling in bushes, the grumble of beach pebbles and breezes funnelling through the defiles. Rivers of spring flowers and long, soft grass flowed down the two tiny valleys leading inland. There was no habitation in sight.

The reason for thinking we might remain alone was that Órmos Polais was not a place to shelter in much of a wind, uncertainty enough to put off most holidaying sailors. Cautious as always, we nosed around a while between the beach, the reef and the cliffs before committing ourselves to dropping anchor. Adèle steered. I stood by the forestay, anchor in hand and forty metres of chain and rope flaked at my feet. Black-blue water became turquoise, then green. The sand floor revealed each detail. It was time.

Diving overboard, we were easily able to see the anchor buried in the sand twenty metres away. How good it felt, silky water over the skin, to swim under the keel and look up at *Shamaal* with a fish's eye. Already we'd attracted a John Dory, the black spot under his dorsal fin like a target. Further along we found coral in the shape of tiny, orange brooms and white petals. A slight puff of sand betrayed the presence of a flounder, then another. Tiny glum-faced fish I'd never seen flitted between wrack and rocks, perching like birds and oblivious to the inquisitive, jerky progress of a red and green wrasse.

Once the sting left the sun we made an expedition ashore in the dinghy, timing our landing on the rocky foreshore between thumps of small waves. The waves came from a swell rolling in gently past the reef, though where the swell came from we couldn't tell. There was barely a hint of wind. 'Probably just from the ships out there,' Adèle said, and I agreed she had to be right. Many ships and large ferries used the channel between Kíthnos and Kéa, and their wash, albeit with a long delay, was bound to work its way into our cove.

In the centre of the beach stood a high wedge of rocks, marking the start of a ridge that separated the two small valleys. From the sandy bottom, a path wound up through huge stones towards the top of the hill. On all sides nature began to close in. Boulders created narrow passages. Spiders the size of snails wove giant cobwebs above our heads. Thorns, thistles and thickets of purple weed grabbed at our feet. By the time we ducked through bushes around the last boulder we were high enough above the beach to see the whole cove. Then, leaping up a couple of rough stone steps, we found ourselves on a level area and, to our amazement, in the ruins of a temple.

We'd heard that ruins of some kind were to be found in Órmos Polais, but from the sketchy description expected little. Columns and capitals lay in the usual haphazard way across the grass. Foundation stones unmoved since before the birth of Christ stood in repose. A row of rectangular, stone-lined pits faced the sea – graves and by their size, it seemed, the graves of children. Continuing up the path we reached another similar piece of flat ground, now at the top of the little hill. Here were the bones of a fairly substantial temple, its foundations intact and columns askew.

For a long time we didn't talk, instead sitting down on a slab that might have been an altar to pull at a bottle of wine and nibble bread from a backpack. The solitude we'd felt on arriving deepened, but with it the creepy, contrary sensation of not being completely alone. The only way of getting to the temple, apparently, was by boat or a dirt track heading inland, and there were no signposts or attendants. Someone had recently come here with a machete and hacked back the worst undergrowth, but nature gave every sign of preparing to return twofold. The spiders which we now saw everywhere – in every tree, between the columns, all over the face of the cliff – were already on the move.

The romance of the setting – the ruined temple, the cliffs overlooking the sea, *Shamaal* at anchor – mingled with growing uneasiness. The graves, long opened and robbed, pointed accusingly at the sky, and I wondered whom they had once contained. Certainly Kéa had its share of ghosts. During its democracy, as described by Aristotle, the fanatical drive to purge society of weak elements extended to *koniazesthe*, the taking of hemlock, a pact in which people on reaching seventy had to commit suicide. *Keion nomimon*, the law of Kéa, this was called. Could some of the doomed have looked out on this cove before drinking their last?

Adèle, who has a phobia of spiders, pointed in disgust at the nearest web, a magnificent construction a metre in diameter. Watching it shake and spring, it occurred to me how much wind there was. Funny we hadn't noticed it before, but it was coming in steadily. So was the sea. *Shamaal*, which had been lying so gently earlier, rocked like a toy horse against her anchor chain. Better get down, Adèle said. We could always return in the morning.

The oil lamps swung so badly we put them away and ate dinner in the dark that evening. The wind was much quieter down here, but the swell crashed ponderously on the beach and the cliffs where we'd swum earlier that day. We tried to sleep, but the motion of the boat, now plunging and jerking against the anchor, made it difficult to lie still. The idea was to ride out the night. And because the wind did not seem strong, we hoped the waves would die. They didn't. Our stern was only a couple of dozen metres from one of the reefs and, as the sea surged, so did *Shamaal*, pulling the anchor chain rod-taut before springing forward. Glancing from the forehatch at the starlit red cliffs, I tried to gauge whether we'd dragged. The nearest rocks flickered with phosphorescence, and the roar of breaking water seemed to herald disaster. About midnight, we decided to escape.

Leaving an anchorage in the dark against the waves takes care. There was no moon and nothing, other than ribbons of surf along the beach, to be seen. Though the wind was strangely quiet, the motion of the boat and noise were terrible, waves roaring on the rocks close behind, motor thudding and the clank-clank of chain as I hauled it up on to the deck. The key was to leave with enough speed to deal with the incoming sea, while being sure in the dark we did not head for rocks. Fortunately that afternoon we'd taken the precaution of noting the compass bearing to the open sea. As soon I had the anchor lashed, Adèle put down the throttle and, with an eye on the compass, gunned *Shamaal* out.

The mystery of the waves was soon solved. In the cove there'd been enough shelter from the wind to give the illusion of calm (though not up at the exposed temple), but the sea, as it often does, still managed to sneak in. Now we had both – waves and a gusty old west-south-westerly wind. Pausing briefly at a safe distance from shore, we set reefed sails and laid a course for Loutra, a small harbour on the north-east side of Kíthnos. We glanced back towards the temple, but night had erased even the cliffs. Until the white flashes of the north Kíthnos lighthouse, five miles due south from here, there'd be nothing but darkness.

Pursuing skies

Outside the certainties of the meltemi season, you can never guess what sort of wind you'll see in the Cyclades. The pilot books give a few tips, but the exceptions outnumber the rules and, as the radio forecasts made clear, even the experts are often at a loss. In the jumbled mountains and island corridors of the crazy-paving Cyclades, one can only be sure of surprises.

The morning we left Loutra, a hard north-north-easterly blew. Aiming for the bottom end of Síros, about twenty miles to the south-east, would put us close to the wind, but without having to tack. We reckoned Force 6, though it was difficult to judge the waves in the dark. Many sailing boats have an anemometer at the top of the mast giving constant readouts to a cockpit screen, but ours was a little battery-operated thing that had to be held in the air and it saw little use. First, someone had to go down and fish it out. Then, who needed it? Anemometers only say in knots, metres per second, averages and maximum speeds what your eyes and ears have already told you in whitecaps, waves, spray and splashes. The sea contains mystery, but also answers.

Sunrise, as so often happens in the Mediterranean, gave a new edge to the wind, and by breakfast we had a Force 6 gusting every few minutes to 7. At this point the escalation in the Beaufort scale becomes marked. The waves in a Force 7 are large. Mantles of thick foam cap breaking crests, and thin streaks stain the waves' backs. The noise and motion aboard are also qualitatively different, particularly in a small boat on a close reach, where the bow either crashes through waves or rides over the top, often to slam down on the other side. Fortunately, we were not on the closest possible reach and many of the waves hit more on the side than the bow. Although this brought constant soakings, it meant we were able to keep our speed. In fact, we flew. Kíthnos subsided and Síros emerged from the white-chipped sea faster than seemed possible. The spinner we trailed for the speed log, seen so often of late sinking into the undisturbed sea, whirred so quickly it had trouble staying submerged. Six miles an hour would be desperately slow on land. In leaping, breaking seas, six knots felt as if we'd been shot from a sling.

Watching water flow steadily over the bow and down the side decks, I remembered the bow leak we'd spent so long trying to fix. Checking there were no ships about and leaving the wind vane to steer, I went below for a look. Adèle was in the first part of the cabin, fast asleep in her sloping bunk and oblivious to the theatre outside. But to get to the leaking area I had to crawl on my belly past the anchor chain locker right to the forepeak, where the steel rods holding the forestay came through the deck. Every now and then the boat lurchēd and I was thrown on to my side. With only a centimetre or so of fibreglass separating me from the sea, the water seemed to swirl and explode about my head.

It didn't take long to find the problem. In one spot, I discovered a pool of water that would lead directly to our clothes locker. I could also see water drip in several places. This did not mean, though, that I'd found the source of the leak. Water, like wind, has no need of straight lines. I knew for a fact that on the outside of the deck there were no holes above the places from which water was dripping on the underside. I was pondering this, trying to hold myself steady and thinking it was time I got back on watch, when I heard a roar. The incongruous thought came to me immediately of a dump truck shedding a cargo of rubble. A crash in the cockpit followed, and *Shamaal* went over on her side. Just as suddenly, she flipped back. This all happened very quickly. Then a scream. I shouted: 'Adèle! What's wrong?' I was disentangled now and back in the main cabin. Adèle was crying, barely woken and in shock. 'The wave came over us. I looked out and you weren't there. I didn't know you were in the bow. I thought you'd gone in the sea.'

The cockpit was half-filled with water and, though the drain was starting to take effect, I took a bucket and bailed. *Shamaal* was fine, still on course, still chasing six knots through a scarred, broken sea. Leaning back down the main hatch, I cracked jokes to pull Adèle from her fright, but her tears left me deeply moved, and for a second not the boat, nor the Cyclades, nor the greatest sea seemed to matter a damn. It is in these unrehearsed moments that we relearn things we should always have known.

The wind dropped as we approached the southern tip of Síros at Ákra Velostasi, and the sea, now buffered by the island, became smooth. The events of that morning seemed distant. We raised sail, dried clothes, munched sandwiches and discussed.

Sliding peacefully up the green, protected southern shores, we came across an odd sight. Coming towards us was a sailing boat with the wind from the *other* side. In other words, our wind blew from the north and theirs from the south, yet we were close enough to see the crew on deck. Seemingly impossible, but happening: both boats should have been leaning the same way and they were not. More or less at the same time, *Shamaal* and the other yacht hit a calm zone, sort of a buffer between the two winds, I supposed, and then, slowly, started to catch the opposite breeze. Now we had the wind from the south and they from the north.

This example of opposing winds – what in Spanish were called *contrastes* – was only an introduction to the oddities of southern Síros. A mile further up the coast we saw more yachts approaching. The wind had done another about-face and once more blew out of the north but, whereas we were ghosting through light airs, the vessels ahead seemed to be in a minor gale. The water up there was churned white. By now we had a French ketch sailing parallel in the same direction and, as we crept towards the 'gale', we got in the habit of looking over to each other, with the occasional shrug, as if to say, 'What can you do?' Once more we entered a calm zone, but all eyes were on the frothy sea now just 100 metres ahead. Exchanging bemused looks with the French, we reefed our sails and struggled through the last of the turbulence to the waiting wind.

This was exactly the kind of moment the anemometer had been made for – witness to a freak of nature. The white water approached like the starting line at a race and, as Adèle steered us across, I held the small machine over my head. The recorded result? We went in two minutes from six knots of wind, a Force 2, to thirty knots, a Force 7. From near calm to a near gale. A metal dish, a book, a loose pencil, all relics of the previous hour's hopeful, lazy sail, flew across the cabin. The steel rigging struck up its melancholy music, and *Shamaal* heeled, sprinting.

On arrival in Ermoúpolis late in the afternoon, we were asked by people how we had got in. Although sheltered from the north, gusts periodically swept through the harbour, flattening the water and straining the yachts at their moorings. A café table had capsized on the quay just as we tied up. 'What was it like out there?' a woman from a nearby Dutch boat came to ask. The wind had been terrible, she said, boats stuck all day in harbour and probably the next day, too. A charter yacht from Páros had been dismasted.

But by then our minds were elsewhere. Ermoúpolis was a fine place that had learnt to live with declining importance (it was a major shipping hub in the nineteenth century) and make the most of an enormous harbour. Priests in stumpy, black hats chinwagged with fishermen. Crowds gathered, dispersed and regrouped around the jaws of arriving and departing ferries. Naval cadets, like flocks of seagulls in their white uniforms, marched this way and that. Adèle noted octopuses drying on a line along the quay. Whiffs of aniseed reached us from an *ouzeria* . . . Leaving Ermoúpolis was going to be harder than arriving.

Several days passed before we departed, stocked with squid, fruit, *loukoumi*, nougat and, for the time I'd come to grips with that bow leak, a serious new electric drill. The light breeze evaporated almost as soon as we left harbour, so, rather than motoring non-stop to Míkonos, our next destination, we dropped in on the uninhabited island of Gaidharos to wait for the wind.

The anchorage was a crescent of sand between two low, scrubby hills with clear water that magnified the seabed. We had no chart of the cove and only a few pilot notes which proved inaccurate, possibly because a storm had rearranged the underwater landscape since the original survey. So after digging the anchor into a likely patch, we rowed about in the dinghy with a leadline and made an inspection of our own, confirming by the end that, whichever way the wind blew, *Shamaal* would remain clear of the rocks.

Friendly as it looked, with a large lighthouse facing Ermoúpolis and fringes of crumbling cliffs, the island was home to a large colony of seagulls that had strong feelings about intruders. The beach, where we cooked our dinner over a driftwood fire, marked roughly the limit set on our movements. A hike to the lighthouse filled the sky with hundreds of wheeling, shrieking birds. A few, probably the parents of the baby gulls we saw cowering in ground nests under bushes, tried to frighten us by whooshing over our heads. The lighthouse and former keeper's cottage had also been taken over. Gulls nested in the portholes of the tower. Bones and guano carpeted the surrounding ground. Harried at every step, it was a relief to return to the neutral beach.

Under a full moon we drank retsina and took turns to read stories of shipwreck and voyaging from *The Aeneid*. Out on the water, a white lamp swung slowly from *Shamaal*'s boom, a warning in the dark to any others of our position. But no others came. For two days we were alone with the gulls, and they were beginning to get used to us when finally a breeze picked up out of the west. Our cue to leave Gaidharos. Without switching on the motor, we raised anchor, wore the boat around and headed east.

Míkonos was plainly visible most of the day. Settlements of white houses stood out for miles and the hills, picked bare by wind and goats, shimmered in the heat. Yet it was not until evening that we arrived, first abandoned by the fair breeze, then baffled by a series of calms and gusts that put *Shamaal* on her side several times before we could enter Órmos Pánormos, a jaw-shaped bay on the north coast.

Here was a Greece that had sold its soul and just about anything else that could be moved. Tourist developments crouched behind security walls on sterile hills. In front of us, a new 'village' was under construction, and every couple of hours came the dry cough of explosions as engineers tried to make it fit – a real war against the landscape. But thirty-six hours passed before we dared sneak out, thirty-six hours of stiff, unforecasted south-westerlies that made *Shamaal* tremble at the end of her line. Nudists huddled along the beach, trying their best to ignore the sand moving in thin curtains. The water became cloudy. The rigging whistled tunelessly. Thirty-six hours! Our consolation was that conditions on every other side of the island had to be doubly fierce.

So we were in for a surprise on eventually rounding the exposed west coast and entering the marina for Míkonos town. 'Strong winds? We've had a rather pleasant couple of days,' said George, our new neighbour. I checked for sarcasm, but George, a bluff Englishman with an old-fashioned motor cruiser that Adèle and I put under the category of 'pipe-smoker's boat', was not the type. How strong had the wind been? 'Force 3, 4, maybe. Not more.' There seemed to be no explanation other than that in Órmos Pánormos we'd entered a kind of trap, the winds rising gently from the south-west side of the island, cooling at the peaks, then accelerating in a rush of chilled air down into the north – katabatic winds, in other words.

Míkonos got its own spell of strong winds the next evening, giving George reason to look at me a little accusingly. As in Órmos Pánormos, we were protected from waves, but the wind, a Force 7, entered unimpeded. In Mediterranan style, yachts moored here by securing one end of the boat with ropes to the quay, the other to an anchor dropped in the middle of the harbour. It was an arrangement that worked well when the wind came either from the front or back of the boat, and not so well, as in our case, with wind from the side. As the line of yachts sagged under the force of the wind, sailors scurried to add new ropes and fenders. Only our rubber dinghy, squashed by now into a grotesque pretzel shape, stood between *Shamaal*'s bow and the stone wall. It would take just a couple of the boats' anchors to lose their grip and the whole row of yachts, like a set of expensive dominoes, could collapse.

The near gale lasted two days and, while Adèle went off filming, I attacked the bow leak, taking apart everything fixed to the forepeak, blocking holes, redrilling, strengthening the fibreglass and putting everything back. These were slow, tedious jobs, mostly spent lying in impossibly small spaces in a cloud of poisonous fumes, dust and dripping resin.

All this time, I'd overhear the conversation from George's boat next door. He had installed some particularly advanced weather service and so became much in demand with various groups of nervous European sailors. Dregs of their exchanges would filter down. 'My information is . . . Do you have latest wetter reeport? . . . At zero four hundred hours . . . 7 becoming 4 . . . is it better to wait?' Sometimes Adèle, with her gift of tongues, would be called upon to interpret.

The actual town of Míkonos – the famous white cubist houses, wrinkled alleyways, boutiques and nightclubs – was out of sight around the curve of coast and out of mind. Míkonos was a distraction, a flash seen from the corner of the eye, and soon lost amid an infinitely greater light.

Delos

A first glimpse of the ruined city on Delos will always catch the breath. Ours was through binoculars from the neighbouring island of Rhinia. We were at anchor, once again the sole boat, in a horseshoe cove surrounded by sunburnt moors. Somewhere on the low, mostly barren island there were supposed to be a few farms, though we never saw them. In our cove, a kindly crone and her bright-eyed husband lived in a one-room cottage. There was nothing else – only the underwater ruins of a long disused breakwater, relic of a time, or so I was told, when this had been a quarantine station. Rhinia was five miles from Míkonos, but might have been 100.

Looking east, the naked eye detected nothing unusual about Delos, other than occasional, light-coloured marks of what may have been buildings. With the binoculars I initially aimed at the wrong area and, on seeing nothing other than the usual scruffy Cycladic landscape, almost gave up. Then I noticed a first set of columns. I shifted my focus and was rewarded with another set, then another and another. Ruins of temples, markets, dwellings and theatres practically tumbled over each other, their smooth, gentle forms contrasting with the harsh land on which they'd been built. Still staring across the water to the city, I handed the binoculars to Adèle.

We sailed over to Delos early next morning, dropped anchor and rowed to a breakwater, the spine of what two millennia ago had been the most affluent, privileged harbour in the western world.

Having arrived early, we had an hour or so before large numbers of tourists would begin to arrive – time and peace enough to become lost in the details. Geckos struck miniature monster poses at the edge of a sacred spring. Poppies decorated corridors formed by column upon fallen column. Fragments of inscriptions in Greek on marble blocks poked from luxurious early summer grass. Marble debris on the west shore marked the lines of something very much like a showy, modern seafront. Rows of more humble dwellings suddenly brought to mind the street life there must have been in a community of 30,000 people. Then the coolness of the museum, its pride of wind-worn lions, Boreas ravishing the Athenian princess Oreithyia, and the collection of memorials to sailors whose vessels 'could not withstand the waves'. On a bare, white wall appeared the text of a sixth-century BC hymn to the sea:

> I call Tethys, the sea-green eyed nymph of the Ocean,
> The lady of the dark veils, who walks gracefully in swift waves,
> Who surrounds the earth with sweet breezes,
> Who breaks in big waves in seashores and rocks,
> And becalms in smooth roads,
> The one who rejoices in the ships, you water-travelled,
>   fish-breeder,
> Mother of Aphrodite, mother of the dark clouds . . .

At its peak, Delos hosted citizens from all over Greece, Italy and the Levant, the original high temple of Apollo being joined by shrines to the likes of Anubis, Isis and the deities of Arabs, Jews and the Romans. But how such an unpromising little island could have become the hub of the Mediterranean world is not entirely clear. The accepted version is that the location made it a perfect stop on the international shipping lanes, even if Delos has shortcomings as a harbour. The mythical explanation is that Poseidon used diamond pillars to anchor the floating island of Adelos in order that Leto might give birth to Artemis and Apollo, the twin gods of light. It was thus that Adelos (invisible) became Delos (visible), a place of such sanctity that during the great Persian invasion of 490 BC, Delos, alone in the Cyclades, was left in peace.

Rhinia, where we now returned, had eerie beginnings of its own. Simply to be in such proximity to the stupendous riches of Delos must have been odd on such a poor island. Then – in 100 BC, let's say – it wouldn't have taken binoculars to see the extraordinary city to the east. But the relationship was stranger, for under Athenian rule in the middle of the sixth century BC it was decreed that no one should die or be born on Delos, meaning by default that Rhinia became the maternity ward and death room of its sacred neighbour. What awe the name Rhinia must have inspired as the sick and elderly were hustled through their brief, final sea journey.

Our anchorage in Skhinou bay, a natural harbour where no doubt many of those troubled cargoes arrived, was enlivened by the presence of Dimitri and Spirodula, the two ancients in the cottage. For nine months of the year they lived here in complete independence, sharing their cottage and adjacent hut with hens, a magnificent white cockerel, ducks, a spaniel gun dog, cats, kittens and geese. The tiny fishing boat used each day to lay nets was their only means of communication with the wider world.

Otherwise, Rhinia was stark, without a trace of softness in its stony, sun-scraped ground. Any sign of life looked somehow out of place. Walking south we found a flock of sheep squeezed pathetically into the hot shadow of a wall. Inland, a tiny chapel clung to rocks in the middle of a desolate field. Its walls were covered in silver votive offerings depicting human arms, hearts, livers, sometimes entire women, children and men, the latter shown in stiff suits and shirts – evidence of a seemingly impossible number of ailments on the sparsely populated island.

My favourite part of Rhinia was below sea level, and it was here that I tried to spend my time. Shimmering water made the sea floor appear closer than it was, tempting me to where I knew I'd have trouble saving enough breath to return. Repeatedly I took the bait. The clarity of the water, the submerged former harbour walls and the rippling carpets of white sand created the impression of the ruins of a huge house through which I could swim room to room. From the coral-flecked black rocks to the sea-grass field, every corner hid secrets – green-striped fish and orange stars, ormers gleaming in mother-of-pearl and clams the size of books. All this, but also, on occasion, the mute, fragmented evidence of events forgotten long ago. One last dive, my blood vessels fit to crack, and I paddled back to *Shamaal*, calling Adèle. With one hand I held the gunwale, with the other one of these heirlooms, an offering for Adèle from the sea: the worn, serpentine handle of a clay amphora.

Meltemi

From Rhinia, passing Delos again and pausing in the cheerful port of Náxos, we came to the small island of Iráklia.

The sole harbour consisted of a cove with a short but substantially constructed quay, fifteen or so minor fishing boats and a welcoming, pine-shaded crescent of beach. The village – one shop, one *taverna* and one café/post office/ferry agent/phone booth – started behind the trees and petered out shortly after.

Anchoring in the turquoise cup of the harbour, just beyond the quay, we were sorry to know in advance that we could only stay a couple of days, but so it had to be. The meltemi, great ruler of the Aegean summer, loomed and we wanted to be through the Cyclades and around feared Cape Maléa to begin the journey west before it came. We were now past the first week of June, meaning we supposedly had about ten days to go. Time to stop in Iráklia for forty-eight hours, then Sífnos and maybe Mílos, too, but not long – the meltemi was breathing down our necks.

The general predictability of the meltemi is explained by the wind's relationship to the monsoon rainy season centred in these months over Pakistan. The low pressure in Asia contrasts with the equally dependable high pressure found at this period over the Balkans, and a strong wind (high pressure flowing into low pressure) results. The ancient Greek name 'etesian' referred to the fact of the wind's *annual* appearance, and even the exact date of the meltemi's arrival invites cautious predictions. Aristotle pinpointed its arrival to the days after the summer solstice of 21 June. Most modern guides agree with Aristotle that it is unlikely before the last days of June, at least at full strength, which is generally reserved for July and August. The ancient Greeks called the softer June versions of the meltemi *prodromoi*, or 'heralds'. Once the meltemi blows, according to popular wisdom, a watch may be set by its rhythms: stirring at ten in the morning, blowing hard around two, dying at six and calm by eight. 'If there's one thing you can depend on,' I'd heard from an old hand on the other side of the Mediterranean a year before, 'it's the meltemi.'

So what were the flies in our cabin trying to say? The first was a passing distraction, the second annoying, the third an invader. They kept coming, and I stopped counting. The flies were over-energetic and agile as all flies, but with a difference. Rather than chase food, which in any case was well hidden, they seemed obsessed only with staying in the cabin. I could do nothing to get them out or, if I did, to stop them from coming back. At first we thought Iráklia, unusually for the Cyclades, might be infested. Yet a brief inspection found no flies on the quay or among the trees or in the handful of streets. It was *Shamaal*'s cabin they wanted – our very own '*prodromoi*'.

Twelve days passed before we finally left Iráklia. The first bout of hard wind hadn't worried us, but when the wind didn't stop, or ease, a fisherman soon confirmed our suspicion: an early, even very early meltemi was upon us – and a stiff one at that.

Some days the wind blew from the north-east, making the cove rough and driving a fast-moving swell against the little beach. We moved and tied *Shamaal* alongside the protected side of the quay, but there were times when waves came right over the wall, flooding the quay, before withdrawing with a rush and sucking sound. On other days, the wind blew from the north-west and when it did the cove, now fully protected, became calm.

On days of north-east wind, the swell stirred the sandy bottom, making the water in the harbour opaque. I passed the time making running dives from the quay into the oncoming waves, swimming around to the protected side and climbing up to dive again. But on north-west days the water cleared, and I'd put on a mask and search for shells to give Adèle. Never in the Mediterranean had I seen so many: shells like open fans, petals, hand mirrors and musical instruments. There were striped Venus', dog cockles, cowries, helmet shells and murex, the spiky snails whose purple dye once made the Phoenicians, or 'purple men', as they became known, so wealthy.

On days of north-east wind, loose items such as flip-flops, a bikini or hat often blew overboard, but then on the north-west days Adèle and I would go out with snorkels to bring them back. It was on these searches that we found, in addition to shells, a handsome set of amber worry beads, probably dropped from a fishing boat, and a navy-blue polo shirt inscribed with a little drawing of a yacht and the words 'Klaus – crew member'. After a freshwater rinse, the shirt looked new and I wore it often. I doubted, should I ever run into Klaus, that I'd agree to its return.

Only seventy people live on Iráklia, and we quickly became familiar with many of them. Because little happened, particularly during the meltemi, life on the island resembled a very slow-moving play, already deep into what was a record-breaking run of nobody knew how many seasons. In formulaic Greek scenes, old men played cards or backgammon outside the café, fishermen repaired their gear, donkeys stood in the shade, a young man blasted his motorbike through the half-dozen streets. Nothing unscripted took place, at least not in public, and the village was all the more peaceful for the fact.

Most of our time was spent at the *taverna*, where a huge, circular marble table had been built on the terrace around the thick, living trunk of a pine. Here we ate rarely, but sipped coffees, watched the sea switch between dark green and blue, and listened to the wind in the bulrushes and bamboo. From here, we could also study the village characters: the shy, intense fisherman; the sullen local beauty and her bucktoothed beau; the entrepreneur with the shop, the big boat, a small hotel and a pair of remarkably sensual eyes; the village idiot (when he wasn't asleep in the street); the obese, show-off doctor and his ladies; the jovial, red-bearded priest; the chorus of emaciated, goat-eyed cats.

Only the arrival several times a week of *Skopelitis*, the small ferry from Náxos, shook Iráklia out of its slumber. Sailings were supposed to be cancelled when the wind reached Force 8, but most days it blew at Force 7 and, even when it was reported to be 8, *Skopelitis* sailed. The ferry worked to a tight schedule and ten minutes at best were given for tourists, tractors, aged locals and the all-important supplies either to embark or disembark. The islanders loved those ten minutes. Indeed, there was a buzz on the quay absent at all other times. The whole community from the priest to the gloomy fisherman became animated, yelling, running from ship to shore, and exchanging news with the *Skopelitis* crew – even, through excited shouts, after the ferry had begun to pull away.

One day *Skopelitis* arrived with the meltemi blowing from north-east right into the harbour. Now, in addition to commercial constraints, there was real danger of damage or shipwreck, and the usual friendly rush became a performance worthy of a circus. The anchor meant to hold the ship's bow into the sea dragged. The heavy stern heaved up and down a hair from the quay, sparks spitting as the iron boarding ramp slammed on the concrete. A truck attempting to enter the ferry slipped repeatedly on the moving ramp, only succeeding with the help of much pushing and even more shouting. Crates of bananas, beer, soap, frozen steaks and ice cream sang through the air to waiting hands. Men struggled with barrels of diesel. Finally, half a dozen pale and frightened tourists, no doubt regretting having bought tickets for Iráklia, were pushed and dragged on to land. Much more shouting, clouds of engine smoke and *Skopelitis* made off. Less than five minutes had passed. For a moment everyone on the quay gave vent to their relief, laughing and gesturing as they relived the drama. Then the locals vanished, taking with them the tourists and crates of supplies, and the quay, like the whole island, fell back into deep sleep. As did we.

An old Mediterranean rule says an absence of dew signals strong winds, and sure enough every morning the decks were dry as the trunks of the eucalyptus trees. There was no need for weather reports up in the village. Force 7, Force 8, north-west, north-east: they never changed, and we had all stopped caring. Mornings we swam, afternoons we ambled through the *garrigue* and ordered beers at the *taverna*, looking down at the sea and joking lazily how we might never leave. The textbook meltemi was only meant to *start* in another week – then keep going all summer. After, came winter. We might still be here next year, by then probably playing cards in front of the old café. Already we'd been on Iráklia long enough to get to know, by face at least, almost every local – even, from our afternoon walks, the poor pig, which reappeared one night on the *taverna* menu.

On the tenth day, just as Adèle and I finally began to rebel, there came the first rumours of an end to the gale. As always the fishermen knew first. Maybe in two days, they said, maybe three, but it would slow to Force 6, then calm right down. The following morning on the track between the shop and the café, one of the old men, a former merchant navy officer, asked where we were headed. Cape Maléa, I said.

'Ákra Maléa? Wait until the day after tomorrow,' he told me. 'Then it will be grego blowing. With grego, you will be fine.'

The flies left the shelter of our cabin. Dew sprinkled the deck. The wind, warm and manageable, veered from north-west to north-east, or grego, and in front of half a dozen well-wishers we sailed from the cove, waving until the quay, beach, the pines and the village became one.

It was only on rounding the corner of the island that I fully realized what a turning point this was: Iráklia marked our east-ernmost position and from here, give or take a few deviations, we'd always travel west. In an almost-enclosed sea, this was a moment every Mediterranean journey eventually reached – this was the outward path of Greek civilization, of the pioneering Phoenician merchants, even, once its circuit was complete, of the sea water itself. In the Mediterranean, to turn west was destiny.

Cape Maléa

'He who passes Maléa says goodbye to his homeland,' the proverb goes. So the first finger of the Peloponnese was the Pale of the ancient Greeks, where voyages were often doomed to end or, at least, as in the cases of Menelaus, Odysseus and many others, to go astray. In *The Odyssey*, Maléa and its satellite island, Kíthera, are the last places on whose modern location all can concur. 'I should have reached my own land safe and sound, had not the swell, the current and the North Wind combined, as I was rounding Maléa,' Odysseus laments. It is from that point, begin-ning with the magical land of the lotus-eaters (possibly Jerba, off Tunisia), that his wanderings take shape.

Even if the old maxim about homeland hardly applied, it was still with a sense of occasion that we sailed towards the famous landmark. Almost 1,500 nautical miles lay between Maléa and Gibraltar via the Balearics, 1,500 miles sure to stretch relentlessly in the calms and contrary winds of high summer. In a cabin filled with the aromas of round Náxos cheese, rosemary sprigs from the Iráklian hills and the last of our nougat, this target of Gibraltar seemed fantastically remote. Yet quietly, almost without effort on our part, the focus had started to shift. Charts for the western Mediterranean were working towards the top of the pile, and I might, in a quiet moment, begin flicking through the pilot books for Spain. Our horizons were widening. Secret coves and days swimming among fish would soon be only a memory, and so, too, the constant, shepherding presence of land. Soon, only the great headlands and corners of the Mediterranean would matter – and Maléa was the first.

The Cyclades send-off was characteristic. Rough seas left from the gales tossed stomachs grown soft on Iráklia and the contents of the cabin equally. Surprise katabatic gusts off the south side of Síkinos launched *Shamaal* into the seemingly impossible speed of ten and a half knots before we managed to reduce (and probably save) the sails. A paraffin bottle broke, spreading a malodorous slick across tools, food and clothing. We ran across an orange lifebuoy apparently lost from the rails of a big ship – '*MARIAM, ST JOHNS,*' it read in black lettering – and lashed this trophy to the top of the deck. We watched the volcanic scoop of Mílos, then the islet and lighthouse of Vrak Ananes sink into the dusk. Briefly the scimitar fins of six bottle-nosed dolphins cut a path through the sea. And then we were alone with the wind.

At daybreak we found ourselves exactly where we wanted to be – a few miles off Maléa and moving quickly west. Notwithstanding our lucky timing and the clement conditions, we'd read or heard enough warnings about the cape to approach warily. Maléa is notorious quite simply because about half of Greece's bad weather systems travel between it and Crete, along with a great deal of shipping, which up until the opening of the Corinth Canal had no other route. A pilot guide from a century back mentions gusts 'sent down the mountains with north winds which are strong enough to rip your sails apart, break the mast or even cause the boat to capsize'. A modern Greek pilot book that I'd examined while in Iráklia also talked of dangerous whirlwinds and rebounding seas. The Greeks claim to be able to read the clouds in the region as clearly as smoke signals from a fire: a hat-like cloud over Maléa meaning north wind, a cloud smothering the top of the cape meaning north-east, and so on. In practice, this lore might be very much less reliable to newcomers than the neat diagrams of clouds and mountains suggest. The advice of the English pilot guide we carried was to be prepared both for calm and gale. Which one might not discover until the last minute: 'You can only use your nose.'

In the event, we only glimpsed the mysteries of Cape Maléa, *Shamaal* under reefed sails, banking and swooping like a shearwater in strong seas. A Russian-flagged tanker passed east. The crew came out on to the bridge and waved, so close we could see their excited faces, and we waved back, shouting *'Privyet!'* and bursting with pride that our little, blue boat had made the sailors happy. But Maléa was not so simple. No sooner was the tanker astern than the wind stopped and the sea fell flat. Then an area of strange, slapping little waves, and wind, or rather winds, for they all blew and simultaneously so that we began to turn in circles – a fresh north wind, a weak westerly and gusts of north-east . . . Yet we had got past, glad not to have made the same trip on a less lucky day.

A warm breeze from the south-west sprang up and leaving Kíthera, Aphrodite's birthplace, to port, and Elafónisos, the grave of Agamemnon's dead captain, to starboard, we sailed on into the silvery haze. Under the headland of Saint Marina an oddly coloured set of rocks stood out – ochre and at an awkward slant that suggested a house on its side. We changed course to sail closer: those strange boulders of ours were the shattered, rusting stern and bridge of a mid-size merchant ship.

The crooked middle finger of the Peloponnese, half a day's sail from Elafónisos, beckoned across the wide waters of Lakonikós Kólpos. The closer we got to Yithion, the main port on the far side, the stronger that comforting sensation of return to familiar ground. Adèle and I had come here several times on holiday from our jobs as journalists in Moscow or London, driving from Athens down through the orchards of Arcadia into the Mani region. We'd come for the outrageous harshness of the Taïyetos mountains, the ghostly tower villages, the unruly history of piracy and rebellion, and the all-pervading presence of the sea. We'd been happy on land, but, even then, hankered in the manner of dreamers at a window to discover the blue spaces beyond. How often we'd looked down the saw-toothed coast and wished one day to return by boat.

Yithion exuded the confidence gained in surviving a few thousand years. Here, secluded on the pine-scented islet of Kranai, Helen and Paris passed the first night of the elopement that would consume an entire world and, if nothing so grand had happened since, no one cared. Yithion was an oasis. Maniots rode in from stony villages on pick-up trucks, the men maybe to sell a little produce, but mostly to sit in corner cafés, while the women hit the markets and spent a little extra on pampering their hair. We, too, gathered our delicacies – baklava dripping through its cardboard box, a blood sausage to hang in the cabin, grapes to eat with hard Taïyetos cheese. Then, like the Maniots on land, we cast off, dropping south.

Our next stop, Kotronas, lay only a few headlands further along, but the appearance of gaunt defensive towers in the cedar and olive groves signalled that an unofficial border into the deep Mani had been crossed. Having no chart, we nosed into the cove, following the seabed and sounding frequently until anchored in golden sand. Above water our bearings were surer, for Kotronas had been one of our regular stops. There, exactly as we remembered them, bobbed the wooden caiques. The seafront cemetery was a little fuller, but the candles we remembered flickered on. The street urchin who'd spent his childhood dangling bait over the quay was still around, only fatter, swarthier, in glasses and now carrying a trident. The madman who used to bound in that chaotic, noisy way to Adèle with flowers – we didn't see him, but in the café hotel where we used to stay they were all there. The son with his baskets of fishing nets, the father in string vest, the mother and, slouched at the same table, with the same striped shirt, suede shoes and ornamented cigarette holder, the village lush. How happy we were to see the mother, as kind and, in her own fashion, regal as ever. We sat with her under rows of cobwebbed bottles inside the café for the football

World Cup final, or a little of it, for she fell immediately into deep, noisy sleep. The television reception, taking life at a similar pace, lasted only slightly longer.

On we sailed. Clustered stone towers built over the centuries by feuding families, evocative names like Áyios Ilias, Exo Nimfi and Kokala, and memories of our first days together escorted us south. Desolate hills rolled ever higher from the sea and from them the winds rolled back down. Here, at last, were the Maniot gusts about which we'd heard so much. Again, they were of the katabatic type, good Force 7s, but without accompanying waves and so, once the sails were reefed, easily handled. Ahead lay the second great cape of southern Greece, Ákra Tainaron. A little further we'd find our beloved Yeroliménas. This night, though, called for shelter and we were lucky, for at hand was the best natural harbour in the region, the oddly named Porto Kayio.

Horseshoe-shaped, with anchorages facing three different directions, the bay of Porto Kayio was precisely the kind of lair that for so many centuries made piracy a flourishing concern in the Mediterranean. Indeed, the sea's geography favoured the buccaneer as much as a modern-day yachtsman and for much the same reasons: shipping lanes were predictable and cover in the jagged shores and islands plentiful. The traditional modus operandi was to hide behind some key junction, such as Ákra Tainaron, and strike from fast, light craft. After an attack, whether against ships or seaside villages, that same maze of crooked bays, coves, caves and innumerable nooks pulled the pirate back into its fold. 'They do most mischief with their Feleucca, which commonly Rows with 12 Oars, and carries 6 Sitters,' recounted an Englishman, remembered only as Mr Roberts, after being press-ganged by Frankish corsairs in the Aegean in the 1690s. 'For at Night they leave the Ship, and get under the shoar before Day, and go ashoar, where they way-lay the Turks.'

Mr Roberts's ordeal occurred at the peak of Mediterranean piracy, a period of several centuries when the Barbary states of North Africa were pitted against Maltese raiders and other Christian counterparts. Only in the nineteenth century would French occupation of Algiers and then American intervention finally bring the seas under control. Even as late as 1895, Joshua Slocum was warned against sailing near North Africa, then found himself being chased through the Strait of Gibraltar.

The roots of Mediterranean piracy were extraordinarily ancient. The dangers of the Mani were already notorious to the Greeks and Romans. The lagoons of the Adriatic were greatly feared, so, too, the coasts of Albania and all the Turkish seas, but also the south of France, the sandy Kerkenah Islands and the Balearics, where men attacked from swarms of small rafts. The most modest pirates could be chancers out to see what they could snatch between collecting their nets or planting meagre crops. At the other end of the scale were the Cilicians, a tough tribe whose reach extended from one end of the Mediterranean to the other. A young Julius Caesar was briefly their hostage, and there is a story that he vowed to crucify his captors for failing to show sufficient appreciation of his early writings. He also complained at the insultingly low ransom demand of twenty talents, which was consequently raised to fifty, and, when Caesar later tracked down and duly crucified the brigands, he cut their throats first in gratitude for agreeing to the increase. Another story suggests that the Cilicians may have invented the precursor of that most emblematic of pirate punishments, the walking of the plank. The Cilicians, Plutarch recounts, had taken hostage a Roman citizen and, on noting his outrage, 'pretended to be dumbfounded and afraid . . . and begged his pardon'. Next, they dressed him up in a toga and, with further mockeries, invited him to leave the ship and return to Rome, even dropping a ladder into the sea for his benefit. 'If he refused they would push him into the water and drown him.'

Time was when a boat wouldn't have sailed so blithely into a place such as Porto Kayio.

*

The sun was already sinking behind the Taïyetos as we entered the bay. Inside, the surrounding cliffs and deep water lent the atmosphere of a volcanic crater; however, despite the excellent shelter, the title 'Porto' was a misnomer. There was no port, only the bay with two adjoining restaurants on the beach, a few scrappy houses and the inevitable towers, sentinel-like on the hills. As for 'Kayio', that stemmed from the quails for which the cape has long been a crucial stop during migration. Yet whether it was Porto Quaglio of the Venetians or Port aux Cailles of the Franks has never been established. These linguistic tangles run all along the Hellenic seaboard, evidence, as much as the visible layers of ruins, of Greek, Roman, Frankish, Venetian, Genoese and Turkish influence. Wind names in modern Greece are especially rich – appropriately so, as it was the winds that stirred the melting pot in the first place. Even today, Greek and Latinate words are freely interchanged (like *zephyros* and *pounentes* for west wind), as well as exotic names such as *sorokos* (the sirocco), which stems from Arab for 'east' and entered Italian, in addition to numerous other nautical terms, as far back as the seventeenth century. *Meltemi* is a Turkish word for a gentle breeze, but has taken on more vigorous connotations in Greece, where some would claim a Venetian origin, insisting the word began as '*bel tempo*'.

Regardless of its foreign name, Porto Kayio was pure Mani, a lugubrious setting in which it was not hard to imagine the dark days when the Maniot reputation was fierce – 'a cruel people, without faith, without humanity', according to a French traveller of the mid seventeenth century.

A few of the older people we'd met in the Mani told us that crimes of honour – avenging insults or a woman's reputation and so on – had taken place within their lifetime, but that now the feuds were finished. Here, the leftovers of this warlike energy had been channelled into a dispute between the two restaurants, which, despite being owned by relations and separated only by a thin wall, refused contact. Sipping coffee in one of the *tavernas* –

we, too, had to take sides – our host joked this was almost how it had been in the old days when minor wars erupted between families in the same village. 'Then, of course, we would have gone up to our towers and begun shooting.'

Cape Tainaron, which we rounded the next afternoon, is one of the traditional entrances to Hades, and it does resemble nothing more than a scene from the End of the World. Wildfires blacken the few patches where anything grows. Everywhere else consists of sun-yellowed rock. But if the cape leads to hell, then the Devil was out on call, for we slipped past in a calm under motor. Only a patch of unprovoked, disorganized mini waves, the fruit of currents colliding underwater, hinted at the powers of this salt- and wind-worn place. Spinning a silky wake, we passed a chapel built from blocks of a former temple to Poseidon, a weather-stained lighthouse and the various holes and crevasses that might once have been, maybe still were, portals to the Underworld. By dusk we were creeping under the sheer cliff walls of Yeroliménas and, after poking gingerly around (again, no chart), dropping anchor.

Yeroliménas had always been at the heart of our trips to the Mani. Nestling under cliffs, the village exudes a spookiness that just occasionally – perhaps at the howl of a dog or simply the night-time lap of waves – borders deliciously on menace. There is only one true street, but fishermen's cottages and ruined stone houses perch all around the cove. Hauled on the beach, which consists of egg-smooth grey and white pebbles, lies the abandoned hulk of a large Arab fishing boat, its fading paint, cracked planking and plundered cabin suggesting a variety of unhappy ends to what may well have started as a hopeful voyage. 'God have mercy,' reads the inscription in swirling Arabic over the boat's name, *Hamada*. In the Maniot way, the locals are initially taciturn, but with the politeness and formality of an inherently proud people, and over our various visits we'd come to count a few almost as friends. In autumn the hunters come, roaming the seafront cafés in camouflaged gangs before taking their guns and dogs into the *garrigue* above the cliffs. At night, the few orange streetlamps are overpowered by the immensity of the sea and night sky.

It was here Adèle and I had spent longest on earlier trips, blinking, after Russia, at the lack of trees and marvelling at the dreamy, restorative power of the sea. The first year, we came from Moscow with Patrick Leigh Fermor's marvellous book *Mani*. Written in the late 1950s, when there were almost certainly more donkeys than cars in this remotest part of Greece, *Mani* revealed a lost world of clans and feuds, but also of honour and hospitality. I'd been travelling a good deal in Chechnya at the time and found both the book and the region struck an immediate chord. The values of a people so stubborn in their independence, the complex rules of the vendetta, the dirges, even the famous towers – so much of what was now folklore in the southern Peloponnese lived on in unsoftened form in Chechnya and the Caucasus I loved. I might read a page of *Mani* and realize I had witnessed that very scene more than 1,000 miles to the east a short time and a few plane trips before. Indeed, we were so taken with the Mani, with Yeroliménas in particular, that we'd fantasize about buying a tower, keeping goats and a donkey, growing figs, and something more – belonging. Yes, here, in the blinding emptiness, it seemed to us we might belong. Here was a place where the sea beckoned, but the land would always welcome us back. The freedom of wind and comfort of land: it seemed that we could have it all. Looking now from *Shamaal* across to Hotel Akroyali, the place where we used to hatch our great plans, we could afford a smile.

At dusk we rowed up to the Akroyali and took our old table on the terrace. The owners, Georgy and his brother, greeted us warmly and offered a jug of wine. They were as we'd remembered. But there was no sign of the Mad Old Gentleman, the impoverished yet dapper fellow who used to argue loudly with everyone, even people at other tables when there was no one at his own. Also absent was the young priest who used to make eyes at Adèle. Most of all, *we* were different: just as in love, but no longer able to believe in such simple endings – and the richer for it. I understood now what Kavafy, the nineteenth-century Greek poet, meant when he said the journey to Ithaca, not Ithaca itself, was what mattered. 'You must pray that the way be long,' he wrote. Looking back at *Shamaal*, I found myself thinking not about the Akroyali, the towers or the tiny, bunker-like chapels on the hills, but the urge to up anchor and continue the voyage.

We left Yeroliménas the following morning.

VI

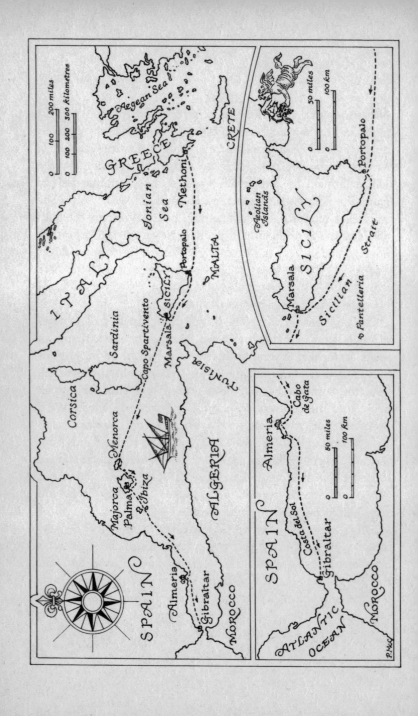

Seas of the setting sun

Hanging from the tip of the third finger of the Peloponnese, the fine old Venetian castle at Methóni faces the widest, emptiest quarter of the Mediterranean. Only to the north does the Ionian narrow, framed by the green Greek coast on one side and the Italian foot on the other. Due west there is nothing for 320 nautical miles, when you scrape into southern Sicily. South, the sea bulges endlessly, swallowing huge bites of Africa in the gulfs of Gabes and Syrtes before extending eastward to the Levant. So not an ocean, but the biggest of the Mediterranean's internal seas – a good North or Black sea, or a couple bays of Biscay. It is here that the westward-travelling sailor, riding on the current of Greece's history, must breathe deeply and leap.

Our turn came at 2 a.m. The castle quivered in the half shadows of town lights as we manoeuvred through the silent shapes of boats at anchor. Several yachts were meant to be leaving for Italy, but they were still there, just recognizable by their silhouettes. Some people had been waiting at anchor for a week because of the contrary west and north-westerly winds. We'd been more lucky, arriving two days before from Yeroliménas to receive forecasts earlier this day of a change to strong winds from the north. A rough but fast reach west, it seemed, and we wanted to gain every mile before that changed. A lighthouse led us out of the bay, where we skirted the shoals, straightened up and aimed for Sicily, far across the moonless sea.

Sailing west has always been the great problem of the Mediterranean. For all its irregularity, the tendency of the wind is to blow from west or north-west and, the further towards Spain and France one goes, the truer this is. That flow, beginning with the poniente pouring through the Strait of Gibraltar, serves the eastbound traveller well. As the Arab geographer Ibn Hawqal remarked in the middle of the tenth century, from Gibraltar 'one is pushed by a single wind to most of the places in this sea'. But how to return? Once at Sicily and beyond, the sailor is trapped in the landlocked sea like the fish in a purse seine.

The compass light had burnt out recently, but we only occasionally used a torch to check our bearing, steering instead by the stars that hung like lanterns in the rigging. The Big Bear cartwheeled in slow motion over our shoulders. A little higher, the Small Bear peeked from its cavern and, hidden in the polka-dot night, Polaris maintained its steady check on our progress. The exact course mattered little, provided we went west, and it was with a certain greed that I ticked off the miles made good.

But the sea was grudging. The previous week's west winds had set up a contrary current that continuously stole a knot from our apparent speed. Romping along at six knots, this might hardly matter, but it was rough and *Shamaal* staggered in the waves, arrested a split second each time she hit her stride. *Shamaal* was also heavy, burdened with ten days' supplies, including the quantities of water that must accompany any Mediterranean passage in summer. If the speed log read a respectable four knots, I knew that after tax we were really only going, at best, three.

As so often during our voyage I found myself wondering how anyone managed in the past. Not easily would be the answer in the sixth century AD. The account of an army sent by Emperor Justinian from Byzantium along this same route to fight in North Africa is filled with fear of the wind and sea. After gales at departure in 533, the cumbersome fleet has to row around Cape Maléa in a calm. 'A great piece of luck,' wrote the admirably frank author, a nephew of the Byzantine general in command. 'If the wind had got up, whether favourable or contrary, it seems to me that the sailors would have had trouble in saving their lives and their ships.' At Methóni, the fleet is becalmed and the army waits helplessly while many of its soldiers die of disease. Then progress across the Ionian is so slow that it takes fifteen days to reach Sicily, by which time water supplies have run out. It is now, with the crossing to Tunisia and fighting against the

Vandal enemy to come, that the expedition verges on mutiny. 'The soldiers were deeply worried about a naval battle and warned without the slightest shame that if they could disembark onto enemy territory they would try hard to act bravely in combat, but that if the adversary made any naval attack they would flee, because, they said, they could not fight the enemy and the sea at the same time.'

For early mariners, these difficulties encouraged coast-hopping and lengthy, roundabout journeys along the shores of Italy or Africa. No one was more daring than the Phoenician traders who left their eastern homes eventually to penetrate the Strait of Gibraltar, reach northern Europe and, possibly, even circumnavigate Africa. Yet that great push west, starting with Libya, then Carthage and Sicily, was largely the work of galleys that stuck close to shore. Only with medieval improvements to ship design and especially to the Arab lateen sail did tacking become more feasible, and the great spaces of the Ionian, the Sardinian sea and Spanish–African channel began to shrink. Gradually, ships became capable of manoeuvring handily in any direction – the triangular lateen best for working upwind and the ancient, more primitive square sail unsurpassed for going downwind. Medieval Genoese traders started regular runs in large *naves* to Flanders, while caravels, the sprightly little ships developed in Renaissance Portugal, would soon conquer the furthest reaches of the Atlantic. But, ironically, it would not be until after the invention of the engine that sailors produced today's familiar Bermudan rig: that on *Shamaal* and just about every other modern yacht – and the easiest, most efficient sail design ever seen.

By dawn, Greece was reduced to a golden sliver and the waves were slight. For me, the psychologically hard part of the voyage, the initial break from land, was over. We were in open sea, moving more quickly now and chasing the setting sun.

By the time the fair north wind finally petered out, as it was bound to do, we were prepared. Back to the age-old battle of wits: contrary winds here, a good breeze there, then calms, a thunderstorm, a day of tacking and once more tearing west with reduced sails, before the next, inevitable sticky calm. It was with equanimity that I watched the 320-mile straight line to Sicily unravel.

It took a second day to reach the margins of our last detailed chart of Greece and sail into the no-man's land of the planning chart for the eastern Mediterranean. Gone the intricate details of mountain heights and harbour depths, of what lay on the seabed and where ships had been wrecked. Out here, at a scale of 1:2,250,000, the picture resembled something one might draw on the back of a napkin. There were archaic subaqua place names: the Herodotus Seamount, Archimedes Seamount and the Ionian Abyssal Plain. There were sobering indications of depth – three to four kilometres in most places, but 5,121 metres in the pits of the Hellenic Trench. Mostly, there were large white areas, blank but for the occasional depth reading that in any case was useless to us bobbing along at the top.

In such a wasteland, it seemed a good time to resume training on my sextant. The instrument allows one to look simultaneously at the horizon and, via two mirrors and a few eye-saving coloured shades, the sun. A measured arc then records the angle between. This is called 'shooting the sun', and from a pitching boat it does feel like shooting – the targets being the weaving and dipping yellow orb and, ultimately, one's location. There follows a notoriously arcane exercise in which the recorded angle is pushed through a thicket of formulae and tables to emerge on the other side, maybe twenty minutes of mind-numbing work later, as a feeble line across the chart. You are somewhere on that line – or not, as even the pros accept that their magic line will usually be a couple of miles out of place. As a novice I'd drawn lines through Ukraine, the Atlantic and the Sahara, but now my shooting was homing in. Checked against the GPS, my plots were regularly within eight miles of our real position, often five, occasionally far less – a workable margin of error in open seas.

Settling the oddly shaped instrument in my hand, my eye in the viewfinder, I'd experience that unmistakable thrill of the chase. Until the day we dropped the GPS overboard or ran out of batteries, there'd be no practical need for the sextant, but in the twenty-first century there was no *need* to be crossing the sea under sail. In terms of giving an exact position, the sextant could not compete with the GPS, yet it compensated by telling us things that the cold coordinates left out. For example, that the summer sun had already started to tiptoe to southern climes, a little further from us each day. That the sun hit high noon later with every mile west, belying the insistence of our watches that time had not changed. Above all, that every measurement, like every judgement, depends minutely on the circumstances in which the measurement is made.

Plotting the latest sight that afternoon (sextant angle: thirty-one degrees and two minutes), a fragment of Catallus came to mind, that:

> I, a newcomer, was given
> A place among the ancient stars of heaven.

On the third day, the empty quarter filled suddenly. So far we had encountered exactly one ship, one tuna, one dazed sea turtle and, of all creatures least likely to be alone, a single locust that contrived in the middle of this emptiness to crash into our mainsail and from there drop into the water. But now we'd entered shipping lanes, and tankers and cargoes were our constant companions, the low drone of their engines noticeable long before the ships themselves broke the horizon.

These were not shipping lanes in an up-and-down English Channel kind of way, for vessels came and went at every conceivable angle. Some sailed close to *Shamaal*, often out of curiosity it seemed. Most ploughed straight from one horizon to the next, but some altered course abruptly in the manner of cars that have missed a turning. On the fourth day a trawler steamed past, no one visible either on deck or in the steering house. Later our old friends in one of the surveillance planes flew overhead. We were nearing land.

The dreamy planning chart gave way once more to its pedantic, detail-obsessed alter ego covering no more than eastern Sicily. Then on the fifth night, after 400 nautical miles, we entered Porto Palo, dropping anchor, in the manner of salmon or sea turtles, at exactly the spot next to *Mare Chiaro* that we'd left on our departure to Greece eleven weeks before.

Bruto

The lads from *Mare Chiaro* greeted us in the morning with shouts of '*Ciao, Shamaal!*' Though there was little we could say to each other, everyone was happy. They came in the dinghy, shook hands vigorously over the gunwales and gave us another crate of shrimp, squid and baby octopus. We offered a pot of Maniot honey. We discovered that *Kochab*, a big steel ketch we'd seen in Methóni, had also arrived, getting in just a few hours before.

Next day we were keen to get going north-west up the Sicilian coast, but, when *Mare Chiaro* came in from fishing, the captain signalled with an up-and-down motion to indicate heavy waves. '*Mare bruto*,' he shouted, and although this word did not appear in my multilingual glossary of maritime terms, it was clear enough what he meant. Noticing *Kochab* about to leave, I rowed over to tell the skipper, a rather grave Serb called Goran, what I'd heard. He shrugged and left anyway. 'We have our forecast and it's giving the wind as south-west, so it should be a good ride along the coast.' But Goran was wrong. The wind blew from the north-west – in other words, right down the Sicilian shore, and so hard later that day that even in harbour we found it almost impossible to row the dinghy. The following day the wind still came out of the north-west, but down to Force 5. Not wanting to be delayed any longer, we left.

Now we really discovered what it means to head the wrong way in the Mediterranean. *Bruto!* Even if the wind were manageable, the sea was appalling, a stomach-turning wasteland of holes and hillocks in which *Shamaal* crashed and shuddered, awash for hour on hour, water slewing across the deck in pale-green rivers. When the wind got up, we reefed the sails to compensate, but then hadn't power to drive through the waves. The current set in train by the wind was strong, and we found whatever progress we did make remorselessly reduced. One step forward, often one sideways or back. By nightfall *Shamaal* was at a standstill and, barring retreat to Porto Palo, with no alternative other than to keep pounding away.

So it continued the next day and beyond, including an entire night of tacking to pass Castello di Falconara – nine hours to advance *one* mile along the coast. Spirits rose briefly off Punta Tenna when, to our delight, we recognized *Kochab* – the only boat except for fishing vessels we saw those days – approach on the opposite tack. Turned out, we heard over the radio, that they'd had enough soon after leaving Porto Palo and put into a small port (where they ran aground). Just as we came along, they'd gone out again. The hours passed more easily in company. *Kochab* was a fifty-foot two-master that had sailed around a good part of the world, and it was fun trying to keep up, tack for tack, mile for mile. We were doing well until Goran, evidently exasperated, ignited the motor and beelined at astonishing speed up the coast. We tried copying, but *Shamaal* couldn't handle the waves head on and, if we didn't go straight, there was no point in using the engine. Back to tacking.

There were lulls, and we used these to cover as much ground as possible under motor, but, by the time we passed inshore of Terrible Bank and the mysterious Graham Shoal, tempers were as foul as the sea. Four days after leaving Porto Palo, feeling irascible and emotional, we limped into Marsala. Over roughly the same time it had taken us to cross the Ionian, we'd covered just 169 miles of coastline.

Pacified by the fug of fermenting Marsala that enveloped the harbour, Adèle and I had just time to drain a reconciliatory glass of the sweet stuff before tumbling into sleep.

The north-westerly – maestrale, as it was called here – became news. Ferries to the outlying Isole Egadi and the supply ship for Pantelleria were cancelled, and hoteliers fretted as holidaymakers avoided sand-blown beaches. This was nothing compared to events in the fishing harbour of Mazara del Vallo, just south of Marsala. Here, the sea surged in, abruptly raising, then dropping, water levels by almost a metre, although somehow sparing moored boats from damage.

The phenomenon, known to Sicilians as the *marrobio*, has been recorded as far apart as Crete and Menorca, sometimes causing severe damage in packed harbours as the boats and pontoons are hoisted, then dumped, several times in a row. Numerous explanations have been put forward, but the *marrobio* is a form of seiche, a chain reaction occurring in enclosed bodies of water, whether the Mediterranean or large lakes. Strong winds set the sea piling against one end and, with nowhere to go, the waters eventually flow back. Sometimes encouraged by shifts of atmospheric pressure at different ends of the area, the sea can literally begin to slop back and forth, like water in a tray.

One of the more feasible explanations of the Jews' famous escape through the Red Sea is that a seiche briefly drove the waters from one end, allowing the Israelites to cross, then flooded back, swamping the Egyptians just behind. If one accepts that the crossing was not of the Red Sea itself, but of Great Bitter Lake to the north of the Gulf of Suez, this becomes possible. The lake runs south-east to north-west, and water levels would certainly be affected by a south-easterly khamsin gale (Exodus says the wind came from the east).

An even more violent wave is the tsunami caused by underwater earthquakes or the eruption of a volcano – a rare but entirely possible event in the Mediterranean. It is thought that the impact of such a wave from the island volcano of Thira might have triggered the mysterious and sudden collapse of Minoan civilization on Crete in about 1450 BC.

But in the Mediterranean it can be hard to separate fact from fond theory or fable. Consider what the fishermen in Greece – and in Sicily, too, we'd heard – said about the moon. When a new moon forms in vertical position, the weather that month will be good, but a horizontal, galley-shaped moon signals the winds will be strong. So why, having started July with the most upright of moons, had we just taken such a pasting from the maestrale?

A clutch of us in the harbour was hoping to head west, some to Sardinia, others Corsica, Spain or the south of France, and there was considerable frustration along the pontoons as the days blew by. For once, though, Adèle and I were model prisoners, happy with our enforced stay in this soporific town where the air, whatever the time of day, smelt as if it had just been released from an empty wine cask. We ate watermelon, drank Marsala and dozed through afternoons in the fusty splendour of the old streets.

As so often in the Mediterranean, there was little other than fierce wind, snatching and whistling through the harbour, to suggest bad weather. The clouds, a parade of sugary cumulus, were spectacular rather than grim. So, too, the snow-white and cobalt patchwork of the sea. There was not a hint of rain and, although the cooler air alarmed the Italians, the lowest temperatures were still in the high twenties. It was a storm – in port anyway – where only the sound had been switched on.

Watching Adèle try to film around the harbour, I was reminded of the constant challenge the wind, under its cloak of invisibility, poses any observer. Adèle had shot fifteen digital cassettes over our journey, but you cannot film the wind any more than a person's thoughts. The best you can do is capture what lies in its path – swaying trees, a dislodged hat, a collapsed umbrella or snapping sails. Even to write about wind presents problems. It is like describing music or the taste of something not only invisible, but also without feel. Again, you must concentrate on tangential information, the effects rather than the cause.

Look in the Cycladic Art room of Athens' National Archaeology Museum. The earliest sculptures – angular, mostly female marble statuettes, much like those that would re-emerge 5,000 years later as 'modern art' – are frozen. In an underwater scene etched on a pan of the same period, there is motion of sorts: four fish swimming anticlockwise around a series of spinning whorls to represent waves. But then water was easy to show – waves are *visible*. It was not until the sixteenth century BC that the Cycladic artists, helped by their more brilliant Cretan neighbours, made the startling discovery of how to portray air. The big-eyed bird on a clay jug from Mílos balances, claws open, wing and tail outstretched and body perfectly weighted. There is no air or wind to see, but anyone who has watched a bird lean against this invisible support knows it is there. On another piece of pottery, a flower stem ripples. On another, poppies bend back from their roots around the curve of the jug. Three and a half thousand years later, you feel the breeze.

Though wind, motion and life may not be the same, the skills needed to show them are related. Is it coincidence that the Greek word *pneuma* should mean equally 'spirit' and 'wind'? A kind of miracle had taken place in the workshops of those small, impoverished islands – literally, as if wind had breathed life into art.

Sometimes, staring into the sky, I tried to imagine what it would be like to see the wind. As if there might be special glasses to understand its secrets – the paths used to reach seemingly impossible places, the mystery of opposing airs and the drama of the katabatic wind. In laboratory simulators and computers these things can be re-created, but to ordinary men they remain as inscrutable as any god. Imagine standing on deck and being able to watch jet streams swoop through the upper skies. Or the slow-turning wheel of low-pressure systems. Or the avalanche of a squall. How would winds look if each were in colour? Sometimes we obtain glimpses. In sandstorms wind blows yellow, in snowstorms white, a tornado black. A friend told me once of sailing during snowfall and how the wind, illuminated by snow, swirled and curled around his sails. It was the first time he understood properly what drove the boat forward. Just a glimpse . . . I was surprised to be so lucky in the Mediterranean.

We had gone to spend the day in Erice, an old Aragonese village at the top of Mount San Giuliano, a little north along the coast from Marsala. It is a peculiarity of San Giuliano that the summit is often trapped in cloud, regardless of the sunny heat elsewhere, and, as the bus climbed from the coast up coil on coil of mountain bends, the fog grew denser and the temperature lower at every turn.

The village itself sat hunched in permanent defence, its warren of stairways, alleys, fortifications and religious establishments as impenetrable as the cloud in which all was wrapped. The largest alleys were wide enough to admit a small car, but there were almost no cars and few people. Discreet locals appeared and disappeared through heavy grilles and tiny medieval doors. A few tourists, shivering in their sea-level holiday clothes, shuffled in a bemused way from one locked church to the next. A group of nuns, white habits billowing like spinnakers, struggled across a square. Only the wind, moaning and hissing, had free rein, though there were defences against this, too: special slit-like passages called *penule*, in which the pedestrian could shelter. Sometimes the wind carried the taste of marzipan and melted butter, a homely touch all the more unexpected in this stony gloom.

From Erice's ramparts, famous for spectacular views on clear days, we saw only the swirling movement of cloud as it worked its way over the mountain. Like pipe smoke it twisted and turned, surging from lower slopes, cutting through trees and storming the ramparts of Erice in unstoppable waves. Every moment of the cloud's erratic progress could be traced. How it circled a tower, curled through crenellations, blew up one street and returned down another. How it struck the bastion, broke in two and rejoined on the far side. Not a detail was missing. At last, the face of the weather that had tormented us so long, the veil slipped – the face of the wind itself!

There were good tidings back in Marsala. No more maestrale. 'Wind: south-easterly, Force 3,' said the forecast. The news shook up the harbour. Some of us had started to take on a semi-permanent look, like that of the stateless families I used to see camped in the halls of a Moscow airport, waiting, without hope, for asylum or passage to third countries. The forecast, accompanied by the usual celebratory strike of a harp, was like the arrival of a smiling customs officer. Passports, tickets, visa – free to go.

Liberty brings complications. The dour Breton in a boilerplate boat suspected a trick. 'I don't know if I trust the south-east wind.' The Italians going to Sardinia wondered if they'd be able to get back. The chatterbox bon vivant from Marseille wished there'd be *no* wind. 'What my wife and I prefer is calm seas so we can motor!' We were just happy to escape.

An hour before we left, a gleaming sixty-foot yacht, crew screaming, skipper powering forward when he thought he was powering back, came within a hair, a thin hair, of dismasting and crushing *Shamaal*.

Our beautiful blue boat, poised in the wind like the Mílos bird, and in one terrible instant almost robbed of her wings.

We said goodbye fondly to Marsala, but were glad to go.

Dog days

Favignana and Levanzo shimmered in the afternoon sun, but it was dusk before we came across Marettimo, last of the Isole Egadi. A feeble pinprick of light flared from the purple-blue flanks – the lighthouse on Punta Libeccio. Night fell, the island disappeared and the light suddenly sparkled. By dawn, the steep, lonely island was gone.

The Balearics were about 430 miles to the north-west, the last really long, open-sea crossing of our voyage. If the weather turned, Sardinia would offer refuge halfway along, but there seemed little chance of sudden change. Summer had entered its deepest, most docile stage. Under quivering skies the sea rose and fell with the rhythm of a sleeper's breath. Shafts of sunlight penetrated far underwater, dividing and reflecting. North African sand stained the damp sails and deck, and a clammy stupor filled the air.

We sailed slowly. When *Shamaal* stopped moving we motored and, the moment wind tickled the stitched and re-stitched edges of the Red Ensign, we sailed again. There were really no other decisions or actions to take. The August lassitude was infectious. Soon we could barely be bothered to read. Navigation became cursory. It was with only the greatest effort that I could rouse myself to eat. Drink we did and not as much as we'd have liked, for, although there was a lot of water on board, we kept to rations. Even to tempt trouble on that front seemed foolish. There were plenty of oranges for extra juice, grapefruits, too, but these required peeling and were far too much like work. A huge watermelon – the biggest in a pile of about 500 being sold by the road in Marsala – was finally manhandled on deck. Now this was a fruit made for hot, lazy people. I had only to plunge the knife for the entire fruit to split. We made no attempt to slice or cut pyramids, instead attacking each half with a spoon in the manner of a giant bowl. After tilting this monster back for the juice I threw it over the side. Adèle's followed. The melon halves floated well and for the longest time remained fixed in our wake.

Each evening the crimson sun appeared to collapse rather than set, pulling Sirius, the rest of Canis Major and the burnt-out remains of the day into the sea. In place came florid orange half-moons, green meteors and star fields thick as snow. Only far from land can the night sky be so vivid. Draco at the feet of Hercules. Cassiopeia floating in her chair through the Milky Way. Gangly Pegasus galloping past. Gathered in almost solid patches, stars spilled into the sea, enveloping our entire world. Sometimes these lights from above mingled with the strange blobs of luminescence we stirred up below. All became one, a world without horizons, beginning or end, a world in which even waking hours seemed a dream.

Then, about midway, the wind blew up strong and steadily from the north-east. We were off, sailing at pace past Sardinia and reclaiming all the progress lost in the ambling hours of the previous night. How good the wind felt. Infinite silence filled the air the moment the motor was extinguished. The sea breathed again and so, too, the skin. Fresh sunlight ricocheted off the cliffs of Capo Spartivento, then Capo Teulada, then the gnarled, black knob of Isola Toro . . . Poor Sardinia – it did look as if we'd done our best to ignore this island, screaming past the east coast in a gale last summer and now the south coast in not much less of a hurry. Having finally found such fair winds, how could we stop?

Even when the wind fell off again some hours later, we took care not to protest too loudly. After more than a year's absence, we were back in mistral territory. In fact, while we cruised this magic zone, all manner of mayhem blew to our north and south-west. According to the radio, the old master was hammering through the Golfe du Lion and Corsican sea at that moment. Big seas and high winds were reaching parts of Sardinia only sixty miles to the north. And although the Balearics were quiet, strong winds buffeted the desert coasts of Almería just beyond. 'The weather pattern . . . is affected by many different systems. It is largely unpredictable, quick to change and often very different at places only a short distance apart,' warned the Spanish pilot book. Now, Sardinian radio dropped from range. Spanish radio took its place. The reports were always the same: fair winds for the Balearics, foul everywhere else.

Midmorning after our sixth night from Sicily, we sighted

Menorca's fuzzy, green hills. Sorting out navigational details for landfall down in the cabin, I was a little shocked to see how few unused charts we had left. The miles were rolling past, the seasons, too, and a journey that had once seemed limitless would soon come to a close.

It is a truism that one should avoid the Mediterranean, particularly Spain, in August, but it is a truism of the jet age, while our calendar had been set by the archaic concerns of wind, seasons and sea. Spring, when wild flowers carpet the soft heathland and nests fill the great cliffs, would be the time to see the Balearics. The *calas*, overlooked by the surprisingly homely entrances of prehistoric dwellings, would be empty and glitteringly clear. Gentle towns such as Mahón would brim with pre-summer optimism. We tried to be hopeful: given the number of anchorages in the serrated edges of the Balearics, it seemed impossible even now that one or two couldn't give shelter from the crowds. But we were wrong.

The deserted idyll of Cala Covas on the south side of Menorca, for example, had become a regular crowded harbour. Twenty-five yachts lined up side by side between the rocky walls of the gorge. Errant turds dotted the water, mobile phones chirruped across decks, and the sound and smell of other people's lives, knowing no frontiers, belied the convention in which all of us obstinately pretended to be on our own. Cala Covas had at least been saved from the developers, but in numerous other *calas* those same cliffs and ravines hid the tentacles of holiday complexes and purpose-built villages, often hidden from the sea and so all the more disappointing a discovery on closer inspection. In Cala de Son Saura, warnings of severe winds kept us at anchor for three days, uselessly as it turned out because, apart from squalls and an ugly sky, the weather was benign. (Sailing to Mallorca on the day the same forecasters announced an improvement, we hit a near gale.) Otherwise, we and the Balearics passed each other by like leaves in the wind.

Only Palma, soft, sensuous city of Arabs and Catalans, held us. Drinking *horchata* under ancient olive trees, climbing the back streets in search of ship's supplies, and taking breakfast at bars where already men in overalls devoured *jamon* and frosty glasses of rosé, I discovered or rediscovered scenes of my father's boat days twenty years past. His schooner *Scarlett O'Hara* would once have been moored close to where we now had *Shamaal*, probably just along the main drag there with the other big yachts. I used to come visiting on school holidays, one or two times to Mallorca, a few others to the Caribbean – wherever the boat, which my father ran as a charter business, might be based. Naturally, my peers were jealous, but I was stubbornly ungrateful, setting myself against anything to do with sailing and dreaming out loud of more prosaic homes – the kind that stayed in one place. There were some anguished moments between father and teenage son in those exotic locales, maybe, if I cast my mind back, even right here in Palma. That was a long time ago now. How the tables had turned – me afloat, my father ashore wishing I would settle down! All I wondered was this: had the seeds of this visit been sown then, when Palma was my ephemeral home, or was this journey really my own? A little lost in the forest of masts in the great harbour, I gave up trying to answer and turned instead to the easier matter of the sextant.

The instrument had taken a knock during the rough weather off Menorca, and the fragile mirrors used to rope in the planets and stars were out of line. To fix it required turning a tiny Allen key in a series of adjusting screws while aiming the sextant at a distant object, in this case the Moorish castle on the hill above Palma. As long as the mirrors remained out of sync, any object viewed through the sextant appeared disjointed – too long, too short or even separated – but once the mirrors, via the screws, had been tilted into their correct place, the sextant view would match that of the naked eye. For a peaceful hour I sat on *Shamaal*'s cabin rearranging the castle this way and that. A turn of one screw and another tower sprouted, a turn of the other and the long crenellations concertinaed into a single, neat hump. With another slight adjustment, I could make the castle – main tower, graceful arch and all – levitate into the clouds. It was a little wistfully that I finally brought the edifice and myself down to earth. We still had a passage to make.

We missed Ibiza entirely, dropping anchor for a night off Formentera instead. This, according to the guides, was so unspoilt that even in summer a degree of peace might prevail, but crowds smothered the bare island. In the sheltered waters off the west shore, weekend yachts, superyachts and small ships floated back to back. A catamaran bringing tourists from Ibiza was so overloaded that not everyone had room to sit. Clinging to the mast, the railings and each other, they made an uncanny double of those sad pictures of immigrant boats picked up off the shores of southern Spain. For the first time in the Mediterranean we were in a place where the traffic of high-speed motor boats made swimming from *Shamaal* to shore more dangerous than it was worth. Uniformed men from the gin palaces howled when we got in their way. So did the girls on jet skis. So, too, the nude men in that dinghy. Did we not understand that the sea was for speed! I dived for shells in vain.

Blustery easterlies delivered us the next day from Formentera back into the otherworldly August sea. Once more the old rhythms, the steady advance across the white spaces of the chart, watch-keeping under the sun and moon, a necklace of bubbles and swirls in our wake. This, after more than fifteen months, was the Mediterranean we belonged to and that belonged to us – *mare nostrum*. But how much longer? Parchment coloured Spain would soon fill the horizon. Cabo de Palos, Punta de Media Naranja, Almería, Cabo de Gata, the Costa del Sol, glimpses southward of Africa: the path led inexorably to the Pillars of Hercules, the end of our voyage and of the Mediterranean itself.

The easterlies faded, died, and in their place an overwhelming calm in which *Shamaal*, motoring south-west, had never seemed slower. The water took on the dense, slippery consistency of mercury. The sky became smoky. The most minor disturbances, ordinarily incognito between the creases of waves, were laid bare and exaggerated. The glass neck of a jettisoned bottle leant into the sky, dominating the sea for miles around. A patch of pale blue rippling under the aquamarine made one think a plastic bag might be the most beautiful thing in the world. Each encounter seemed full of portent. Tiny concentric rings and a gathering of bubbles told us we were being watched from below. Three or four gentle waves rolling lazily past signalled a ship over the horizon. Half a lemon, blinding yellow against the water, was followed a short while later by the other half, bringing to life the whole scene of the ship's cook, his fish stew and the final twist, perhaps before he wiped his sweating brow and went out by the rails. Was that his cigarette? Someone had smoked it right to the filter before flicking it overboard. What detritus of shipboard life we passed: a packing crate, a football, a paintbrush covered in a distinctive billiards-table green and, as if in parody of the mariner's abandoned lover, a rubber doll, her stubby, semi-inflated hand reaching up from the sea.

Every moment we expected the wind to return, to cover the sea's nakedness and fill our sails. It never came. Hour on hour we motored, through two glaring days and two milky nights, where the beams of the full moon shone like spotlights. At last, the double-flash of the Cabo de Palos lighthouse: we had reached Spain.

Still motoring, a diagonal run took us the remaining ninety miles to Cabo de Gata, behind which hid Almería and the last stretch to Gibraltar. Already Atlantic currents began to make themselves felt, sometimes holding us up, sometimes curling around in counter-currents from astern. Maybe that mix of seas, new Atlantic water coming in and old, salt-rich Mediterranean water trickling out, was what brought so much life around *Shamaal*. Jellyfish like plucked eyeballs stared up in their hundreds. The head of a loggerhead turtle (*Caretta caretta*) peeked cautiously, unaware perhaps that the dappled armour of his body was not only visible underwater, but magnified as well. A second and a third turtle led to a group of six, scattered like stepping stones across the surface. Tuna, silvery skins taut and hard, lanced through the sea in pursuit of flying fish. These made desperate, bullet-like flights a few centimetres above water, sometimes covering considerable distances before physics dragged them down. Finally, there were the dolphins. Never had we seen so many at once. They shot past in sixes, torpedoing in and out of our wake, performing backflips, leaping into the still air and sliding under the keel, where their pearly bodies turned pale green.

There are stories about dolphins dating back many centuries, not only concerning their games, but also their apparent willingness to aid those in distress. Herodotus recounts how Arion, a star musician of his day, was rescued by dolphins after brigands forced him into the Ionian. Before going overboard, Arion asked the pirates permission to play a final song on his lute, and it is this that was supposed to have attracted his saviours, long believed to have enjoyed human music. There are also tales of dolphins, like mermaids and mermen, making tragic attempts to stay with their human friends on land. Arion's dolphin refused to leave his side and, after a brief spell of luxury, died ashore. In *Mani*, Patrick Leigh Fermor reports a reliable account of dolphins flocking to the sound of concert music from a radio on a small boat off the Aegean island of Andros. 'Carried away by the crescendo they grew more boisterous and leapt out of the water, banging the side of the boat and even attempting to join him on board.'

Modern fishermen have little time for dolphins, which poach fish from nets and tear holes in the mesh, and when they see one they will pelt it with stones. All over the world, multitudes suffocate and drown in tuna nets. Nevertheless, they are protected by many countries and the enthusiasm of humans for attempting to save beached whales, which are cousins of the dolphin, suggests that among ordinary people the ancient bonds remain strong. For me, the hollow whoosh of breathing alongside *Shamaal* was the happiest of sounds. The dolphin was the sprite of the Mediterranean, its muse and jester, the guardian of its unchanging spirit and, as one of the few mammals to live like fish, a link for all of us to all seas.

After a record number of hours under motor – more from Formentera than during entire months in the past – we pulled into Aguadulce, our first port on the Spanish mainland. Thorn- and stone-covered hills occupy much of the Almería region's coast, one of the wildest in Europe. Yet wherever the terrain flattens, man has come with his prefab concrete, tarmac and tracts of plastic greenhouse sheeting. Aguadulce is one of those resulting creations. The name means 'sweet water', but the impression given by the purpose-built tourist town was of some- thing stagnant and quite possibly poisonous. Nearby Almerimar, our next stop, proved no better – all breeze-block walkways and empty themed pubs – and so we decided to wait for the levanter, the easterly wind of these parts, then cover the remaining 130 miles to Gibraltar in one leap.

The vigil for the wind gave me the chance to reopen my tattered copy of *The Odyssey*, as I'd long meant to, and in this suitably transient setting contemplate that founding story of voyaging and return.

Sometimes bitter, sometimes joyful, often unpredictable, the themes in Homer resonate with travel in any age. I remembered a chat with Goran from *Kochab* while we were in Methóni. He'd only recently returned to Europe more than two decades after sailing from France in his then new steel boat for Brazil. In that time, he'd navigated by stars, survived great storms, swum through walls of bright-coloured fish – done the things that make one dream. Only he no longer dreamt. I was intrigued to hear that in Tahiti he'd met Bernard Moitessier, the man who in the late 1960s sailed one and a half times around the world without pause, becoming guru of the permanent odyssey. All these years later, this was what Goran remembered: 'Moitessier made a lot of people believe the sea was a beautiful place, but, you know what, it is not. It is hard and difficult.' In Goran's weary, bearded face, I was reminded of that line from Homer: 'I tell you, there's nothing like the sea to break a man, however strong.' In Menorca, Adèle and I had met two Canadians desperate to end four years' cruising. 'The sea is all sameness now . . . Some people seem to have luck with weather, others don't – we don't . . . We're so tired of having to watch the sky all the time . . . The sea is just so damned *salty*.' Again I thought of Homer. His Mediterranean was 'wine dark . . . grey . . . foggy . . . vast . . . foaming . . . cruel'.

Travel is double-edged. As the early twentieth-century Greek poet George Seferis wrote, 'men of inconstancy, of wanderings and of wars, though they differ and may change in terms of greatness and value . . . always move among the same monsters and the same longings'. In other words, we are all on Odysseus' galley. We thirst to make voyages, yet crave home, and we know it is a difficult, probably impossible balance to maintain.

Adèle and I had already made our choice. *Shamaal* would spend the winter at a boatyard somewhere in or around the strait – Gibraltar, perhaps, Morocco, or near Cádiz. Then, our Mediterranean voyage over, we'd return to jobs and our flat in North London. Only not for long. Many an hour we'd talked about the trip back, our readjustment to city life and the pleasure of seeing old friends, yet already our thoughts were on next summer and where we might go in *Shamaal*. The whole world opened at the Strait of Gibraltar. To the north: Lisbon, Porto and the rias of Galicia. To the south: Essaouira, the Canaries and the rivers of Senegal. Then west . . . The idea of stopping now was inconceivable. And if next summer didn't work, then the one after would do, or the one after that. 'Don't hurry the journey,' wrote Kavafy. Ithaca exists only for those who are ready – and we were not.

Which brought to mind the conclusion of *The Odyssey*. We are told how the traveller returns to his native island, how he overthrows his enemies and rejoins faithful Penelope. The main points of the plot would appear to have been resolved. Except for one glaring question: what then? After ten years of war and another ten wandering, after following the four winds, can we really believe that Odysseus will never again feel the wayfarer's urge? Homer is silent on this most difficult point, only mentioning teasingly that Odysseus will some day have to make a long trek inland to placate his old antagonist Poseidon.

Others have written their own postscripts. In Dante's *Divine Comedy*, Odysseus is unable to resist one last voyage, embarking with his few, now aged friends, to pass the Pillars of Hercules into the Atlantic where finally 'the sea closed over us and the light was gone'. Tennyson's version describes a similar fatal, final journey:

> I cannot rest from travel: I will drink
> Life to the lees . . .
>
> Come, my friends,
> 'Tis not too late to seek a newer world.
> Push off, and sitting well in order smite
> The sounding furrows; for my purpose holds
> To sail beyond the sunset, and the baths
> Of all the western stars, until I die.

Odysseus – perverse, addicted to voyage, insatiably curious, even about death – the ultimate, uncompromising traveller. The idea reminded me of a long-held suspicion: that the fatal day his crew opened Aeolus' sack, unleashing the storm that drove them for ever from Ithaca, Odysseus may not have been so fast asleep after all.

The levanter finally arrived, strong and muggy from the east. The locals preferred the westerly poniente, which was fresh and tasted of the Atlantic. Some claimed to be driven mad by the levanter. In Tarifa, just beyond Gibraltar, there were said to be an unusual number of suicides, in addition to the prosperous industries of wind generators and windsurfing. Travellers, though, are nothing if not selfish (look at Odysseus), and the day the easterly came Adèle and I sailed downwind out of Almerimar with the lightest of hearts. The sea parted as *Shamaal* rode down each wave. We were on the move again.

The edge of the world

Shipping lanes to port, foothills of the Sierra Nevada to starboard, we plied the length of the Alborán Sea, almost without having to adjust the sails. Glowing Málaga and Marbella slipped past, bluish Morocco came into view, and so, one dawn, when the sea was silver and the levanter a whisper, we came across the rock Spain's Moorish conquerors knew as Jebel Tarik.

The Strait of Gibraltar, where Europe and Africa meet in that delicate and regretful kiss, can be daunting when approached from the Mediterranean. Having forgotten the existence of tides, the sailor will find himself in a clockwork sea driven by ocean, wind and moon. A million cubic metres of water pour every second from the Atlantic, lifeblood for a Mediterranean sucked dry by evaporation and poorly resupplied by rivers and rain. To understand the relentlessness of the flow, consider this: sea level at Tanger, just outside the strait, is two to three metres higher than in the Mediterranean just twenty-five or so miles to the east. Alone, this creates a permanent eastgoing current, one knot on the edges, double that in the middle. Pushed by a strong poniente, literally the 'putting down wind', that current may become four knots – easily enough to stop *Shamaal* dead. Hindered by the levanter, the 'rising wind', the current will slow or even reverse, but that collision of wind and water makes for rough seas. Thrown into the mix are powerful tidal streams which, because of the constant Atlantic flow, switch direction at radically different times in areas only a short distance apart. Yet another current, this time old, heavily salted water that has completed a circuit of the Mediterranean, flows constantly, deep under the surface, back into the Atlantic's embrace.

The legend of the Pillars of Hercules, one being Gibraltar, the other Ceuta, testifies to the grip this fearful place exercised on early Mediterranean travellers. Already this was the sole opening from the inland sea, edge of *terra incognita*, border of the Ocean Stream and the location, some say, of Hades. Hercules was on his tenth labour, bound for the island of Erytheia to steal Geryon's cattle, when he arrived. In one version, Africa and Europe were still joined (as indeed they once were) and Hercules forced them apart. In another, the gap was much wider and Hercules, meaning to keep out monsters, pulled it closed. Either way, he raised the two pillars to commemorate his achievement, and from then the strait marked the beginning and end, both physically and spiritually, of an entire world.

Dolphins, which flourish alongside cetaceans and fish of all kinds here, escorted us through the chop around Gibraltar's Europa Point. The wind faltered and tripped over the great rock, then died.

Motoring through ranks of waiting tankers, we crossed the bay, Gibraltar looking all the more an anomaly now that we could appreciate the flatness of the surrounding Spanish coast. Then, just short of the colony's airport runway, which is also the border with Spain, and almost 5,000 nautical miles since leaving England, we dropped anchor.

Gibraltar does not wear the years well. Overpopulated and blighted by English municipal architecture, this scruffy outpost of history should really only be seen from the sea or the summit. This, we reached by foot and cable car that afternoon. Following the human crush in the town below, the dignified faces of the Barbary apes were surprisingly reassuring. The air was fresh and, from the railings of the highest terrace, the views of the

Mediterranean, Africa and the Atlantic made my head spin. How far east the sea stretched. How far we'd come. In the glassy blue I could almost trace our wake, a foam line snaking past Spain, Italy, Greece, Malta, Tunisia, Corsica, the Côte d'Azur . . . But when I turned west, how much further that sea, deeper blue now, almost black, went on.

I thought of the first voyagers to arrive out of the east, that fabulous, self-contained world, and find themselves standing on this peak. From Egyptians in their lotus-shaped boats to Cretan chieftains and sharp-minded traders of Phoenicia, all the pioneers of European navigation and exploration had started in the east. It was in the Levant that cautious experiment became innovation, that coast-hopping led to open seas. It was from that base that the first mariners expanded, describing ever widening circles, a circuit, in fact, of their world – the world that for a long time would be *mare nostrum*. With the winds catalogued, the furthest coast colonized and the widest quarter mastered, what feeling of completeness this early Mediterranean sailor must have enjoyed. Like a blind man negotiating an unknown room, he'd felt out each wall, each island of furniture. He knew its pitfalls, its comforts, its gods. He knew and loved this room so well he neither wanted nor would ever need to leave: it was home. Then rumours of the door to another, unimaginably greater space. Perhaps he found it himself. The idea terrified. Only a very few, the Phoenicians first, summoned courage to pass. Others declared this place off limits, 'the untraversed sea beyond the Pillars' in Euripides' words, 'the end of voyaging, where the Ruler of the Ocean no longer permits mariners to travel on the purple sea'. *Ne plus ultra*, the ancient motto claimed: 'There is nothing beyond.' But the secret was out and with it the challenge.

Along with so much else, the Mediterranean gave us this great, unsettling lesson – a lesson of travel and life. That each sea leads only to the next. That the end of the labyrinth is, in fact, the beginning of a far greater system. That the wind, as Ecclesiastes says, 'goeth toward the south, and turneth about unto the north;

it whirleth about continually, and the wind returneth again according to his circuits'.

The tide was on the flood when we rowed back. *Shamaal* tugged at her anchor. Stars unfolded. Adèle and I sat in the cockpit, sipping the last of our Marsala. Early September and all around the southward migration was again under way. For storks, Gibraltar was one of only two routes, the other at the far end of the Mediterranean across the Bosphorus. Heavy birds with wings like sails, they'd need the thermals of a hot day to carry them into Africa. Light crosswinds, too, if they were to avoid being driven to sea. In the marshes, cork oaks and grass hills of Andalucia, they waited, many thousands of them: storks, but also herons, eagles, buzzards, vultures and the small birds, too, the bee-eaters, finches and orioles. Who knew what tomorrow would bring? In darkness, we all waited for the wind.